THE LETTERS
OF
FRANCIS THOMPSON

Francis Thompson. A pastel sketch from life by R. Ponsonby Staples, dated 1897. (Used by permission of the Humanities Research Center, University of Texas.)

THE LETTERS
OF
FRANCIS THOMPSON

Edited by
John Evangelist Walsh

Hawthorn Books, Inc.   Publishers   New York

First Edition: 1969

Designed by Gene Gordon

This volume is dedicated,
with respect and in memory
of our pleasant meetings,
to
Mrs. Percival Lucas,
Mrs. T. Murray Sowerby,
and
Sir Francis Meynell,
who long ago read many of these
letters as they arrived fresh in
the daily post at their father's
house, and who now have aided
materially in their publication.

Books by John Evangelist Walsh

THE SHROUD
The Story of the Holy Shroud of Turin

STRANGE HARP, STRANGE SYMPHONY
The Life of Francis Thompson

POE THE DETECTIVE:
The Curious Circumstances Behind
The Mystery of Marie Roget

INTRODUCTION

Though he was a fluent, if seldom chatty, letter-writer once he picked up his pen, Francis Thompson seems to have been nearly as reclusive in the matter of correspondence as he was in his personal friendships. Indications are that during the twenty years of his working career he wrote probably no more than about three hundred letters, and the bulk of these went to Wilfrid Meynell and his family. Of some twenty other acquaintances it was only with Coventry Patmore, Katie King, and perhaps Mrs. Elizabeth Blackburn that he carried on anything like a regular exchange. Fortunately, in addition to many of those to the Meynells, most of the Patmore letters have survived. Those to Mrs. Blackburn, aside from a few fragments included herein, have not yet been found, while all of those to Katie King were destroyed.

Thompson never really enjoyed letter-writing. He lacked the facility for throwing off letters from shallower levels of consciousness, and gradually he became more and more hesitant about committing himself to what he called "familiar and unguarded" correspondence. In his later years his caution extended occasionally to writing a letter and holding it till the next morning, when he would read it over and then burn it. "Once, I think, two successive letters were posted in this *fiery* fashion," he remarked when trying to explain a careless passage he had written. Even postcards were not always to be trusted: "They are like revolvers," he observed wryly when a card of Mrs. Blackburn's had raised some transient fuss, "too handy for the vent of momentary spleen." Such wariness, it is all too clear, was part of that essential immaturity under which he labored through his life, that pathetic uncertainty of touch—both a cause and a consequence of opium—which ever plagued and limited his personal relationships. While we could wish that he wrote more, to more people and more openly, the few letters of such a reticent nature and so interior a poet will often glow with an intenser fascination for readers than those left behind by more expansive personalities.

While a good portion of the letters to the Meynells were inevitably submerged and lost in the natural flow of things, the elder

Meynell did manage to salvage well over a hundred of them from the constant flood of paper that swirled around his daily existence as editor, writer, and literary adviser. Viola Meynell, in her *Memoir* of her mother, recalled how "the long library table at Palace Court was turned white with papers, the little litter of authorship, the great litter of journalism," and it was into this fragile agglomeration that Thompson's letters dropped when they arrived at the Meynell home. That any were preserved is due to the care of Wilfrid, who bundled them snugly into letter boxes after they had lain for a few months amid the confusion of the table, "and perhaps a few years in the indiscriminate depths of the lockers that made the library window-seat."

Even the scanty number Thompson sent to others exists largely through the concern of the Meynells. For his 1913 biography of the poet, for instance, Everard Meynell collected the eleven extant letters to Coventry Patmore as well as notes sent to such acquaintances as Charles Lewis Hind, Wilfrid Whitten, William Archer, and Alfred Hayes. One particularly interesting item—the long journal-letter of 1890—survives only in a 1909 typescript prepared by Everard; about 1925 Thompson's sister, Margaret, moved by some innocent apprehension, burned the original.

For the years preceding Thompson's first contact with the Meynells no correspondence at all has yet come to light. There were undoubtedly many letters sent to his family from school at Ushaw during 1870–77, which might illuminate for us the youthful pressures that formed so unusual a poet and perhaps also tell something about the actual strains that led to his entrammelment with drugs. But these letters have entirely disappeared, the last of them left behind in Paris in 1940 when Norbert Thompson, the poet's half-brother, fled with his family before the oncoming Nazi army.

During the period 1878–85 Thompson lived at home in Ashton-under-Lyne, while commuting to Owens College, so his letters were probably not plentiful, though he must have written a few, particularly to relatives. With his uncle, Edward Healy Thompson, for example, a sometime teacher of English and a journeyman writer on Catholic subjects, he maintained for a number of years what would have been a revealing correspondence. "He used to write to me," the uncle later explained, "until I gave him some advice, which I suppose he resented, for he never wrote to me again. His letters were all of a literary cast, and showed I thought, no small amount of self-conceit in the way of habitual criticism and fault-finding." The criticism, as well as what the older man called "self-conceit," would be valuable now as a record of Thompson's unusually prolonged struggle to liberate his own poetic identity, but these letters regretfully are still missing.

Perhaps someday they will turn up. In the meantime it is rather appropriate that this initial publication of Thompson's correspondence should begin with that first fateful letter to Wilfrid Meynell. The poet was twenty-seven years old when he wrote it in February 1887, had been dreaming of poets and poetry for a decade, and for more than a year had drifted through a lonely and deepening frustration in London. Eventually, when that first letter had opened the door of the Meynell home to him, he at last found sympathy, understanding, and, it can be said, even life itself.

Of the 188 letters in this volume, 163 are taken from holographs, of which a complete photostatic file is in my possession. To these I have added a number that exist only in copies or in published sources (diligent search having failed to uncover the originals), and each of these is identified in the notes. With one exception, no changes, whether in punctuation, wording, grammar, etc., have been made in letters printed from holographs. The exception concerns Thompson's habitual, though not exclusive, use of "ȳ" for "the," a personal quirk probably begun as a deliberate imitation of De Quincey's script, but which he clung to throughout his life. The usage, obsolete even in Thompson's youth, lends a certain quaintness to the manuscript letters but seems annoyingly irrelevant in print, and the familiar article has been herein substituted.

In letters taken from published sources, where the originals are missing, changes of various kinds may have been made which are impossible now to trace. Study shows, for instance, that Everard Meynell in his 1913 biography customarily made deletions without specific indication, simply explaining at one point that most of the letters in the volume were "abbreviated." In some cases, such dropping of material required him to make a slight rewording of the transitions and surrounding material.

Thompson almost never dated his letters, fittingly enough for a man whose awareness of the passage of time was rarely measured by day and night. But it has been possible to assign fairly accurate dates to nearly all of them by comparative study and by matching the text with known events. In some cases envelopes in association have yielded dates, but these are accepted only when the text confirms them.

My particular gratitude for permissions and various sorts of timely cooperation is extended to: Mrs. Olivia Sowerby, daughter of Wilfrid Meynell and present possessor of most of the letters preserved by her father; Rev. Brenden Connolly, Director of Libraries at Boston College, who made available the many letters in the Terence L. Connolly, S.J., Francis Thompson Collection; Mrs. Joan Harriss and Miss Alice Meynell, daughters of Everard Meynell, who own the long series of notes Thompson sent to their father in 1905; Sir Francis Meynell, who permitted the inclusion of the several important letters in his possession; Harriss Library, Preston, for the valuable letter to Katharine Tynan; and Lilly Library, Indiana University, for an interesting unpublished fragment.

J.W.

Dumont, New Jersey
February 1969

PRINCIPAL EVENTS IN THE LIFE OF FRANCIS THOMPSON

(Compiled from *Strange Harp, Strange Symphony:
The Life of Francis Thompson*, by John Evangelist Walsh)

1859—December 18, born, Preston, Lancashire.

1864—Family moves to Ashton-under-Lyne, near Manchester.

1868—Precocious reading of Scott, Macaulay, Shakespeare, the Apocalypse, etc., along with the usual boy's fare.

1870—Enrolls in St. Cuthbert's College, Ushaw, to prepare for the priesthood.

1876—Literary ambition surfaces, causing disturbance in his religious vocation.

1877—Leaves the seminary on the advice of his superiors. Enrolls at Owens College, Manchester, to prepare for a medical career.

1879—First experience with opium (laudanum).

1880—December, mother dies after a six-month illness.

1884—Leaves Owens College without a degree.

1885—November, quarrels with his father, leaves home for London.

1886—Various menial jobs in London; often hungry and reduced to street dereliction. December, a brief visit home.

1887—February, submits an essay and some poems to *Merry England*; further dereliction on London streets. Summer, befriended by a nameless prostitute.

1888—Spring, attempts suicide. April, first poem, *Passion of Mary*, appears in *Merry England*. May, first meeting with Wilfrid Meynell, editor of *Merry England*. First conception of *The Hound of Heaven*.

1889—Recuperating at a monastery in Storrington, Sussex. Writes *Ode to the Setting Sun*, the Shelley essay (posthumously published), *The Hound of Heaven*.

1890—March, returns to London to write and to assist Wilfrid Meynell with *Merry England* and *The Weekly Register*. August–October, writes *Sister Songs*.

1892—Fall, relapses into drug addiction; December, the Meynells send him to a monastery in Pantasaph, Wales. Writes *Little Jesus*.

1893—Fitful love affair with Maggie Brien, daughter of his landlady; lasts through 1895. November, *Poems* published.

CONTENTS

Introduction		7
Principal Events in the Life of Francis Thompson		11
Note on Abbreviations		21

Letters

Recipient	**Date**	**Page**
	1887	
1. Wilfrid Meynell	February 23	23
	1888	
2. Wilfrid Meynell	April 14	23
	1889	
3. Wilfrid Meynell	February	25
4. Wilfrid Meynell	May	26
5. Wilfrid Meynell	September	28
	1890	
6. Wilfrid Meynell	January	28
7. Wilfrid Meynell	February	30
8. Wilfrid Meynell	early March	31
9. Wilfrid Meynell	March	32
10. Canon John Carroll	Begun in May, finished August 12	33
11. Alice Meynell	July	48
12. Wilfrid Meynell	August	50
13. Wilfrid Meynell	September	50
14. Wilfrid Meynell	September	51
15. Alice Meynell	fall	52
16. Alice Meynell	winter	55
17. Wilfrid Meynell	late December	56
18. Alice Meynell	December 31	57
19. Wilfrid Meynell	December 31	59

Recipient	Date	Page

1891

20. Wilfrid Meynell	January	60
21. Wilfrid Meynell	January	62
22. Wilfrid Meynell	January	63
23. Wilfrid Meynell	March 4	65
24. William Ernest Henley	early	65
25. Wilfrid Meynell	May	66
26. Wilfrid Meynell	July	67
27. Wilfrid Meynell	October	69
28. Wilfrid Meynell	October	71
29. Alice Meynell	December	72

1892

30. Wilfrid Meynell	January	73
31. Wilfrid Meynell	summer	74
32. Katharine Tynan	July 15	75
33. Alice Meynell	late summer	78
34. Alice Meynell	August	79
35. Alice Meynell	September	83
36. Alice Meynell	September	84
37. Alice Meynell	September	87
38. Alice Meynell	September	88
39. Wilfrid Meynell	September	90
40. Wilfrid Meynell (?)	late December	91
41. Mrs. Elizabeth Blackburn	December 29	92

1893

42. Wilfrid Meynell	January 4	93
43. Wilfrid Meynell	January	94
44. Mrs. Elizabeth Blackburn	February	94
45. Wilfrid Meynell	April 3	95
46. Wilfrid Meynell	May	96
47. Coventry Patmore	June 15	97
48. Wilfrid Meynell	mid-June	98
49. Wilfrid Meynell	July	99
50. John Lane	July	99
51. Alice Meynell	September	100
52. Alice Meynell	September	102
53. Wilfrid Meynell	September	103

Recipient   Date   Page

	Recipient	Date	Page
54.	Wilfrid Meynell	September	105
55.	Wilfrid Meynell	September 14	106
56.	Wilfrid Meynell	September	108
57.	Alice Meynell	September	108
58.	Father Adam Wilkinson	October	109
59.	Wilfrid Meynell	October	109
60.	Wilfrid Meynell	November	111

1894

	Recipient	Date	Page
61.	Alice Meynell	January	112
62.	Wilfrid Meynell	February	114
63.	Monica Meynell	February 15	116
64.	Wilfrid and Alice Meynell	April	117
65.	Alice Meynell	summer	118
66.	Father H. K. Mann	summer	118
67.	Alice Meynell	October	119
68.	Alice Meynell	October	120

1895

	Recipient	Date	Page
69.	Editor, the *Westminster Gazette*	spring	121
70.	John Lane	April	122
71.	John Lane	May	124
72.	Wilfrid Meynell	June	125
73.	John Lane	June	125
74.	Coventry Patmore	July	127
75.	Wilfrid Meynell	July	129
76.	Wilfrid Meynell	August	130
77.	Coventry Patmore	August	131
78.	Coventry Patmore	September	132
79.	Coventry Patmore	late September	133
80.	Wilfrid Meynell	late September	134
81.	Coventry Patmore	October	134
82.	Wilfrid Meynell	fall	137
83.	Wilfrid Meynell	December 24	137
84.	Wilfrid Meynell	December 31	138

1896

	Recipient	Date	Page
85.	Alice Meynell	early	139

Recipient		Date	Page
86.	Wilfrid Meynell	February	140
87.	Wilfrid Meynell	mid-March	141
88.	Coventry Patmore	March	142
89.	Wilfrid Meynell	April	144
90.	Coventry Patmore	summer	145
91.	Wilfrid Meynell·	May 2	147
92.	Wilfrid Meynell	May 11	148
93.	Wilfrid Meynell	May	151
94.	Wilfrid Meynell	May	152
95.	Monica Meynell	May 18	152
96.	Monica Meynell	May	153
97.	Wilfrid Meynell	May 21	154
98.	Alice Meynell	early June	156
99.	Wilfrid Meynell	June 11	173
100.	Coventry Patmore	June	174
101.	Harriet Patmore	late June	177
102.	Wilfrid Meynell	July 28	178
103.	Coventry Patmore	mid-August	178
104.	Wilfrid Meynell	August	180
105.	Wilfrid Meynell	September 15	182
106.	Wilfrid Meynell	September 27	182
107.	Coventry Patmore	November	184
108.	Arthur Doubleday	November	185
109.	Harriet Patmore	November 30	186
110.	Wilfrid Meynell	early December	187
111.	Wilfrid Meynell	early December	187
112.	Wilfrid Meynell	December 17	188
113.	Wilfrid Meynell	December 23	189

1897

114.	Charles Lewis Hind	April	189
115.	Wilfrid Whitten	late April	190
116.	William Archer	May 31	191
117.	Charles Lewis Hind	June	193
118.	Alfred Hayes	summer	194
119.	Charles Lewis Hind	November 2	195
120.	Unknown	November 5	195
121.	William Hyde	fall	196

Recipient	Date	Page

1898

122. Arthur Doubleday	January 10	198
123. Monica Meynell	January	200
124. Charles Lewis Hind	late March	201
125. Mary Thompson	March	201

1899

126. Charles Lewis Hind	? 1899	202
127. Charles Lewis Hind	? 1899	203
128. Charles Lewis Hind	? 1899	203

1900

129. Unknown	late May	204
130. Wilfrid Meynell	late June	206
131. Wilfrid Meynell	July 19	207
132. Wilfrid Meynell	September 11	211
133. Wilfrid Meynell	fall	211
134. Wilfrid Meynell	October	212
135. Wilfrid Whitten	mid-November	213
136. Wilfrid Meynell	December 24	215
137. Wilfrid Meynell	? late 1900	218
138. Charles Lewis Hind	? late 1900	219

1901

139. Wilfrid Meynell	January	220
140. Wilfrid Meynell	January	220
141. Wilfrid Meynell	February 12	221
142. Editor, the *Nineteenth Century*	February 12	222
143. Everard Meynell	August 14	222
144. William Archer	summer	223
145. Charles Lewis Hind	November	224
146. Wilfrid Meynell	fall	225
147. Wilfrid Meynell	December 24	226
148. Monica Meynell	late December	227

1902

149. Wilfred Meynell	May	228
150. Charles Lewis Hind	June	229
151. Charles Lewis Hind	September	230

Recipient	**Date**	**Page**

152. Monica Meynell	late	230
153. Alice Meynell	December	231
154. Alice Meynell	December 27	232

1903

155. Wilfrid Meynell	May	232
156. Monica Meynell	June 14	233
157. Wilfrid Meynell	October	234

1904

| 158. Everard Meynell | June 23 | 235 |

1905

159. Wilfrid Meynell	January	236
160. Everard Meynell	January 15	236
161. Editor, *The Academy*	February 5	237
162. Wilfrid Meynell	February 5	237
163. Everard Meynell	May 2	238
164. Everard Meynell	June 12	239
165. Everard Meynell	July 8	240
166. Everard Meynell	July 22	241
167. Everard Meynell	July 24	241
168. Everard Meynell	July 27	242
169. Everard Meynell	August 2	243
170. Everard Meynell	August 3	244
171. Everard Meynell	August 8	245
172. Everard Meynell	August 12	246
173. Everard Meynell	August 14	248
174. Everard Meynell	August 16	249
175. Everard Meynell	August 17	249
176. Wilfrid Meynell	August 31	250
177. Wilfrid Meynell	December	250

1906

178. Mrs. Elizabeth Blackburn	mid-January	252
179. Wilfrid Meynell	early February	254
180. Wilfrid Meynell	late February	256
181. Wilfrid Meynell	March 5	259
182. Wilfrid Meynell	May	260
183. Wilfrid Meynell	May 9	261

Recipient	**Date**	**Page**
184. Everard Meynell	summer	262
185. Everard Meynell	fall	263
	1907	
186. Wilfrid Meynell	February 22	264
187. Wilfrid Meynell	spring	264
188. Alice Meynell	September 14	266
Index		268

NOTE ON ABBREVIATIONS

EM. *The Life of Francis Thompson* by Everard Meynell. Burns and Oates Ltd., London, 1913.

VM I. *Alice Meynell, A Memoir* by Viola Meynell. Burns and Oates Ltd., London, 1929.

VM II. *Francis Thompson and Wilfrid Meynell* by Viola Meynell. Hollis and Carter, London, 1952.

Essays I. *Literary Criticism* by Francis Thompson, ed. by Rev. T. L. Connolly. E. P. Dutton, New York, 1948.

Essays II. *The Real Robert Louis Stevenson and Other Critical Essays* by Francis Thompson, ed. by Rev. T. L. Connolly. University Publishers, Inc., New York, 1959.

1. To Wilfrid Meynell

February 23/87

Dear Sir,

In enclosing the accompanying article for your inspection, I must ask pardon for the soiled state of the manuscript. It is due, not to slovenliness, but to the strange places and circumstances under which it has been written. For me, no less than Parolles, the dirty nurse Experience has something fouled. I enclose a stamped envelope for a reply; since I do not desire the return of the manuscript, regarding your judgment of its worthlessness as quite final. I can hardly expect that where my prose fails my verse will succeed. Nevertheless, on the principle of "yet will I try the last," I have added a few specimens of it, with the off-chance that one may be less poor than the rest. Apologizing very sincerely for my intrusion on your valuable time, I remain,

Yours with little hope,
Francis Thompson

Kindly address your rejection to the Charing Cross Post Office. *The Editor of "Merry England"*.

> Accompanying the letter was the essay "Paganism Old and New" and at least two poems: *The Passion of Mary* and *Dream-Tryst*. Meynell did not read the manuscripts for about three months, and when he tried to contact Thompson there was no response. In a last effort to reach him Meynell published *The Passion of Mary* in the April 1888 *Merry England*.

2. To Wilfrid Meynell

April 14th 1888

Dear Sir,

In the last days of February or the first days of March, 1877, [for 1887] (my memory fails me as to the exact date) I forwarded to you for your magazine a prose article, ("Paganism, Old & New," or "Ancient & Modern," for I forget which wording I adopted) and accompanied it by some pieces of verse, on the chance that if the prose failed, some of the verse might meet acceptance. I enclosed a stamped envelope for a reply, since (as I said) I did not desire the return of the manuscript. Imprudently perhaps, instead of forwarding the parcel through the post, I dropped it with my own hand into the letterbox of 43 Essex Street. There was consequently no stamp on it, since I did not think a stamp would be necessary under the circumstances. I asked you to address your answer to the Charing Cross Post Office. To be brief, from that day to this, no answer has ever come into my hands. And yet, more than a twelvemonth since the forwarding of the manuscript, I am now informed that one of the copies of verse which I submitted to you (i.e. "The Passion of Mary") is appearing in this month's issue of "Merry England." Such an occurrence I can only explain to myself in one way; viz. that some untoward accident cut off your means of communicating with me. To suppose otherwise,—to suppose it intentional—would be to wrong your known honour and courtesy. I have no doubt that your explanation, when I receive it, will be entirely satisfactory to me. I therefore enclose a stamped and addressed envelope for an answer, hoping that you will recompense me for my long delay by the favour of an early reply. In any case, however long circumstances may possibly delay your reply, it will be sure of reaching me at the address I have now given.

I remain,
Yours respectfully,
Francis Joseph Thompson

P.S. Doubtless, when I received no answer, I ought to have written again. My excuse must be that a flood-tide of misfortune rolled over me, leaving me no leisure to occupy myself with what I regarded as an attempt that had hopelessly failed. Hence my entire subsequent silence.

> Thompson had been informed of the appearance of *The Passion of Mary* by Canon John Carroll, an old friend from Ashton. The new address he supplied was the chemist shop of Edward Thomas at 44 Drury Lane. The "flood-tide of misfortune" was his descent to street dereliction. A meeting took place about mid-May at the *Merry England* office, and with Meynell's guidance and encouragement Thompson began his rehabilitation.

3. To Wilfrid Meynell

Storrington Priory,
Monday [February 1889]

Dear Mr. Meynell,

I am, as I expected to be, very ill just now; so that you must excuse me if I confine my letter to what is necessary.

In the first place, Mrs. Blackburn spoke of forwarding me some
boots. If you can do so, I should be very much obliged, for those
I have are completely worn out. In the second place, principally
owing to my boots being worn through, my socks are likewise beyond repair. You did send me one pair on the day I came here: if
you could manage to let me have another pair, no doubt that would,
with care, be sufficient for some time. And I want to make a request
which looks rather like a luxury, but which I believe to be a necessity in my present position. Can you send me a razor? I shall have
to shave myself here, I think; & it would of course be a saving of
expense in the long run. Any kind of a razor would do for me; I
have shaved with a dissecting-scalpel before now. I would solve the
difficulty by not shaving at all, if it were possible for me to grow a
beard; but repeated experiment has convinced me that the only result of such action is to make me look like an escaped convict.
Finally, with regard to the books which Mrs. Blackburn spoke of
your sending. Do not let what I have said regarding my illness delay
you in that. It is true I am not at present capable of writing; but
it would be an absolute mercy to have any books. At present there
is nothing to keep my mind from dwelling on itself. I may say I
shall want even a Shakespeare for the *"Dublin"* article, since I
believe they have not one here. I wish they had. I could easily find
distraction for my mind there. And with regard to my illness, there
is nothing to be alarmed about. It is severer & more obstinate than
I had hoped would be the case; but it is a mere matter of holding
on. And in that kind of passive endurance I am well practiced. I
daresay this week will see the end of it.

I think I shall like this place when I begin again to like any
thing. The want of books is the principal drawback so far as I see

at present. Let me say that I keep on my legs, and force myself to go out as much as possible.

Give my kind remembrances to Mrs. Blackburn. And, oh, please, when you send me anything, let me, if you can, have Mrs. Meynell's article which you promised I should see.

Yours very sincerely,
Francis Thompson

Please accept my warmest thanks for all your kindness & trouble on my behalf. I know this is a very perfunctory-looking letter; but until the first sharp struggle is over, it is difficult for me to write in any other way. Once again, however, there is no cause at all for uneasiness on that account.

> Thompson had been sent to the monastery at Storrington probably because he had shown signs of relapsing into addiction in the early days of 1889. Mrs. Elizabeth Blackburn was a friend and editorial assistant of Meynell. The Shakespeare article was "The Macbeth Controversy" (*Dublin Review*, July 1889), basically a review of a book by Comyns Carr.

4. To Wilfrid Meynell

[Storrington,
May 1889]

The *Dublin* article having been sent I write to ask you for more work, or directions as to work. I am afraid, however, that even if there is room for it the article will hardly be on time, and that through my own fault. I miscalculated the date, from Father Driffield's letter, and seeing no newspapers did not discover my error till I came to post it. Even if I had known, though, I hardly think I could have finished it a day earlier, for I worked so badly to begin with. This is something like a confession of failure, and I am naturally chagrined about it. But I have one comfort from the affair: I not only hope but think (though until I see how I proceed with my next book I will not speak decidedly) that it has broken me to harness. You ask me to write frankly and so I will tell you just how I have found myself get on with my work. At first I could not get on at all. I tried regularly enough to settle myself to writing; but my brain would not work. Then gradually, after long pushing, my brain began slowly to move. It has not gone very fast since nor gone willingly, but I have been able to make it go regularly. During the last four days I wrote at a pretty uniform rate, and wrote so continuously as I have never been able to write before—in fact more continuously than I mean to write again, except in an emergency like this—I began to feel very shaken at the end of it. But the valuable thing is that I was able to make myself write when and for as long as I pleased. If I have indeed begun to acquire the power of working in the teeth of nerves and mood and bilious melancholy, then the fight is half fought. And I think I have. I want some more work now, lest if left to myself I may lose a habit scarcely acquired . . .

The only two ideas in my head both require books. The one is for an article on Dryden, the other an old idea for an article on "Idylls of the King". Very likely my idea with regard to the latter has long been anticipated: so that to prevent any possible waste of labor, let me briefly explain it. I have seen it objected to them that there are only the slightest and most arbitrary narrative links between them and that they form no real sequence. My idea is to show that they have not a narrative, but a moral sequence. (I have nothing to do with the allegory). Tennyson's idea has been to show the gradual disruption of Arthur's court and realm through the "little pitted speck in garnered fruit" of Guinevere's sin, which "rotting inward slowly moulders all." This he does by a series of separate pictures each exhibiting in a progressive style the disintegrating process. Each exhibits some definite development of decaying virtue in court or kingdom. Viewed in this light they have a real relation to each other which is that of their common relation to the central idea. It is a *crescendo* of moral laxity; and throughout, by constant little side touches, he keeps before my mind how all this is sprung from the daily visible sin of the Queen's life. That is the idea: judge for yourself if it is worth anything. If you have any work ready for me I should prefer to do that; I think I could now do work not originated by myself . . .

Quoted from edited versions in VM II, p. 31, and EM, pp. 100–2. The additional paragraph given in EM, p. 102, as belonging to this letter really belongs to another quoted in EM, pp. 103–4 (no. 6 below). Neither of the article ideas was pursued.

5. To Wilfrid Meynell

[Storrington,
September 1889]

. . . I have done so principally because I remember more of him [Shelley] than any other poet (though that is saying little). Coleridge was always my favourite poet; but I early recognised that to make him a model was like trying to run up a window-pane, or to make clotted cream out of moonlight, or to pack jelly-fish in hampers. So that until I was twenty-two Shelley was more studied by me than anyone else. At the same time I am exposed to the danger of talking platitudes, because so much has been written of Shelley of late years which I have never read. I may have one or two questions to ask you in relation to the subject as I go on. Thank you for the American paper. Only the poet feels complimented. Your criticisms on the *Merry England* article were (for once in a way) entirely anticipated by my own impressions. Happy are they that hear their detractions and can put them to mending. With regard to what you say about the advantage of my being in a more booky place than Storrington I entirely agree. Nor need you fear the opium. I have learned the advantage of being without it for mental exercise; and (still more important) I have learned to bear my fits of depression without it. Personally I no longer fear it.

> Quoted from EM, p. 96. The "American paper" (unidentified) may have contained a reprint of *Dream-Tryst*. Three articles by Thompson appeared in *Merry England* in 1889, prior to September: "Literary Coincidence," "Crashaw," and "The Error of the Extreme Realists."

6. To Wilfrid Meynell

Storrington Priory,
Thursday [January 1890]

Dear Mr. Meynell,

How good and kind and patient you are with me! far more so than I am with myself, for I am often fairly sick of the being that inhabits this villainous mud-hut of a body. I received the medicine all right. Lilly's book I will not detain beyond the end of the week, whether or not I am able to get it reviewed by then. I was, for four or five days, much better, but I am sorry to say that it did not last. Having noticed that the attacks come on principally during the half-sleep of early night or early morning, I sat up the greater part of the night in order to tire myself into heavy sleep. The device was successful during the four nights that I kept it up; but the first night that weariness caused me to drop it, the attack returned. I must, however, count it something gained that the consequences are no longer so severe as they were, and I have hopes that the thing may gradually be loosening its hold upon me. I beguiled the four nights I have spoken of, while the mental cloud was somewhat lifted, by writing the verses I herewith send you. If there be no saving-grace of poetry in them, they are damned; for I am painfully conscious that they display me, in every respect, at my morally weakest. Indeed no one but yourself—or, to be more accurate, your-selves—would I have allowed to see them; for verse written as I write it is often nothing less than a confessional, a confessional far more intimate than the sacerdotal one. *That* touches only your sins, and leaves in merciful darkness your ignominious, if sinless, weaknesses. If there be poetry in your verse, the poetry may con-done the weakness; but if there be not—and that means nine times out of ten—it requires some confidence to give anyone the oppor-tunity of becoming acquainted with it. When the soul goes forth, like Andersen's Emperor, thinking herself clothed round with sing-ing-robes, while in reality her naked weakness is given defenceless to the visiting wind, not every mother's son would you allow to gaze on you at such a time. And the shorter of the two pieces especially is such a self-revelation, I feel, as even you have hardly had from me before. Something in them may be explained to you, and perhaps a little excused, by the newspaper-cutting I forward. For some inscrutable reason it has affected me as if I never expected it. I knew of it beforehand, I thought I was familiarised with the idea; yet when the newspaper came as I sat at dinner, and I saw her name among so many familiar names, I pushed away the remainder of my dinner, and—well, I will not say what I did. I have been mis-erable ever since. The fact is my nerves want taking up like an Atlantic cable, and recasing. I am sometimes like a dispossessed hermit-crab, looking about everywhere for a new shell, and quivering at every touch. Figuratively speaking, if I prick my finger I seem to feel it with my whole body.

I gather from her last poem that Miss Tynan is no longer with you, or I should hardly have sent the longer verses; for I feel that I have taken a perhaps unwarrantable liberty in apostrophising her, even in her poetical and therefore public capacity. I can only plead that verse, like "l'Amour" in Carmen's song,

> "est un Boheme,
> Et n'a jamais, jamais connu de loi."

The thing would not write itself otherwise. She happened to set the current of my thought, and I could not quit the current. Let me add, lest I should be accused of insincerity, that although "Moods" furnished me with my test, it was the poet of "Poppies" and the "Dreamers" . . .

> Ms. incomplete. Thompson's review of *A Century of Revolution*, by W. S. Lilly, appeared in *Weekly Register*, April 12, 1890. The two poems that accompanied the letter were *The Sere of the Leaf* and perhaps *Daphne*, or *Daisy*. The illness was some kind of stomach trouble; the medicine was prescribed and sent by his father.

7. To Wilfrid Meynell

[Storrington,
February 1890]

. . . *Shelley* was sent off yesterday. Herewith a few fugitive verses I spoke of. With regard to the article, please take no notice of any writing on the backs of the sheets, and disregard all pencilled writing, either front or back. The opening is carefully constructed so that, if you think advisable, you can detach it, and leave the article to commence on page 10 . . .

> Quoted from EM, p. 96. The fugitive verses were probably *To a Dead Astronomer*, and perhaps *Buona Notte*, but it is difficult to be certain what poems Thompson sent from Storrington since a half-dozen poems written at the time did not reach print until after his death.

8. To Wilfrid Meynell

> Storrington,
> Friday [early March 1890]

Dear Mr. Meynell,

Many thanks for your letter. I write hurriedly to say that I have not money for my travelling-expenses. Consequently unless you can send it me by Monday morning I shall be in a rather awkward position. If you send, please send stamps, as those are most quickly and easily changed.

Nothing preventing, I shall arrive at Victoria 2:33 p.m. Train leaves Pulboro at 12:53, and the train on from Horsham leaves at 1:30—a fast train with but one stoppage.

Surprised about *Shelley*. Seemed to me dreadful trash when I read it over before sending it. Shut my eyes and ran to the post, or some demon might have set me to work unpicking it again. Don't see but what we can easily draw the knife out of your heart by knocking out the praise of Swinburne. Won't grieve you if we leave in the disparaging part of the comparison, I hope? And I dare say you are perfectly right about it. Fact is, don't know much about Swinburne, and I was afraid to abuse him too whole-heartedly. At the same time made the comparison to get opportunity of dropping in two or three "bits."

> Yours most sincerely,
> Francis Thompson

Just met and said good-bye to *Daisy's* sister-blossom—or blossom-sister—Violet. Last four of the family all flowers—Rose, Daisy, Lily and Violet (commonly called Baby). Received an interesting account of how they used to have "thirty rabbits, seven chickens, two pigs, and a *cock-a rooster.*" Now reduced to two lonely rabbits. Inquired cause of mysterious disappearance. "Eaten them." [illegible] (as we used to say at Ushaw) there are nine children in the family.

> Daisy (the original of the poem so named) and her sisters were children of a family named Stanford that lived about a mile from the monastery, at Cootham. Thompson would encounter them going to and from school and sometimes walked home with them.

9. To Wilfrid Meynell

Friday [March 1890]

Dear Mr. Meynell,

For fear you should think that I have been neglecting to see you, I just write a line to say that I called at the office on Wednesday, but found the door locked; so that I concluded you were not coming there that day. I have received the clothes, for which many thanks. Also Mr. Sharp's new *Life of Browning,* which I have about half read already. This reminds me to do what I have been intending to do for a long time past; but whenever I wrote to you, my mind was always occupied with something else which put the subject out of my head. I had better do it now, for even my unready pen will say better what I wish to say than would my still more unready tongue. It is simply that I wanted to tell you how deeply I was moved by the reading of Browning's letter in *Merry England.* When you first mentioned it to me, you quoted loosely a simple sentence; and I answered, I think, something to the effect that I was very pleased by what he had said. So I was; pleased at what I thought his kindliness, for (misled by the form in which you had quoted the sentence from memory) I did not take it more seriously than that. When I saw *Merry England,* I perceived that the original sentence was insusceptible of the interpretation which I had placed upon your quotation of it. And the idea that in the closing days of his life my writings should have been under his eye, and he should have sent me praise and encouragement, is one which I shall treasure to the closing days of *my* life. To say that I owe this to you is to say little. I already told you that long before I had seen you, you exercised, unknown to myself, the most decisive influence over my mental development when without such an influence my mental development was like to have utterly failed. And so to you I owe not merely Browning's notice, but also that ever I should have been worth his notice. The little flowers you sent him were sprung from your own seed. I only hope that the time may not be far distant when better and less scanty flowers may repay the pains, and patience, and tenderness of your gardening.

As for the book, I am sorry to say that Mr. Sharp must have rushed it through the press in a way that only pecuniary necessity could justify any writer in doing. His characteristic defects run riot in a way that it is only fair to ascribe to breathless haste. One painfully conspicuous trait, however, cannot be ascribed to haste. Will no one suggest to Mr. Sharp that Holofernes in *Love's* . . .

> Ms. incomplete. The letter was written soon after Thompson's return to London from Storrington. His review of William Sharp's life of Browning appeared in *Merry England*, July 1890. Browning's letter to Wilfrid Meynell, written on October 7, 1889, in which he called Thompson's prose and poetry "remarkable," was printed in the January 1890 *Merry England*, with Thompson's name deleted. Browning died on December 12, 1889.

10. To Canon John Carroll

25, Third Avenue, Queen's Park, W.

A.D. 1890
Finished August 12. Begun,
Heaven knows when. [May]

Dear Canon,

I must beg your and everybody's pardon for my long silence. The fact is that I have been for months in a condition of acute mental misery, frequently almost akin to mania, stifling the production of everything except poetry, and rendering me quite incapable of sane letter-writing. Some of the productions which have been inflicted upon Mr. Meynell would bear ample witness to this, if you could see them (which, thank heaven, you can't). It has ended in my return to London, and I am immensely relieved; for the removal of the opium had quite destroyed my power of bearing the almost unbroken solitude in which I found myself. I am now just recovering from an attack of Russian influenza—comparatively mild, but sufficient to leave my digestion very disordered, myself easily tired, and my head apt to get sodden after an hour or so of use. I am sorry to hear that you have been so ill, and hope you may now be quite better. The medicine which Papa sent me was effectual. Which cured me I don't know—I took both, one after the other, and gradually recovered. As for my prospects, unfortunately the walls of the Protestant periodical press remain still unshaken and to shake. I have done recently a review of Lilly's *Century of Revolution* for the *Register,* which has, I fancy, appeared, but in some number which I have not seen. Poor work, and I don't want to see it. Also a review of Mr. Sharp's recent *Life of Browning* (a little book in Walter Scott's "Great Writers' Series") which may or may not appear in the *Register*—it is only just finished. No doubt you saw in the famous January "Merry England" Browning's letter about me. It is, I see, alluded to in Mr. Sharp's "Life". Sharp's book has been remarkably successful, no doubt because it has come out just during the Browning boom, and has no rival. But it is badly written, and therefore very difficult to review. He is a young poet, a friend and disciple of Rossetti, of whom he published Reminiscences which gave me a kindly feeling towards him. He is also a personal friend of Mr. Meynell; so that literary sincerity becomes impossible to me. You don't know how one is hampered in these ways. As for the verses published in this month's "Merry England", I don't know why they were published at all. Mr. Meynell told me himself that he did not care particularly for them, because they were too like a poem of Mrs. Browning's. (You will find the poem—a poem on Pan making a pipe out of a reed—where it first appeared; namely in one of your two old volumes of the "Cornhill Magazine." There I read it; and it is a great favourite of mine. The last two stanzas, with their sudden deeply pathetic turn of thought, are most felicitous, I think). The verses on Father Perry in last month's "Merry England" were the first verses of mine that attracted any praise from Catholic outsiders. An old priest wrote from Norwich expressing his admiration; and Father Philip Fletcher (who contributes the pleasant, gossipy signed articles to the "Register") also praised them to Mr. Meynell. This must have been grateful to Mr. Meynell, for his previous experience had been very different. Good Uncle Edward (whom I shall write to after you, now that I am taking up my arrears of correspondence) writing about my first two little poems, liked "The Passion of Mary", but styled "Dream-Tryst" "erotic". I charitably suppose him to have merely meant that it was a love-poem; though the word more often bears a not very pleasant signification. As a matter of fact, however, "Dream-Tryst" is not even a love-poem (though I admit it reads like one). Anyone can see that it is an utterance of genuine personal feeling; therefore it could not be a love-poem, for I never in my life was in love. Every love-poem that I have written has been a failure, showing clearly that I cannot write dramatically. But the *Ode* brought Mr. Meynell a genuine annoyance, at which he did not merely smile. (Please consider this letter strictly confidential, and let nothing in it, which involves anyone besides myself, go beyond you and my father. The ramifications of Mr. Meynell's acquaintance extend over England, and things would quickly filter back to him if talked about, besides the mischief they might do him with others. Therefore in giving you the intimate private details which I am giving you, I am writing as to one whose discretion I can absolutely rely on). Who do you think chose to put himself in a ferment about the "Ode"? Canon Toole! When the editor of the "Tablet" was in Manchester, Canon Toole attacked him about the article on me which appeared in that paper. What, he asked, was the "Ode" all about? He couldn't in the least understand what it was all about. But even if he had understood it, he was quite sure that it was not a thing which ought to have appeared in a Catholic magazine! And Mr. Meynell subsequently received an anonymous letter, which he believes (though he does not know, for he has no proof) to have been inspired by Canon Toole; and in it he was warned against publishing anything more of mine, since it would be found in the end that paganism was at the bottom of it. This with regard to me, who began my literary career with an elaborate indictment of the ruin which the re-introduction of the pagan spirit must bring upon poetry! A person of only ordinary intellect might have supposed it neither wise nor charitable to attack what he confessedly did not understand; but Canon Toole is apparently not a person of ordinary intellect. As for the "Song of the Hours", to which you referred, Mr. Meynell was greatly pleased with it; but considered that while it avoided the violence of diction which deformed the "Ode", it was not equal to that in range of power. He has another poem of about equal length which he thinks has "some very fine things in it"; but though a month ago he thought of publishing it, he has apparently altered his mind.

I am not sorry; for the poem, addressed to Miss Tynan (of course in her public capacity) contained some very over-coloured eulogy. I have lost hopes of Miss Tynan, and am no longer in the mood to pay her so tremendous a compliment as this poem. Since she published her . . .

The article on Shelley which you asked about I finished at last, with quite agonising pain and elaboration. It might have been written in tears, and is proportionately dear to me. I fear, however, that it will not be accepted, or will be accepted only with such modifications as will go to my heart. It has not been inserted in the current issue of the "Dublin"—a fact which looks ominous. Firstly, you see, I prefaced it by a fiery attack on Catholic Philistinism (exemplified in Canon Toole, though I was not aware about him at the time I wrote the article), driven home with all the rhetoric which I could muster. That is pretty sure to be a stumbling-block. I consulted Mr. Meynell as to its suppression, but he said leave it in. I suspect that he thoroughly agrees with it. Secondly, it is written at an almost incessant level of poetic prose, and seethes with imagery like my poetry itself. Now the sober, ponderous, ecclesiastical "Dublin" confronted with poetic prose must be considerably scared. The editor probably cannot make up his mind whether it is heavenly rhetoric or infernal nonsense. And in the midst of my vexation at feeling what a thankless waste of labour it is, I cannot help a sardonic grin at his conjectured perplexity. Mr. Meynell's opinion was couched almost exactly as follows. "*Shelley* is splendid; all except the Swinburne passages, in which your praise of the [word illegible] sounding verse of Swinburne, stabs me to the heart. The lovely little lyric in this month's *Merry England* (by which he meant "Daisy") is worth all the *Poems and Ballads* put together." So the passages praising the author of *Poems and Ballads* were eliminated before sending the article to the *Dublin*. Mr. Meynell paid me a pretty compliment about the said *Daisy* on the night of my return to London. I was at his house, fighting a losing battle on behalf of Swinburne, when little Monica Meynell entered the room. He introduced me to her, and asked, "Is she taller than Daisy?" I thought that she was, a trifle. "Mr. Thompson", he explained to her, "has a friend called Daisy, and he has written some very beautiful poetry to her, which

I wish had been written to you, my dear!" One little bit of praise, too, I got, in connection with the Shelley article, which I valued a great deal, because it was in reference to something outside my own province. In a footnote I had remarked, "Is not Brahms the Browning of music?" As I have no technical knowledge of music, and little knowledge of Brahms, I thought that the comparison might be false. So when Mr. Meynell began to question me as to where I had heard Brahms, I asked what he thought of the comparison. "I am no judge in the matter", he replied, "but I will tell you what one who is a judge said. I read your article to Mrs. Meynell; and when I came to that bit, she cried at once, 'Oh, how exactly true.'" I wonder what she does not know! A mistress of poetry, an exquisite art-critic, she knows, besides, music, Latin, Greek, Italian, French, German, and all kinds of multifarious things at which I can but dimly guess.

And now I hope this letter is long enough to make some amends for all the letters which you ought to have had. With kindest remembrances to all,

I remain, Yours sincerely,
Francis Thompson

July

Since I wrote the foregoing pages a considerable time has elapsed. How long, I do not know, for they were written at intervals, and so were not dated. My health has been consistently bad; though I have had, and have, nothing definite the matter with me, except dyspepsia and constant colds. My writing powers have deserted me, and I have suffered failure after failure, till I have been too despondent to have any heart for writing to you. Much, no doubt, is due to this infernal weather. Confined to the house and deprived of sunlight, I droop like a moulting canary. It was not so when you knew me; but my vital power has been terribly sapped since then. Only air and exercise keep me going now. I was told by Mr. Meynell that you had been in London. He unfortunately forgot to mention to you that I had left Storrington, or perhaps I might have had the pleasure of seeing you. As to the literary enterprises alluded to in the early part of this letter, they have successively failed. The Browning article proved dull. What Mr.

Meynell has thought at all presentable appears in the *Reviews and Views* of the July "Merry England". I do not suppose that he would have thought it worth while to do so much, but that Mr. Sharp is his friend, and it was necessary to give the book some notice. There can now be no doubt that the "Dublin Review" has rejected my article on "Shelley". Nothing has been heard of it since it was sent. I only hope that they have not lost the MS. That would be to lose the picked fruit of three painful months—a quite irreparable loss. Mr. Meynell's remark was,—"Well, if they reject that, it will be a commentary on the condition of Catholic literature." I am not surprised, myself. What is a poor ecclesiastical editor to do when confronted with something so *sui generis* as this—my friends' favourite passage, and the only one which I can remember. I had been talking of the "Cloud", and remarking that it displayed "the childish faculty of make-believe, raised to the nth power". In fact, I said, Shelley was the child, still at play, though his play-things were larger. Then I burst into prose-poetry. "The universe is his box of toys. He dabbles his hands in the sunset. He is gold-dusty with tumbling amid the stars. He makes bright mischief with the moon. He teases into growling the kennelled thunder, and laughs at the shaking of its fiery chain. He dances in and out of the gates of heaven. He runs wild over the fields of ether. He chases the rolling world. He gets between the feet of the horses of the sun. He stands in the lap of patient Nature, and twines her loosened tresses after a hundred wilful fashions, to see how she will look nicest in his poetry." The editor sees at once that here is something such as he has never encountered before. Personally, I recollect nothing like it in English prose. In French prose I could point to something not so dissimilar—in Victor Hugo. But not in English. De Quincey is as boldly poetical, and his strain far higher; but he is poetical after quite another style. The editor feels himself out of his latitude. He is probably a person of only average literary taste: that is, he can tell the literary hawk from the literary handsaw when the wind is southerly. The poor man feels that discretion is the better part of valour. The thing may be very good, may be very bad. But it is beyond or below his comprehension. So he rejects it. Twelve years hence (if he live so long) he will feel uncomfortable should anyone allude to that rejection. Unless he has lost the MS. In that case the thing is gone for ever. Possibly, also, (as I am inclined to think) Canon Toole may have spread his opinions of me in high quarters, and so my writings may be regarded with suspicion. He has certainly frightened the editor of the "Tablet". I had a commission (through Mr. Meynell) to write an article for the jubilee number of the "Tablet"; but the editor took fright at its tone, and would have nothing to do with it when it was written. I had said that Cardinal Wiseman too often wrote like a brilliant schoolboy, (I *might* have said that, as regards his style, he seldom wrote like anything else;) with other sins of omission and commission which Mr. Cox clearly thought likely to bristle the hair of the Canon Tooles. My only available revenge was to describe him to his own sub-editor as "a Philistine with the chill off"—a description which the said sub-editor thought decidedly accurate. I admire more highly than ever the courage and resource which Mr. Meynell holds on his course through the dense sea of Catholic literary ignorance. He has, in my opinion—an opinion of long standing—done more than any man in these latter days to educate Catholic literary opinion. I was myself virtually his pupil (and his wife's) long before I knew him. He conciliates, and insinuates soothingly his opinions; while I, with my vehement manner of writing, drive a furrow straight ahead, ploughing up prejudice on every side. I recently learned, by the way, that I had a narrow escape when I sent my first MS. to him—was literally snatched like a brand from the burning. He glanced at my MS.; the title, "Paganism Old and New", did not attract him, and he put it away. "We don't take much notice of contributions from outsiders, you know," he said to me. The MS. lay neglected for a long time. At last he was making a general clearance of accumulated MSS.,—"going to have a grand bonfire" as he said; and was looking over them to see that there was nothing of importance among them. His eye was caught by the poetry which accompanied my prose article, and he began (I suspect in jest, though he did not say so) to read it aloud; "with growing astonishment." The sequel you know. Here I must pause tonight: my last productions I will speak about when I conclude this *mega thauma* in letters.

The lines on Father Perry have taken hold of "Merry England"

readers as nothing else of mine has done. Mr. Meynell had several
letters from ecclesiastics (including one from the head of a monastery—I forget where or in what Order) expressing admiration of the
poem; and the sub-editor of the "Tablet" had one from some
priest in Liverpool. A Mrs. Donnet (who must, Mr. Meynell thinks,
be a sister or some other relation of Father Perry) asked permission
to print the verses on cards for private circulation, as the best
memorial of the Jesuit astronomer. *Quod factum est.* Mr. Vernon
Blackburn's judgment of them I think true. He said he was decidedly taken with them: they did not rise very high, but then they
were not meant to do so. Quite true. I meant the thing merely for
a pretty, gracefully turned fancy; what the Elizabethans would have
called an excellent conceit. That it is nothing more, I quite agree
with Mr. Blackburn, whose judgment I much value. In the first
place he generally represents Mrs. Meynell's judgment, who is his
guide and friend in everything—and such a guide and friend no
other young man in England has. In the second place he has an
excellent judgment of his own. As a critic, he is far in advance
of me; when he reaches my age he will be far in advance of me as
a prose writer. And not improbably he may then be far in advance
of me as a poet, though his poetical development I feel at present
less able to forecast. The poem published in this month's "Merry
England" Mrs. Blackburn thinks the best I have done. Her judgment is certainly good, but I am as yet not sufficiently acquainted
with it to know what may be its limitations; so I give this simply as
her individual criticism. Of Mr. Meynell's opinion, I know merely
that he dropped me a post-card saying the poem was "very fine".
Another very small poem on Shelley, Mrs. Meynell (according to
Mrs. Blackburn) has pronounced "a little masterpiece." The expression, however, may have been hastily and inaccurately reported
by Mrs. Blackburn: I prefer to take it with caution. Yet a third
poem, a sonnet, I have heard nothing about; but I have never really
succeeded with a sonnet. A fourth poem, which I might have
written and did not write, has got me in great disgrace. It was to
have been as long as, or longer than, the "Hound of Heaven". But
there was prose waiting to be written, and I thought that my duty
to Mr. Meynell imperatively required I should sacrifice the poem,
since the "Hound of Heaven" had already engaged me longer than

I had looked for. During a week I struggled with the impulse, which was so strong as to prevent me from writing prose, though I would not yield to it. Then at last I stifled it; and as a result I can write neither prose nor poetry, and have made myself unwell. Mrs. Blackburn strongly disapproved of what I had done. Poetry was the special gift that God had given me, and when I had the impulse it was my duty to work it out. "Ah! if I stood alone!" I said, "but it is injustice to Mr. Meynell." She rejoined that she could quite understand that consideration making me unhappy; but that if there was loss now, it would be repaid him ultimately. "With regard to some of his *protégés* I think, and sometimes tell him, that he is wasting support and encouragement on worthless people; but I have no such feeling at all with regard to you." I acknowledged that I had had a strong impression that the poem would be for mere beauty—not for power or thought—the best that I had done. "Then write it, by all means." "I can't now; the impulse is past." "There, you see!" she said. Then I confessed that it was to have been addressed to two of Mr. Meynell's children; and she was downright vexed. "Oh, I wish you had written it," she said. "Oh, you horrid boy! To think that those creatures should have been so near immortality. I hope it will come back to you." I shook my head and said that if ever it did, it would not be while this weather lasted: it would need air and sunlight to rekindle the poem. She has informed me since that when Mrs. Meynell was told of it she "simply wrung her hands"; and Mr. Meynell said that I had acted very foolishly, and was never to do such a thing again. "I told them you had had a good scolding for it; and so there was no more to be done", said Mrs. Blackburn. I had no idea that it would give them any particular pleasure, or I would not have throttled it. I thought I should be consulting only my own selfish pleasure in writing the poem. Now I am miserably endeavouring to resuscitate it; neither able to write it or leave it alone. And I am despondent and wretched. One of Mr. Meynell's children, by the way, was the heroine of one of the funniest child-stories I have heard for some time. I was at his house the other night, and he was upstairs saying good-night to the children. Presently he came into the drawing-room, and said (addressing his wife by her familiar name) "——, do you know that your daughter Prue means to carry her tale-bearing habits into the other world?" "What do you mean?" asked Mrs. Meynell, laughing. "Why, she and Dimpling were saying their prayers; and she caught Dimpling smiling. 'Dimpling', she said, 'you ought to be ashamed of yourself. You're a year and eight months older than I am, and yet you're laughing at your prayers. *I shall tell God of you when I get to Heaven!*' "

August

I have been re-reading what I said regarding my rejected Shelley article, and I see that you might possibly interpret my language as referring to its *merit*. This would make my words read arrogantly in the extreme. When I said that I knew nothing just like it in the language, I was speaking of its *kind*, its style. As to the *merit* of that style, I have ventured no opinion of my own, but simply given you my friends' opinion. I am so poor a judge of my own work, that they never pay any attention to what I think about it. Please always bear this in mind. You may be sure that in speaking about my own work I always follow the same rule, to tell you merely what my friends say as to its merit. As to the little poem on Shelley of which I have spoken, whether or not Mrs. Meynell used the expression "a little masterpiece", there seems no doubt that they particularly admire it. So far as I understand from Mr. Blackburn, they prefer it to the "Hound of Heaven". You are hardly likely to see it however, for there are reasons why it might give offence to touchy members of the Catholic constituency. Mr. Meynell has been away for his holidays; and during the first week of his absence, the editor of the "Tablet" was likewise away. During that week the two chief Catholic papers, one Tory and Unionist, and the other Liberal and Home-Rule, were edited by mother and son; for Mrs. Blackburn edited the "Register" and Mr. Blackburn the "Tablet". As a result, I did a little minor work on the "Tablet"—part of the Chronicle of the Week, and two or three of the Notes, including a paragraph on Rudyard Kipling and a ferocious little onslaught on the trashy abomination which Swinburne has contributed to the "Fortnightly." That man is a melancholy instance of what comes from insincerity. Some of his early work was beautiful, as even Mr. Meynell will admit in individual instances. You saw, I suppose, Mr. Blackburn's admirable little article on Henley in a recent "Tablet"—the very best thing he has yet done. It marks his literary puberty, if I may use such an expression. His style in it is not yet original; it is strongly influenced by Henley himself. But every young painter graduates from some school; Raphael's early pictures were Peruginesque; and Mr. Blackburn has used his master's style with an individual vigour and cleverness which make it a compliment to Henley to be so imitated. It is very distinguished work for so young a man. He is only twenty-four; yet I consider that in this article he has quite passed the average of my own prose. A little while back I thought he would beat me when he reached my age; and I think he has already done so. He had an excellent letter, up to the same average of style, in last week's "Scots Observer"; in which also appeared an exquisite little poem by Mrs. Meynell—the first she has written since her marriage. A long silence, disastrous for literature! The poem is a perfect miniature example of her most lovelily tender work; and is, like all her best, of a singular originality in its central idea no less than in its development. It is quoted, by the way, in this week's "Tablet". In the current "Scots Observer" she has a little sketch (the product, I hope, of her holiday) finished like an ivory carving. This, like all the four articles she has at times contributed to that paper, should go down to posterity among the very choicest prose-morsels in the language. I hope it was the result of her holidays because unless done under conditions of unusual health, it will have made her ill, as the production of these gems always does. That is why they are so lamentably few. Even after she has written her various art-criticisms on the opening of the London art galleries, she is generally in bed with violent headache; and her ordinary journalistic work is sufficient tax on her frail health. Her soul has indeed "fretted the pigmy body to decay"; but fragile she must always have been. Her youthful portraits show a beautiful, spiritualised face, with musing, saddened eyes; the head, in most portraits, drooped as with the weight of thought. Yet the mournful sweetness of the countenance is preserved from anything merely weak and poetessish (Mrs. Meynell is a poet—something very different from that unendurable creature, the poetess) by its contained quiet. A face which is a poem as beautiful as any she has written. Nor is this prejudice. In the first of these portraits which I saw, I did not recognise her. Yet

I once cried to myself: "What an ideal face that would make for a female poet!" It is a rare thing. Most women of genius—Mrs. Browning, George Eliot, Charlotte Bronte—have been decidedly plain: Mrs. Browning, indeed, alludes to her husband's penetration in seeing beyond "this mask of me"; and Charlotte Bronte, as you know, shows herself painfully conscious of her own plainness. Mrs. Meynell will not attain any rapid notice like them. Her work is of that subtly delicate order which—as with Coleridge, for instance —needs to soak into men for a generation or two before it gets adequate recognition. Nevertheless it is something to have won the admiration of men like Rossetti, Ruskin, Rossetti's bosom-friend Theodore Watts, and, shall I add, the immortal Oscar Wilde? (A witty paradoxical writer, who, nevertheless, *meo judicio*, will do nothing permanent because he is in earnest about nothing). Known or unknown, she cares as little as St. Francis de Sales would have cared what might become of his writings. To return to myself. (When I happen to mention Mrs. Meynell, you must always be prepared for a fervid *excursus*). I am going to try to pierce the barriers of the "Scots Observer", but I anticipate no success. It is a pity; for Henley's paper is not only the most brilliant literary review now appearing, but it is the one periodical where genuine literary style on the part of an unknown writer will not frighten the editor. As he says himself, anything like the style of the pre-journalistic days is caviar to editors. He ought to know, for I believe in his time he has been rejected by every magazine in London. But unfortunately for me, he has most crotchety tastes; as Mr. Blackburn's article will have told you. An admirable critic where he is sympathetic; but given to unexpected, exasperatingly wrong-headed likings and dislikings. Besides those of which Mr. Blackburn has accused him, I may mention that he sets Christina Rossetti far above her brother Dante, and Swinburne far above Shelley; he is impatient of Shelley, and contemptuous of De Quincey. Moreover he hates exuberance in style, he likes short sentences, and detests preaching, philanthropy, sentiment. Now Shelley is my pole-star in poetry, De Quincey in prose; I am given to exuberance, long sentences, sentiment, philanthropy, (in the form of believing goodness to exist even in outcasts), and sometimes to preaching. Clearly, therefore, he ought to detest me. And in fact, I know he dislikes my poetry (says it "reeks of Shelley"), and I expect him to dislike my prose—when he gets any. At present it is like a lady about whom Mr. Blackburn told me—renowned for her Malapropisms. A friend met her in Paris, and was about to address her when the lady put up her hand: "Hush, don't recognize me! I am travelling in embryo." So is my prose article. For the rest, I have made considerable progress with my poem to Mr. Meynell's children—though as to the quality of what I have written I am in the dark. And now I think this letter should be big enough to cover a multitude of sins of omission in my correspondence. I see that you and a number of our friends were at Ushaw for the Exhibition week. The death of my old master, Mr. Formby, to which you referred in your post-card, I saw in the "Register". I was deeply sorry. Wishing not to bring myself under anyone's notice until I felt my position more assured, I had abstained from following my first impulse, which was to send him a copy of the magazine containing my Ode, and accompanying it by a letter. Now I wish I had pocketed pride, and done so. Not knowing my circumstances, he may have thought I had forgotten him. But I had not forgotten him, as I will venture to think he had not forgotten me.

Since I penned these lines (on Friday; it is now Monday), I have written some little verses to Mrs. Meynell, which I submitted to Mr. Blackburn. He returned them with some criticism wonderfully alert and sure-footed for his age (he is certainly my master in criticism!) and when I have made the pretty numerous alterations which he acutely suggests—a delicate, difficult, and anxious task— he is going to try the "Scots Observer" with them. I have really no hope, myself, of the result. He confesses that he is afraid Henley may read the poem once, say "I don't know what the fellow's driving at!" and toss it aside. "For I don't know whether you're aware of it", said Mr. Blackburn, "but one has to read your poetry over twice to understand it. I always have to." I smiled, and said that I should have expected he would require to read most of it more than twice. It was inevitably so, from the abstract nature of the thoughts and subject-matter. At any rate, we shall try the experiment on Henley; but I am prepared for failure. Mr. Blackburn thinks the conclusion of Mrs. Meynell's little sketch in the current

"Scots Observer" one of the very finest things in English prose-
literature. So do I. The whole article should ultimately take rank
among the choicest prose-morsels of the language. With perhaps
one exception, it is the most quintessential prose thing she has
written—the very attar of style. That exception must be made, however, for "The Rhythm of Life" in relation to its different subject-
matter was as exquisitely perfect as this little character-sketch. With
best love to my father, and to Polly when you next may see her
(Maggie, I suppose, will by this time be beyond the reach of
messages), I remain,

Yours affectionately,
Francis Thompson

P.S. My address is still that given at the beginning of this letter,
which is so enormous that I shall have to send it in two envelopes.
I am afraid that you will have to read it by easy stages, unless you
subdivide labour by calling in your curate. By the way, I spoke of
my lines on Shelley as being risky for a Catholic audience. Let me
explain the reason, lest you should suppose something worse. They
are founded on a letter given in Trelawney's "Recollections"; a
letter from Jane Williams to Shelley two days before his death. The
poem is put into the mouth of the dead Shelley, and is supposed to
be addressed by the poet's spirit to Jane while his body is tossing
on the waters of Spezzia. Now Jane Williams was a married woman.
I have carefully avoided anything which might not be addressed by
one warm friend to another; but Catholic readers (witness Canon
Toole) are apt to shy sometimes at shadows. It was, of course,
wrong for Shelley to entertain even an ideal and platonic passion
for another woman while he was himself married, and married to a
woman who truly loved him. But apart from that, I can find no
reason at all for supposing there to have been anything criminal
between them. Had Shelley been unmarried, I should have considered the thing absolutely innocent. When a poet writes love-
verses to a lady, and gives them to her husband for her, it is surely
evident that neither pistols nor divorce-courts are necessary. Now
that is what Shelley did. By the way, if you want the most vivid
and life-like picture I have come across of what both Shelley and
Byron were like to those who knew them intimately, you should

read Trelawney's "Recollections of Shelley, Byron, and the Author." It does not shrink from showing Shelley's unpleasant side, any more than Byron's, and gives the impression of being an unflinching account of the writer's actual experience with them. It makes you almost feel as if you had yourself been in personal communication with the two. By the way, Lady Shelley has in her possession a casket or locket (I forget exactly what) or something of the kind, containing locks of hair of Shelley himself and of all his friends, including Trelawney. When the latter's book appeared, she wrote to him saying that she supposed he would wish to have his hair removed from the collection, since after what he had written he could no longer count himself among Shelley's friends. So she told Mr. Meynell. A clear proof that he has nothing extenuated.

I have just received (Tuesday) a suggestion, which is virtually a request, from Mr. Meynell, that I should write a poem on Newman for the "Register" or "Merry England". To write verses to order in that fashion precludes all chance of its being poetry, and ensures the probability of bad verse. But of course I must do it.

Wednesday—Knocked off three little stanzas for Mr. Meynell. Am going to post this letter, as soon as I see how many envelopes it wants. Will be necessary to number the pages for you. Excuse its being written on scraps of paper. It is such a length that it would have ruined me in note-paper.

> The original of this letter, long in the possession of the Thompson family, was destroyed by Margaret Thompson (Mrs. Richardson) sometime about 1925, while she was living in Canada. Copies, however, had been made by the Meynells in 1909, with the permission of Mary Thompson. A portion of it, containing some frank and uncomplimentary remarks on the poetry of Katharine Tynan, was withheld and is now lost. The extensive quotation of this letter in EM, pp. 123–28, deletes many of its passages without indication, and one whole sentence is probably an interpolation: "That Mrs. Meynell is not like them you may judge from 'Her Portrait'." These words do not appear in the typescript source, though they do reflect the sense of a passage in the same paragraph, not quoted by EM, immediately preceding the sentence. The poem, *Her Portrait*, however, was not written until 1892.
> The poem "published in this month's *Merry England*" was *Daphne*. The poem on Father Perry was *To a Dead Astronomer*.

"Good Uncle Edward" was Edward Healy Thompson. The ode objected to by Canon Toole was *Ode to the Setting Sun*. The *Song of the Hours* appeared in *Merry England*, January 1890. The poem to Miss Tynan, *The Sere of the Leaf*, did not appear until January 1891, in *Merry England*. The Shelley article was rejected by the *Dublin Review* and not published until 1908, the year after Thompson's death. It attracted much attention and sent the magazine into an extra edition for the first time in its seventy-five-year history. The rejected *Tablet* article was *Our Literary Life*, published in 1948 in *Literary Criticisms*. Vernon Blackburn, son of Mrs. Blackburn, was music critic of the *Pall Mall Gazette* and a friend of the Meynells. The poem which Wilfrid Meynell thought "very fine" was *The Hound of Heaven*. The "little masterpiece" was *Buona Notte*. The "fourth poem" which Thompson stifled and then resuscitated was *Sister Songs*. The "little verses to Mrs. Meynell" were either *To a Poet Breaking Silence* or *Before Her Portrait in Youth*. "Polly" was a nickname for Thompson's sister Mary, then a nun in a Manchester convent. The poem on Cardinal Newman was printed in *Weekly Register*, August 16, 1890.

11. To Alice Meynell

[July 1890]

Dear Mrs. Meynell,

I have been haunted by the thought that I may (yesterday afternoon) have seemed to you little grateful for the thoughtful and delicate sympathy which led you to interpolate in the *Register* the notice of my M.E. poem. It was like yourself—one can say no more —and I was deeply touched when I discovered it. If you wished to give me pleasure, you indeed succeeded.

I have been reconsidering Vernon's objection to the "walk the fables"; and I have come to the decided conclusion that I attach little weight to it, because he manifestly argued for victory, not for truth. Before we discovered what passage he had attacked, he assigned one set of reasons for his attack; when we discovered the passage, and assailed his criticism, he substituted a directly contradictory set. I have made a tabulated analysis of this procedure; and I appeal to your memory if it be not accurate. He first based his objection

A
on these grounds
(a)—I had been led astray by classical idiom, and had better shake off classical influences as soon as possible.

(b)—I had used a Latin construction, foreign to the English language, and incapable of being comprehended in a tongue without inflections.

(c)—What I had used was really an ablative after the verb, as would have been seen had I written in Latin. Then, with a consistency that fills me with admiration, he proceeded to sustain his objection

B
on these grounds
(a)—I had been led astray by a loose English idiom, and had better have guided myself by a consideration of classical grammar.

(b)—I had used a construction impossible in Latin, and foreign to every language *except* English. (As for the "inflections" objection, that was dexterously shuffled up his sleeve.)

(c)—What I had used was really an accusative after a preposition, as would have been seen had I written in Latin.

If Vernon will assure me that he has submitted these compatible grounds of objection to two persons whose opinion he values, and that they both entirely agree with him,—then I shall be pleased to ask him what is the extra value of 001 over 1.

Seriously, it is not the first time I have found this little weakness in our dear Vernon. The instinct (in conversation) of carrying his point is stronger for the moment than the desire for truth or consistency. Time has yet to teach him how much a critic's authority ultimately gains by the simple avowal of felt error. If you get him in writing, he is different. Then he is usually fair enough. On the second line to which he took exception, I think him right.

I hope Viola fulfilled my commission to say good-bye for me to yourself and Mr. Meynell last night.

Yours ever,
F.T.

The poem noticed by Mrs. Meynell in *Weekly Register* was *The Hound of Heaven*. His discussion with Vernon Blackburn probably concerned the same poem.

12. To Wilfrid Meynell

Monday Evening [August 1890]

Dear Mr. Meynell,

I cannot let you leave without writing to you to thank Mrs. Meynell for the gracious note which she sent me. I had no opportunity of expressing my thanks personally; for I hate displays of feeling in company. If she derive any pleasure from the knowledge that she has given pleasure to others,—but that must be a thing of every day with *her*—then you can tell her that she has given me deeper than pleasure.

I sincerely hope that the weather will improve for the holiday you must so much need. But there is always some wretched Saint somewhere, some spoiled child of the Eternal Father, praying for rain to suit some selfish benevolence of his own; and the Almighty is weakly indulgent with these people. As I told a monk at Storrington, it is not fair that any body of men should possess such undue influence at the Court of Heaven.

With all best wishes,

Yours very sincerely,
Francis Thompson

Mrs. Meynell's note probably offered thanks and congratulations on *To a Poet Breaking Silence* and/or *Before Her Portrait in Youth.*

13. To Wilfrid Meynell

Sunday [September 1890]

Dear Mr. Meynell,

I called at Palace Court on Friday, and, finding you were gone, started to follow you to B.&O.'s. Unfortunately I fell into composition on the way; and when I next became conscious of matters sublunary, found myself wandering about somewhere in the region of Smithfield Market, and the time late in the afternoon. I am heartily sorry for my failure to keep my appointment, and hope you will forgive me. I thought I had disciplined myself out of these aberrations, which makes me feel all the more vexed about the matter. If there should still be any room or occasion for my services in connection with the catalogue, I will call at B.&O.'s to-morrow.

Always yours,
F.T.

Thompson's excessive abstraction at this time was probably a result of his immersion in the long poem *Sister Songs*. Wilfrid Meynell, in addition to his function as a magazine editor, served as a reader for the firm of Burns and Oates.

14. To Wilfrid Meynell

Wednesday [September 1890]

Dear Mr. Meynell,

I have had to let the review of Dr. Hake stand much as I first wrote it, with but a few modifications: for better acquaintance disappointed the favourable expectations awakened by my chance dips into him. If I had re-written the notice in the light of my present knowledge I should have had to speak much more un-favourably; and that I understood from Mrs. Blackburn was not desired. If this is a fair specimen of Dr. Hake, I must be ranked among the non-elect in his regard. What I have said about him is abominably insincere according to my present feelings. On the other hand, the notice of Mr. Yeats is my absolute opinion: indeed, I have reined in a little the warmth of language to which I was disposed, lest my pleasure and surprise should betray me into ex-treme praise. If the reviews are not very brilliant, you must excuse me if you can; for I myself am not very brilliant just now. Fact is, the dearest child has made friends with me in the park; and we have fallen in love with each other with an instantaneous rapidity not unusual on my side, but a good deal more unusual on the child's. I rather fancy she thinks me one of the most admirable of mortals; and I firmly believe her to be one of the most daintily supernatural of fairies. And now I am in a fever lest (after the usual manner of fairies) her kinsfolk should steal her from me. Result—I haven't slept for two nights, and I fear shall not recover myself until I am resolved whether my glimpses of her are to be interdicted or not. Of course, in some way she is sure to vanish: elves always do, and my elves in particular. This individual little elf is a Catholic, by the way; which partly accounts for the celerity of our mutual confidence. And her kinsfolk see the *Register* every week; which ought to throw for you a new and agreeable light upon Elfland—almost sufficient to compensate you for the infamous attempt of the P.M.G. to create you a Doctor.

F.T.

Thompson's reviews of *The New Day* by T. G. Hake and *The Wanderings of Oisin* by W. B. Yeats appeared in *Weekly Register*, September 27, 1890. The "Park" was Queen's Park, located within a few blocks of Thompson's lodgings in Third Avenue, then, as now, a neighborhood haunt for mothers and children. The "P.M.G." was the *Pall Mall Gazette*.

15. To Alice Meynell

31 Elgin Avenue,
Saturday Night [fall 1890]

Dear Mrs. Meynell,

I have been musing a little on the theme mentioned between us this afternoon; and some frequent thoughts have occurred to me— or rather I should say, recollections of frequent experience. (The theme I mean, is the difficulty of communicating oneself. By the way, R.L.S.'s theme is more distinct from yours than I quite realised this afternoon. *His* is sincerity of intercourse. Yours is rather adequacy of intercourse. And the two, though they may overlap and react on each other, are far from identical.)

But the thoughts of which I speak (they are but one or two) are as useless to myself, as pebbles would be to a savage, who had neither skill to polish them nor knowledge whether they were worth the polishing. So I am moved to send them to the lapidary. If anything should appear in them worth the saying, how glad I would be it should find in you a sayer! But it is a more possible chance that poor thoughts of mine may, by a bountiful caprice of nature, stir subtle thoughts in you. When branches are so richly laden as yours, a child's pebble may bring down their fruit.

First, then, there is one obstacle to communication which exists little, if at all, for the generality; but is omnipresent with the sensitive and meditative who are destitute of nimble blood. I mean the slow and indeterminate beginnings of their thought. For example, such a person is looking at a landscape. Her (suffer one to use the feminine pronoun. It takes the chill off the egotism of the thing, to assume, even by way of speech, that in analysing my own experience I am analysing yours.) her companion asks her—"What are you thinking of?" A child under such circumstances (to illustrate by an extreme antithesis) would need no questioning. Its vivid, positive thoughts and sensations take to themselves glib and unpremeditated voice. But she? She is hardly thinking: she is feeling. Yet "feeling" is too determinate and distinctive a term: nay, her state is too sub-intellectual for the term to be adequate. It is sensoriness instinct with mind; it is mind subdued to sensoriness. She feels in her brain. She thinks at her periphery. It is a blended twilight of intellect and sensation; it is the crepuscular hour of thought. It is a state whose one possible utterance would be music. Thought in this subtle stage cannot pass into words because it lacks detail; as the voice, without division, cannot pass into speech; as a smooth and even crystal has no brilliance. To that "What are you thinking of?" she can only answer, "Nothing," or "Nothing in particular." And not unlikely, her companion, seeing that she was full of apparent thought, is discouraged at what seems her unsympathetic reticence. Yet she longed to utter herself, and envied the people who, at a moment's notice, can take a rough pull of their thoughts. If one could answer, "stay awhile, till my thoughts have mounted sufficiently to burst their dykes"—But no: by that time his interest would have faded, and her words would find him listless. She towers so high to stoop on her quarry, that the spectator loses sight of her, and thinks she has lost sight of *it*. And the habit so engendered makes one slow of speech apart from slowness of thought. One cannot at the first signal *mobilise* one's words. How one wonders at the men who, with an infinitely smaller vocabulary, have it always on a war-footing, and can instantly concentrate on a given subject.

Another point is that power of communication in oneself is conditioned by power of receptiveness in others. The one is never perfect; neither, therefore, can the other be. For entire self-revelation to another, we require to feel that even the weak or foolish impulsive things we may let drop, will be received without a chill,—nay, even with sympathy, because the utterer is loved. That priceless "other's" principle must be (to parody Terence without an attempt at metre) *Tuus sum, nil tuum mi alienum puto*. But such an "other" is not among men—no, nor women either. The perfectest human sympathy is only the least imperfect.

Then again, when we *can* communicate ourselves by words, it may often become a sensible effort to a sensitive person through the mere dead weight of language, the gross actualities of speech:—exactly as to delicate *you* a lovely scene loses half its attraction if it must be reached by the fatigue of walking to it.

Finally, I think there is the fact that, in what concerns their veritable spirit, all mortals are feminine. In the mysteries of that inner *Bona Dea*, speech is male, and may not enter. We feel that we could only admit to them the soft silence of sight. But then,—we cannot say: "draw aside my flesh and see." Would we could!

That reminds me of what you alluded to about the inefficiency of the eyes. I am so glad you mean to touch on that. I see much about the superior eloquence of eyes, etc. But it always seems to me they have just the eloquence of a foreign tongue, in which we catch only enough significance, from the speaker's tone and the casual sound of some half-familiar word to make us pained and desperate that we can comprehend no more.

There is a turn in Seneca:—

> Illi mors gravis incubat,
> Qui, nimis notus omnibus,
> Ignotus moritur sibi.

"On him death lies heavy, who, too known of all, dies unknown to himself." "Too known of all!"—With myself I am but too intimate; and I profess that I find him a dull dog, a very barren fellow. Your Delphic oracles notwithstanding, a man's self is the most unprofitable acquaintance he can make; let him shun such scurvy companions. But, "nimis notus omnibus!" If *this* were the most likely terror death could yield me, O Lucius Annaeus!—Who is known to *one*? In that *Mare Clausum* of our being, sealed by the con-venting powers of birth and death, with life and time acceding signatories, what alien trafficker has plied? Far heavier, *Luci mi,* death weighs on him, who dies too known of himself, and too little of any man.

I have bored you, I feel, unpardonably. But impute the fault to yourself. Your remedy is to prove, for the future, the imperfections of human communication, by not communicating to me the subjects of your articles. Really, I never did this kind of thing before, and—please, I will not do it again.

Repentantly yours,
Francis Thompson

But my repentance does not extend to suppressing the letter, you observe. A most human fashion of penitence!

> Thompson took up lodgings at 31 Elgin Avenue, Paddington, in October 1890. For some further remarks by Thompson on "the eloquence of eyes" see letter 100.

16. To Alice Meynell

31 Elgin Avenue,
Tuesday [winter 1890]

Dear Mrs. Meynell,

Memory still holds some seat in this distracted head.

You are talking of the moon, and you say: "Constancy in approach and departure is the reason of her inconstancies. Juliet will not receive a vow spoken in her invocation."

Now I do not venture upon any assertion with regard to this. For in the matter of grammar, I have most completely the Socratic wisdom of knowing that I know nothing. But does not the second "her" grammatically refer to Juliet? So I took it when I first read the sentence, though of course I quickly perceived your true meaning.

Vernon objected to me another defect in the article: *viz.* "Their joy is flying *away* from them on its *way* home." Seeing that this trivial blurr can be erased by just running your pen though the superfluous "away" (it seems to me unessential to the meaning), I cannot perceive how he should think it an effective plea in supporting his preference for one article over another. His preference is very likely right and mine wrong; but it is not the casual clash of two vowel-sounds, nor yet a casual grammatical slip (if such it should prove), that will dip the balance on either side.

Pray excuse the very unmetrical "lapses and ebbs" of my hand-writing. When you write on a chair, because you are too lazy to bring your table within reach of the fire, the result is apt to become "elliptically or parabolically or hyperbolically curved."

Yours most sincerely,
Francis Thompson

Thompson is discussing Mrs. Meynell's essay "The Rhythm of Life." She did not take his advice about the superfluous "away" in future printings, but did alter the sentence referring to Juliet.

17. To Wilfrid Meynell

[late December 1890]

Dear Mr. Meynell,

I leave with this on the mantelpiece (in an exercise-book) the poem of which I spoke. If intensity of labour could make it good, good it would be. One way or the other, it will be an effectual test. I have taken the advantage of a theme on which I have never yet written ill; if from it I have failed to draw poetry, then I may as well take down my sign.

I hope you will both have enjoyed the Academy, and that the renewed cold may not affect you. I was afraid you were by no means well yesterday evening.

Always yours,
Francis Thompson

This was the covering note Thompson left at the Meynell house with the manuscript of *Sister Songs*, probably on Christmas Eve.

18. To Alice Meynell

31 Elgin Avenue,
Dec. 31, 1890

Dear Mrs. Meynell,

Warm thanks for your letter. I only hope there may be a quarter as much merit in the poem as you incline to think. I do not fear your sincerity; I fear only that you may let your feelings bias your judgment. Above all, do not suffer me to think that I have wrought a beautiful bracelet (if such be not the case), merely because you never saw so many jewels set in the same space before. *That* of itself will not secure a beautiful bracelet, as you know, and I know. And do not treat me as did Dr. Todhunter the other day at Chiswick. Wishing to ascertain the impressions of a favourably disposed man new to my poetry, I mentioned the objection which had been made against me that I accumulated imagery until I became obscure and inartistic. He hesitated—a tell-tale hesitation—and then said, "Well, but what a splendid fault! And your imagery is often so unexpected and surprising." Perhaps you could hardly say a more dangerous thing to a man. How can you expect that he will keep a very severe guard upon a "splendid fault"? This is what will too probably happen. Next time he composes, says conscience—"Hold your hand: you have enough imagery, far too much imagery, already; sacrifice that one you are about to use." "Oh," he rejoins, "but it is such a beauty! to sacrifice it would be a pity; I can hardly harden my heart against it. And if I retain it—after all, it will be a 'splendid fault.' People will easily pardon it. Just this once!" By degrees he really comes to think that a "splendid fault" is brother to a virtue, and absolutely cultivates it. Swinburne has cultivated his "splendid faults"; and the result is not splendid. So none of this correction-and-sugar, please. If my Muse rouges, tell her so; though she vow and protest that it is no more than all fashionable Muses use.

I am glad you liked the stone nymph. It was one of my own special favourites when I wrote it; and I can say so the more freely because only a quarter of it belongs to me. The credit for the remaining three quarters must go to another Francis—him of Sales who is my patron-saint. You are not of course likely to remember that in the *Song of the Hours*, which I wrote at Storrington, I compared Time to a fountain showering down in hours, and went on

"Some a dragoned Trouble
    May spit from its writhen jaw;
And some our babble and bubble
    From the urn of a Joy may draw."

Both that fountain and this are from a common source. I came across it when I was about 19 in Leigh Hunt's *Indicator*. The essayist had just discovered St. Francis de Sales, by means of a little volume of selections, and delightedly communicated his discovery to the public. He thought St. Francis a polite and gentlemanly Dr. Johnson. Among his quotations was a saying addressed by the Saint to his episcopal Boswell, which specially struck Leigh Hunt, as it did me. I forget the exact words, but they were to this effect. "To bear affronts with patience and cheerfulness, is to draw good and sweet water out of the mouth of a brazen lion." Henceforth, when you meet any of these carven founts in my verse, you will know where they come from.

I have been reading Kipling's poem for myself, and admire it more than ever. In two particulars this reading has changed my mind. I *like*, not dislike, the "gentleman unafraid." And I rather come round to Mr. Meynell's opinion about the last line of the poem. But if it be a fault, it is a very slight one in so fine a thing. I sent Mr. Blackburn a note about the poem; in which, as usual, I managed to introduce something extreme and unjust in regard to Henley. So when you see Mr. Blackburn, please tell him that I retract my words of Henley. I am mortified at that man's ability to irritate me. By a single sentence he can make me tingle to the scalp with antagonism. And how, I know not. It is not his frequent wrong-headedness, it is not his violent utterance. Ruskin can say things as wrong-headed; Ruskin can say them with as intolerant a violence: yet at Ruskin I only stare or smile. But there is some secret, inexplicable provocation in Henley's language, which would make a snail butt its horns at him.

> Always yours sincerely,
> Francis Thompson

P.S.—As for your estimate of yourself—God help any *but* yourself who had uttered it! I could, 'an if I would—but I will not, till I know your revised judgment on my poem; lest what I said might appear a bribe to the judge. This much I will observe now. It is to me as if the moon should wonder how Messrs. Brock can have any respect for her, when they possess all those beautiful fireworks. After such an astonishing declaration from you, I shall presently begin to surmise that Artemis thinks herself a turnip-lanthorn. Please never say such a thing again: it pains me.

> The letter was written in response to Mrs. Meynell's praise of *Sister Songs*. For Thompson's most effective use of this fountain imagery, see his sonnet, *A Double Need*.

19. To Wilfrid Meynell

December 31, 1890

Dear Mr. Meynell,

I forward you the Lewis Morris Ms. If you think it too extravagant, I will rewrite it. And of course you can hack and hew as you please.

I have imagined at times, that in certain moments you may be inclined to have certain thoughts, just as I myself have fits in which I see the black side of everything. Will you pardon me if I have not surmised them truly, and pardon me also for what is perhaps, I fear, the impertinence of sending you the enclosed little bit? And will you also *not* think that it is simply a present of blacking for my Editor's boots? As a matter of fact, it was just an attempt to put into a sentence or two what I was thinking this New Year's Eve; when I pondered on the great work I discern you to have done and still be doing. I hope that many a New Year to come will see you spreading it; and wish I could be your right hand in it, not the clog I am. On account of your services to the Angelic

Art in particular, I am sure the angels must be rehearsing a special chorus for you in Paradise. I thought so when I read Miss Probyn's poem.

May they sprinkle every stone in your house.

Ever most truly yours,
Francis Thompson

Thompson's review of *A Vision of Saints*, by Lewis Morris, appeared in *Weekly Register*, January 10, 1891. May Probyn's poem, *A Christmas Carol*, appeared in *Merry England*, December 1890. The manuscript of "the enclosed little bit" is missing, but it was printed in EM, p. 116: "Within the mid girth of banyan was the banyan-spirit, all an-ache with heavy heaving through the years; and he was saddened, because he doubted to what end his weary pain of them had been. For beyond his trunk the banyan spirit looked not. While without the great grove hailed him sire; and from every bird nestling among its thousand branches, Heaven's ear heard *his* voice." This is Thompson's comment on Wilfrid Meynell's selfless character and his role as encourager of youthful talent, as well as head of a large family.

20. To Wilfrid Meynell

31 Elgin Avenue,
Friday
[January 1891]

Dear Mr. Meynell,

Before I talk of anything else, let me thank you *ab imis medullis* for the one happy Christmas I have had for many a year.

Herewith I send you my laggard poem. I have been delayed partly through making some minor corrections, but chiefly through having to transcribe the "Inscription" at the close of it—which I had not shown to Mr. Blackburn. I was resolved, as I told him, that this at least should be seen by you before any one else. Once having received his opinion that the rest of the poem was not a ghastly failure, I was content to take my risk of these last few stanzas being poor poetry. They are, in a measure, somewhat anachronistic;

for the last two of them were written at the end of May, when I first conceived the poem: and since *then* I *have* let fall one or two "unconsidered trifles" of verse in Mrs. Meynell's path. However, *quod scripsi scripsi:* as it stood in May it must continue to stand.

You must form your own opinion of the poem. Mr. Blackburn's you no doubt know. As I gather it, he thinks the second part successful, but the first very much mixed. He has indicated by pencil marks what portions of the first part he admired, and they are not bewilderingly numerous, as you will see. Having no rubber handy, I have been obliged to leave his marks in; so do not take them for my own indications of what you are called upon to admire. By the way, I see he has queried "lovesome." Is there no such word? I never made a doubt that there was. It is at any rate according to analogy. If it is an error, then "lovely" must be substituted throughout, which differs somewhat in *nuance* of meaning.

In conclusion, rather than express my feeling myself I am tempted, for once, to imitate a Dissenting fanatic, and refer you to Scripture—Acts III, the beginning of the sixth verse. (Protestant version, I do not know how it may be numbered in the Douay one).

Always most truly yours,
Francis Thompson

P.S. The title of the affair may puzzle you. It puzzled Mr. Blackburn, though as the latest from College I think he ought to have been up to it. It refers to the *amphicypellon* which Hephaestus, in Homer, bears round to the gods when he acts as cup-bearer by way of joke. This *amphicypellon* the commentators were divided about. It means, of course, literally, "a cup on either side"; and one half of the commentators said this signified a double-cup, while the other half said it meant only a two-handled cup. Now, many years ago, when Schliemann's things from Troy were first exhibited at South Kensington, I remember seeing among them a drinking-cup labelled "Perhaps the amphicypellon of Homer." It was a boat-shaped cup of plain gold, open at the top and with a crescentic aperture at either extremity of the rim, through which the wine could either be poured or drunk. So that you could pour from either end, and (if the cup were brimmed with wine) two people could have drunk from it at the same time, one at either extremity. In a certain sense, therefore, it was a double cup. And it had also two handles, one at either of its boat-shaped sides, so that it was a two-handled cup. You will see at once why I have applied the name to my double poem.

> Thompson is discussing *Sister Songs*. The biblical reference is "Silver and gold I have none, but what I have I give thee." The gold cup found at Troy by Schliemann, the *amphicypellon*, was seen by Thompson at the South Kensington Museum (now the Victoria and Albert) in June 1879.

21. To Wilfrid Meynell

Thursday
[January 1891]

Dear Mr. Meynell,

The discovery of what I have done to my own skates leads me to ask you to warn Monica next time she goes skating. If she wishes to preserve her skates, do not let her climb in them the bank of the Round Pond where it is set with stones. I was careless enough not only to let her do so, but to follow her example, and the edges of my skates are hacked and turned, as I expect hers are. Indeed, she ought not to go on the bank in her skates at all; it is most destructive to them. For which reason, doubtless, I invariably do it myself. But you must make her understand that I am like certain saints,—that man of exalted piety, St. Simon Stylites, for instance,—to be admired for my sublime virtues, but not recommended for imitation. I forget how many feet of sublime virtue St. Simon had; mine defies arithmetic.

If the children had half so delightful an afternoon as I had with them, I shall not have to doubt whether they enjoyed themselves. Cuckoo, considering how new he is to the ice, got on very well; far better than I expected from his delicate frame. He was quite brave about tumbles—and to be sure, Monica did her best to familiarise him with them. As for her, I was surprised at the progress she has made. She can already skate backwards a little—I can't. She can do the outside edge a little—I can't. It is true that her mode of terminating the latter stroke is to sit down rapidly on the ice; but this is a mere individualism of *technique*. It is a mannerism which, as she advances in her art, she will doubtless prune in favour of a severer style; but all youthful artists have these little luxuriancies. Without any jest, I never saw a girl learn to skate so quickly as she has done. Of course she has not yet reached elegance in her skating; but in a homely fashion she can traverse the ice at very serviceable speed, as I found. I raced her two or three times on even terms, and was well beaten. Tumbles do not daunt her, I rather think she seeks them. Perhaps the fascination of skating for her lies largely in the facilities which it gives for this mode of exhilarating delight.

Let me thank you warmly for your kindness in trusting the children to me. Or shall I say trusting me to them? For on reflection, I have a haunting suspicion that Monica managed the party with the same energy that she devotes to her skating.

Do not infer hence that she tyrannized over me. On the contrary, both Cuckoo and she were most solicitously anxious lest I should mar my own pleasure in attending to theirs. A needless anxiety, since I desired nothing better than to play with them. Indeed, they could not have been better or kinder.

Yours most sincerely,
F. Thompson

The Round Pond, in Kensington Gardens, was two or three blocks from the Meynell home in Palace Court. "Cuckoo" was a nickname for Everard Meynell.

22. To Wilfrid Meynell

Tuesday
[January 1891]

Dear Mr. Meynell,

I write a hasty line to say that I fear I cannot, at such short notice, alter the passage which you object to in the poem. So that, as far as I am concerned, the British Public will have to remain in exterior darkness, were is weeping and gnashing of teeth. You see, I accidentally sat up all last night, and did not discover the fact until day came through the blind. Consequently I am suffering for it to-day. As for poetry—I am despondent when I am without a poetical fit, yet when I have one I am miserable on account of my prose. I came lately across a letter of Keats' (penned in the prae-Endymion days) which might almost word for word be written by myself about myself. It expresses exactly one of the things which trouble me, and make me sometimes despair of my career. "I find," (he says) "I find I cannot do without poetry—without eternal poetry; half the day will not do—the whole of it. I began with a little, but habit has made me a leviathan. I had become all in a tremble from not having written anything of late: the Sonnet overleaf did me good; I slept again." I, too, have been "all in a tremble" because I had written nothing of late. I am constantly expecting to wake up some morning and find that my Daemon has abandoned me. I hardly think I *could* be very vain of my literary gift; for I so keenly feel that it is beyond my power to command, and may at any moment be taken from me. I have got fresh cold and a cough; I hope it may be a portion of *your* cold, which, having been exorcised from you, has taken refuge with me.

Yours very sincerely,
Francis Thompson

The printers of *Merry England* are good fellows, they do not "stand upon points." Thickly as you had sown the proofs with corrections, I managed to find some four or five on which to try my own hand. And then I thanked heaven I was not a proof-reader.

> The poem in question was probably *A Hymn to Snow* (*Merry England*, February 1891). It consisted of ninety-two lines, only the concluding portion of which has ever been reprinted; the rest is much inferior. The Keats letter was one written to J. H. Reynolds in 1817. Thompson's quotation of it from memory is a wonderful instance of his well-known powers of retention. The actual passage runs: "I find that I cannot exist without poetry—without eternal poetry—half the day will not do—the whole of it—I began with a little, but habit has made me a Leviathan—I had become all in a Tremble from not having written anything of late—the Sonnet over leaf did me some good. I slept the better last night for it—this Morning, however, I am nearly as bad again."

23. To Wilfrid Meynell

[March 4, 1891]

They have printed the *Corymbus* in one immense stanza, without a break from start to finish! The effect is ruinous indescribable —I thank Heaven I know enough German to swear in, for English lacks adequate thunder! I demand someone's head on a charger.

F. T.

If you see in tomorrow's paper anything about a body being recovered from the Thames, perhaps you will kindly call and identify it?

> This is a postcard. When the poem *A Corymbus for Autumn* was later reprinted in the 1893 volume, it was broken up into stanzas.

24. To William Ernest Henley

[early 1891]

Dear Sir,

Some time ago I sent you an article ("A Threnody of Birth"). As I am now the older by some months, and the wiser by no intelligence, I conclude that you did not like it. Consequently I send you a fresh article which is nothing that the other was. It is not imaginative, it is not over the head of the reader, if he have a head; and for the reader who is without that useful but not (it should seem) indispensable appendage—faith, I can make no account of him. Anyway, read it, *conjure te,* and whether you find it a good article or a bad article, you will certainly discover it to be a devil of an article so soon as you look at the title. It can be understanded of any reader who, like a virtuous Christian, has read his Congreve, his Butler, or his Swift. At last I fear I have damned my little paper. For if you should speak of Congreve to the average reader he would answer—Congreve? C? Never heard he made plays; thought it was only rockets. [Next four lines illegible.]

Yours sincerely,
[no signature]

P.S. If the former article have not gone all the way of all [word illegible], would you have the kindness to return it, for which purpose I enclose a stamp, since I took no copy of it. The present article you can dismiss to the [two words illegible] if it does not please you. It would have no significance in any paper but the N.O.

> The only existing manuscript of this letter is a draft in pencil preserved at Boston College; it may, in fact, never have been sent. "A Threnody of Birth" was not published until it appeared in *Essays II* in 1959. Many passages and images from it, however, were transferred to the poem *An Anthem of Earth*; the germ of *The Making of Viola* also occurs in this essay. The "fresh article" was "Modern Men: The Devil," which remained unpublished until it also appeared in *Essays II*. "N.O." is *National Observer*, the name assumed by W. E. Henley's *Scots Observer* in November 1890.

25. To Wilfrid Meynell

31 Elgin Avenue,
Wednesday
[May 1891]

Dear Mr. Meynell,

I hardly, I fear, gave you even commonplace thanks for the favour you conferred on me in choosing me for your little son's godfather. Even now I am utterly unable to express to you what I feel regarding it: I can only hope that you may comprehend without words. As for the quietness with which I took it on Saturday—for the premeditated utterance of emotion in speech I have an instinctive horror, which I think, you share sufficiently to understand and excuse in me. Besides, the words which one might use have been desiccated, fossilised, by those amiable persons who not only use the heart as a sleeve-ornament, but conspicuously label it—"This is a Heart." One can only, like Cordelia, speak by silence.

I enclose a slightly revised version of the poem I gave you on Saturday. There are a certain number of small verbal alterations, and portions of three stanzas have been retouched—in one case to meet an objection of Vernon's.

I heard that you did not look well yesterday, and I am afraid this weather must affect you. I hope you may benefit by the gleam of sunshine to-day, and that Mrs. Meynell continues to push on the time when we may once more see her. Give my love to Monicella, and Cuckoo, and all the children. As for F.M.M., I doubt the primitive egoism of human nature is still too new in him to care a baby-rattle about my love. And believe me,

Always most truly yours,
Francis Thompson

Francis Meynell was born on May 12, 1891. The poem was probably *To My Godchild*, which Meynell printed in the June 1891 *Merry England*.

26. To Wilfrid Meynell

Tuesday Night
[July 1891]

Dear Mr. Meynell,

The accompanying essay took shape by accident. Towards the end of last winter I came upon a draught of the notices of Patmore and Mrs. Meynell written for that ill-starred *Tablet* article of mine, after I returned from Storrington. The notices struck me as being better than I had been aware of—considering the circumstances under which they were written. So I determined to preserve them by adding a little fresh matter so as to weld them into a single article. I started with the *Preludes* portion, which grew under my fingers, and was about half written when I went to Friston. Then came Mrs. Meynell's Patmore article. Consequently I dropped, on my return, the section dealing with him; and finished only the *Preludes* section. I do not hope that it is an adequate treatment of its subject; but it is the best I can now do. I can at least say that I wrote no line of it to please, and no sentence that I would withdraw or modify (apart from purely literary considerations) if you were all in your graves—*dii avertant omen!* I wrote it, in fact, solely for my own gratification, without admitting to my mind a thought of how it might strike you. And if you will forgive me for having been daring enough to touch the theme, I shall be satisfied.

The other Ms. is that of the verses which I mentioned in my note to Mrs. Meynell on Sunday. Pray excuse the atrociously literal "patching up" of one stanza. It was too much labour to keep writing out the page afresh every time I remodelled the stanza. And do not trouble your patience and aggravate your sore throat by thinking it necessary to read this dismaying heap of manuscript in any hurry. I have taken my time over the writing, and shall not grumble at any one taking his time over the reading.

Ever yours,
Francis Thompson

P.S. I gave your message at Woodfield Place to Mrs. Carr, for she said that Mrs. Blackburn was too unwell to see me. I hope that dear Evvie is better. Tell him I have not forgotten his promised letter: but you see I have not been so vacant of occupation as I seemed. And St. Ignatius now makes claim on one again.

> The manuscript of Thompson's unpublished essay on Patmore and Mrs. Meynell is preserved at Greatham. The Meynell portion of it was reworked for a review in the *Tablet*, January 21, 1893. The "ill-starred" article refers to a commission received early in 1890 to do a fifty-year survey of Catholic literature for the *Tablet*. It was rejected and not printed until it appeared in *Essays I* in 1948. The mention of St. Ignatius refers to his two-part article on the founding of the Jesuits, in *Merry England*, September and October 1891. Mrs. Blackburn's lodging in Woodfield Place was just around the corner from Thompson's room in Elgin Avenue.

27. To Wilfrid Meynell

Saturday
[October 1891]

Dear Mr. Meynell,

I began a letter to you last Wednesday; but it never got finished in consequence of the devotion with which I have since been working at a short article which I have just completed. Unfortunately the feverish burst with which the essay has been put through has worked it no good. I am nothing satisfied with what I have done.

I console myself by thinking that since you knew I was all right, my writing or not writing will have been a matter of unconcern to you, since my letters are not wont to be of fascinating interest.

The weather has been very showery and changeable this week; and now that I feel on my feet again, I am longing to be back amongst you all. Touchstone, with the slightest alteration, voices my feelings about country life. "Truly, shepherd, in respect of itself, it is a good life; but in respect that it is a shepherd's life, it is naught. In respect that it is solitary, I like it very well; but in respect that it is private, it is a very vile life. Now in respect it is in the fields, it pleaseth me well; but in respect it is not in the city, it is tedious." I hope, nevertheless, that I shall not see you long after I return. For I hope that before the season gets too late you will yourself make your escape from that infectious nest of sewer-rats called London. I know how ill you were before I left; and it is disquieting to think that here am I, like the fat weed that rots itself in ease on Lethe wharf, while you are using up body and soul for the benefit of the blubber-brained Catholic public. The *Register* gave me a "turn," by the way, last week. My eye strayed carelessly across the announcements of deaths, and suddenly saw —"Monica Mary." My heart stood still, I think. Of course the next second I knew it must be some other Monica Mary, not she who walks among the poppies—and the restaurants. But just as I am managing comfortably to forget how confoundedly fond I am of the child, comes something like this to show it me.

How, unwell as you must be, you have managed to make such good work of the *Register* & *Merry England*, I don't understand. M.E., in particular, is an excellent number. There is not a poor article in it—except my own, which is dull enough to please a Bishop. Well, perhaps the *Story of a Conversion* flags a little in sustained romantic interest; and—somehow—I don't seem to remember much of the plot. By the way, *who* is the idiot in the *Globe*, who talks about "a curious drawing by the Alsatian artist, Alfred Rethel," as if he had never seen or heard of the once famous twin designs which earned—among others—the praise of Ruskin? Your modern art-critic, like your modern literary critic, thinks that art and his moustache budded together. I am not sure but that he considers it a relation of cause and effect.

Brin's article I think the best of his that I have seen. It is really very good, allowing for the fact that it is essentially imitative writing, and his "make-up" (to speak Thespianly) must have cost a world of trouble. Of course, if that terrible *Michelangelesque* principle (quoted by Fuseli in your article) were applied, he would be left "naked to laughter," and there is no mistaking whither his habiliments would fly. Brin, in fact, has made to himself a pair of breeches from Mrs. Meynell's cast-off petticoats. But it is cleverly done, and I did not think Brin had been tailor enough to do it. There are really felicitous things in the article, though the art of them *has* been caught from her. For instance the bit about the crops "bearing their sheaves of spires" (how *did* Brin contrive to say anything so good? It is imaginatively put), the transformation of the sheep-bells, of weeds putting on "the oolitic immortality of sculpture," *etcetera*. At bottom, doubtless, he has not much to say. But he has said it so well—that it is a pity someone else could have said it so much better.

The Franciscan article is decidedly good. But I am getting a little sick of this talk about "individualism," which only darkens counsel. The writer seems to mean by it not at all what it means to me—and I think to the Cardinal. What *he* calls a regulated individualism many people would call socialism. In fact, some socialists claim the Franciscans as a Catholic and religious experiment in the direction of socialism. It seems to me that you can juggle with words like "individualism" to suit your own whims. What a mortal week it has been to public men! I was astonished when it all came upon me at once through the medium of the *Register*. So Pope Hennessy is dead. Soon all of Disraeli's young men will have followed him into the *ewigkeit*. And none of them all, so far as I remember, have attained first-class political eminence. It is a case of Napoleon and his Marshals. As for Parnell, the poor fellow must have tasted the bitterness of death after Carlow. He must have felt then that the end had come of all. And the end must come of my letter, or I shall miss the post and my tea both. With best love to all,

Ever yours,
Francis Thompson

> This letter was written during a brief stay at the Franciscan monastery at Crawley, Surrey. The death of a Monica Mary Ullathorne was reported in *Weekly Register*, October 3, 1891. The issue of *Merry England* he is discussing was that of October 1891. "Brin" was Bernard Whelan, a friend of the Meynells'.

28. To Wilfrid Meynell

Crawley,
Wednesday
[October 1891]

Dear Mr. Meynell,

I was unable to get in more than the most hurried scrawl to you before post-time last night, after writing my late note to congratulate Mrs. Meynell on her birthday. Therefore I repair the omission now.

I intimated in that note that I found the monastery trying to me in this cold weather; but I must reinforce that intimation after my further experience of it. Today has been simply a day of concealed suffering to me, the cold and damp of the place attack my chest so dreadfully. Father Cuthbert suffers much from his throat, Father Angelo is very unwell, and will have to leave the monastery; and to speak plainly, if I stop more than a day longer, I feel that I shall be seriously ill. We went to see the Carthusian monastery at Cowfold today. There was but very little walking to do; yet

I have returned feeling reduced and exhausted. I must therefore earnestly ask you to let me have the means of returning to London at once—the earliest day, of course, would be Friday, since I can get no answer from you before then. It would not be necessary for me to spend my time at Palace Court; at the British Museum I should be perfectly comfortable during the day. But here it is simply murderous to me, and I look forward with sinking of the heart to facing two more days of it. I told you that Madam gave me neither return-ticket nor money for a ticket-back: therefore I cannot leave till you send me my fare back.

I hope you are yourself well; for though Palace Court is not Crawley, I know you feel cold more than I do. But it is the damp that is so deadly here. If kindness could make my stay pleasant, it would be pleasant. But, truth to say, I was afraid beforehand that I should fail to stand the place in winter; and it has proved very much worse than I feared. With love to Mrs. Meynell and the chicks, and very much to yourself,

Yours ever, dear Mr. Meynell,
Francis Thompson

Mrs. Meynell's birthday was October 11. "Madam" was Mrs, Blackburn. The Meynells lived at 47 Palace Court.

29. To Alice Meynell

Wednesday
[December 1891]

Dear Mrs. Meynell,

I hope Mr. Meynell may be better, in spite of the fresh change in the weather. It has caused me to relapse somewhat; but tell him that I will be at Palace Court to-morrow, if I can be of any service there, and I will have a *Dublin Letter* at the Press before I start in the morning.

I send you herewith the first scene of the comedy on which I have been so long engaged. You will do me a kindness if you will look over it and tell me what it is like, when you have time and inclination. But only when time allows you and inclination has not to be too much forced: there is no hurry about the matter, no matter how long you may be before coming to judgment.

I have put the "Rhymers" into it, as you will see—but glorified "Rhymers," of whom only one figure, *Bradford*, bears any relation to the original (Radford). The N.O. men of the Whibley persuasion come in for some strokes, too. And to finish with even-handed justice, I have in the verse of *Johnson* satirised the more conspicuous defects of my own earlier poetry. And faith! I rather think I have hit myself hardest.

I repeat, don't bore yourself with [this] while you feel indisposed. Only, whether it be bad, good, or indifferent, keep it safe for me; since it would be a dreary labour to recompose it from the *disjecta membra* of the rough draft.

I hope you may yourself be better than I thought you looking on Monday. It is clumsy to say so; but there—I find that I have a dreadful reputation among all the O'Connor girls (for example) of never paying compliments. And truly, I am afraid it is an art I never shall acquire.

I am sick and dejected, and haunted by presentiments—but whether they mean bale or bile, a man may make question.

Always most truly yours,
Francis Thompson

> The comedy was the unpublished *Venus Fly-Trap*, the manuscript of which is at Boston College. The "Rhymers" was a loosely organized club of poets and writers in London during the early 1890's. Thompson was not a member, but attended a meeting in the fall of 1891.

30. To Wilfrid Meynell

[January 1892]

Dear Mr. Meynell,

I don't know what I shall do, or what you will do. I haven't been able to write a line, through sheer nervousness and fright. Confound Canon Carroll! It is he who has put me into this state. I was not in the least in this condition of stage-fright when you first proposed the thing to me. I wish you had never incumbered yourself with me. I am more in a condition to sit down and go into hysterics like a girl, than to write anything. I know how vexed and impatient you must feel to hear this from me, when you had expected to have the thing this morning. Indeed I feel that you have already done too much for me; and that it would be better you should have nothing more to do with me. You have already displayed a patience and tenderness with me that my own kindred would never have displayed; and it is most unjust that I should any longer be a burden to you. I think I am fit for nothing: certainly not fit to be any longer the object of your too great kindness. Please understand that I entirely feel this; and am perfectly resigned to the ending of an experiment which even your sweetness would never have burdened yourself with, if you could have foreseen the consequences.

F. T.

> Thompson's agitation was occasioned by the pressure of his attempt to write, at the Meynells' request, an obituary poem on Cardinal Manning, who died on January 14, 1892. The poem, *To the Dead Cardinal of Westminster*, must have been finished only a few days later, since it appeared in the February 1892 issue of *Merry England*.

31. To Wilfrid Meynell

[summer 1892]

Dear Mr. Meynell,

Will you stamp the accompanying letter and send it off for me? It is only some small verses I am offering the *U.M.*, to compensate for long neglect. They will be too late, I expect; but I shall have vindicated myself from the charge of neglect, whether they are in time or not.

I have been looking at your straw tile, which seems a failure, owing to the enamel soaking in through the interstices. Now the enamel has exactly the appearance of a varnish I used to use for "ringing" microscopic slides. It was a compound of zinc (probably zinc oxide), and set in just the same kind of a surface. If used alone, it would have run in between the slide and the cover-glass, and spoilt the microscopic "object." Therefore the procedure was, first to "ring" the slide with a certain cement, too glutinous to run; then the white zinc varnish was laid on over the cement. It seems to me that the one chance of succeeding with your straw tile is to adopt some similar process: to find some preparation which will coat over the straw and stop its interstices, then lay on the enamel over that. I give the suggestion for what it is worth.

F. T.

The verses probably were *The Testament of Calvary*, published in *Ushaw Magazine*, March 1893.

32. To Katharine Tynan

1 Fernhead Road,
Paddington W.
[July 15, 1892]

Dear Miss Tynan,

It has long weighed on my conscience that I never answered the charming and only too generous letter in which you thanked me for *The Sere of the Leaf*. The fact is, that I am more ignorant than a schoolboy of social conventions, and so I did not know whether it would be *en règle* for me to write to you without a personal acquaintance. When at length I consulted Mr. Meynell, he told me to wait until you came to London, and thank you in person. At that time, you see, he was expecting a speedy visit from you. The result was—unintentionally, I have no doubt, to confirm me in the idea that I should transgress conventions by writing. But you have been so kind and appreciative in reviewing the *Manning* verses and *The Making of Viola* in the *Independent*, that I can no longer resist writing to you. The latter has especially delighted me. I despise the conventional modesty of these days, and see no reason why a poet should pretend to see no merit in his own verse, when in his heart he believes it good. When I find a poet doing so, I always exclaim internally "What the deuce did you publish it for, then? Your only possible justification for cumbering paper with it, is that you honestly believed it poetry." Therefore, I frankly say that I think your criticism of *The Making of Viola* exactly what wanted saying about it, and condensed into a few beautiful words as only a poet could have done it. Not the least among the alleviations of a not very appreciated lot, I count that I should have had some of my poem praised in a few significant words by two poets —yourself and Mrs. Meynell. You have a special right to praise *The Making of Viola*, for you are partly its parent—not on the poetical, but on the metrical side. It is, as no-one is better qualified to discern than yourself, founded on the bold application of a metrical principle which has lain dormant since the decay of the early alliterative metre—which Mrs. Meynell felicitously calls the *tempo rubato* principle. There are traces of it in the Elizabethan poets; and from then to now it has simply dropped out of the knowledge of Englishmen. In late days there has been some revival of it, but it has been an unintelligent revival. Swinburne alone has used it beautifully, though slightly, in a lyric or two; but you beautifully and often. George Meredith has employed it with the most utter and unmusical misconception of its object. Its purpose in the Saxon and early English poets was to vary a set metre. Meredith uses it to *constitute* the metre, and thereby stereotype it in the most obvious and mechanical fashion. The true law is, that you take a metre (the more received and definite the better), and then vary it by the omission of syllables, leaving the lines so treated to be *read* into the given length by pause, and dwelling on the syllables preceding or following the *hiatus*. The omission of syllables is the exception, not the system, of the metre; and the art of the poet is shown in skillfully varying the position and manner of the omissions. In this way the most delightful effects of loving, lingering, and delicate modulation, on the one hand; or airy, dance-like measure and emphasis, on the other, may be compassed. But Meredith regularly omits the same syllables, in the same position, in every single line; producing a pendulum-like monotony of insistent beat, instead of variety which our ancestors employed the device to effect. For instance:—

> "Lovely are the curves of the white owl sweeping
> Wavy in the dusk lit by one large star."

And that triple accent is iterated with clockword precision in every line, till it becomes a horror contrary to the most delicate principles of rhythmic music. Now the true use of the principle was first revealed to me by my beloved *Poppies*. That, and a poem in your *Shamrocks*, sent me to the early English writers, where I studied the principle at its source, till I had thoroughly grasped its various uses. In *Viola* I designed to bring out its capacity for dance-like effects. Its capacity for dainty lingering effects I attempted to work out a year ago, in a poem unpublished. But I find that you have achieved precisely the same effects as this latter poem in St. Francis' hymn in your just published volume. Enough of myself. Only that if there be anything happy in the metre of *Viola*, you were my first mistress in it.

You must allow me to say how charming and dainty I thought your poem, *Sweets*. That delightful art of repetition, so difficult to achieve, is handled in it with fascinating effect. I hear that you are engaged to be married. Let me wish you all the delight that you have given me by your poems. I can well remember my coming into possession of a copy of *Poppies*. I found an old *M.E.* containing it on a second-hand bookstall, and the twopence I gave for it was a truer gauge of admiration than many a sovereign. For at that time I was struggling for mere existence, and a penny spent on aught but the necessaries of life was a plank withdrawn between me and starvation. Once more thanking you for all your kindness, which includes a most appreciated notice of my verses on the Cardinal, I will conclude this letter; which I hope you will neither resent as an intrusion, nor for its lateness, nor yet for the space I have wasted in lecturing you on a point of metre where you are far better qualified to instruct me. Alas! how every recorded syllable of the Cardinal's successor assures us that we have exchanged a genius for a satisfied mediocrity after the great heart of the British Dissenter—in mind, though not in politics. A respectable Stead, whose formula happens to be *moi et l'église*, instead of *moi et le peuple!*

Yours always sincerely,
Francis Thompson

Excuse my writing to you on M.E. paper, which happened to be

the only note-paper at hand when I took up my pen. Forgetting
that I had just changed my lodgings, I unthinkingly began by
putting my former address at the head of my paper.

July 15, 1892

> Thompson's *The Making of Viola* appeared in *Merry England*,
> May 1892. Katharine Tynan's *Poppies* appeared in the same
> magazine for April 1885.

33. To Alice Meynell

Monday Night
[late summer 1892]

Dear Mrs. Meynell,

At the risk of offending you by what you may think officious
interference, I take up my pen to implore you to meddle as little
as may be with the text of *Preludes*. In principle, I think the modern foible of poets for revising in maturity the poems of their youth
to be not only most perilous for the poems tampered with, but a
capital sin against that art which the process is designed to serve,
and by which you set such store. It is fatal to *keeping,* and keeping
is surely all in all to art. You would not retouch your youthful
portrait into the contours of mature womanhood, though they be
absolutely more perfect. And all poetry to a certain degree, but
poetry such as *Preludes in excelsis,* is a portrait. It is a portrait of
your youthful self. By remodelling it according to the mind of
your maturity, you will destroy its truthfulness to the thing you
were, without making it truthful to the thing you are. It will be
a hybrid; it will lose the absolute fresh sincerity of girlhood, without gaining the graver and more reticent sincerity of womanhood.
It will, indeed, be a sin against sincerity. For your poetry was
intended to show yourself; and now you are retouching the portrait
for the public as you would like yourself to have been. It will
lose the value it had for us, and must have had for all men, by
reason of its single-minded utterance of your young self; it will
not have for us any value as an utterance of your matron-self. In
the name of your art, which you are going about to betray under
the notion of safe-guarding; in the name of your poetry, which

we loved for what it was, not for what it should or might have been; in the name of the white sincerity which you have never before falsified; in the name of your admirers, whose instinct for poetry you have not doubted in the case of others; I conjure Alice Meynell to leave us Alice Thompson. Unimproved, unsophisticated, with her weakness and her strength as we saw, accepted, admired and loved her.

In regard to the essays, I would by no means have you put out the admirable *Wendell Holmes*; but I would have you insert the subtle *Patmore*, unmatched from any other pen. I have given you some reasons. I add to them your regard for Coventry himself. Will you leave the one adequate plea which the age has sent forth for that great unknown poet to go down to posterity in the lopped and bedevilled state to which it has been reduced by the devil of a Henley and the devil of a printer?

Be angry, but hear me.

Yours most truly ever,
F. T.

Alice Meynell's *Preludes* was first published in 1875. With revisions, it was republished by John Lane in 1893, along with a volume of her essays.

34. To Alice Meynell

Crawley
[August 1892]

Dear Mrs. Meynell,

The enclosed lengthy document—it can hardly be called a letter —was written last night, but I have had no opportunity of sending it till this afternoon. It was written, as you will see, to explain the personal use I intend to make of my visit here. I hope it will not bore or tire you too dreadfully to read it. I have had my lunch, just seen Fr. Cuthbert, and am waiting for a walk in the garden with him. Then I will enter on the questions explained in the accompanying last-night-written document. Best love to Mr. Meynell and Monnie: tell him I find it very pretty here, and am looking forward to seeing and thanking him for my visit to-morrow.

Fr. Cuthbert sends best wishes to you both. With love to yourself (there are too many "bests" already, and I can't say "bestest"),

Ever yours both,
Francis Thompson

[The following letter was enclosed.]

1 Fernhead Road,
Monday
[August 1892]

Dear Mrs. Meynell,

I hardly know whether to occupy your mind, however briefly, with a subject which I fear, from some late indications in your manner, has begun to weary and overstretch your mind with the tyrannous extent and uncertainty of the questions which it suggests. I don't quite know why I write, indeed, except that I have confided my thoughts to no-one; and before I go to Crawley I feel a necessity of confiding them to someone. I go with very serious purpose, so far as my own mind is concerned. The alleged coincidence of Fr. Cuthbert's system with C.P.'s has simplified and defined immensely the central points on which I want to assure my mind. There are two points in C.P.'s teaching—so little of it, that is, as I have gathered—which I will not away with.

1st His doctrine on the nature of union with God and between souls in Heaven, *as it has been presented to me*, I simply reject; my God-given instincts reject it. The permanence of carnal delight in the Heavenly union would to me make it un-heavenly. Even here on earth, my own instinct as to the typical union—given also the typical woman—would be a union like that of the Virgin and St. Joseph. Provided I were united with her spirit, I would be content to wait for her body till I could be united with it on the same terms—i.e., *as a spirit*, when it was assumed to the dignity of its soul. I recognise that on earth it may not be so for the many; but after—?

2nd The opinions I have gathered—not for the first time—from the *Fortnightly* on the number of the elect. Let him bring me the tale of the stars, and I will listen to him. I do not believe in an exclusive society of Duchesses in either life. I reject the thought that Heaven is a select little spiritual aristocracy. That it *has* its aristocracy, yes—but its commonalty too. I believe in the Commonalty of Souls. I must touch here a subject I never touched before with any person but one. I do so because you, who know that my poetry contains that deeper life of me which passes within closed flesh—you must know this thing of me already, having read those *Manning* verses which I do not like to read again. You know that I believe eternal punishment: you know that when my dark hour is on me, this individual terror is the most monstrous of all that haunt me. But it is individual. For others—even if the darker view were true, the fewness is relative to the total mass of mankind, not absolute; while I myself refuse to found upon so doubtful a thing as a few scattered texts a tremendous forejudgment which has behind it no consentaneous voice of the Church. And I do firmly think that none are lost who have not wilfully closed their eyes to the known light: that such as fall with constant striving, battling with their temperament; or through ill training, circumstance which shuts from them true light, etc.; that all these shall taste of God's Justice, which for them is better than man's mercy. But if you would see the present state of my convictions on the subject, turn to the new *Epilogue* of my *Judgment in Heaven*. (You will find it in the wooden box containing my M.S., where I have lately placed it instead of the old copy. Or Mr. Meynell may have brought back the book of translations, which also contains it.) There I have given the spirit of them, which is better than any letter.

In these two matters, then, I stand implacably aloof from C.P., *if I rightly understand him*. And I go to ask Father C., if his system coincides with C.P.'s in these details, no less than in its general purport. Does he, I shall ask, hold eternal punishment *by eternal suffering*? If so, does he hold, as part of his system, the minute number of the elect? Secondly, does he hold, as part of his system, that other principle which *I have understood* to be C.P.'s? Or does he hold any principle which issues in it? Lastly, if he holds either or both of those two principles, are they integral portions of the system? Will it logically fall to pieces if either of these principles be withdrawn? Should he answer all these in the affirmative

—then this famous common System, though legions of Coventry Patmores stood behind it, and hordes of Father Cuthberts, shall not stand before the instincts of my own soul. I will quarry out of it what truth my mind may think good for building with; but the System itself shall be for me anathema. For what am I a poet, but that my soul's instincts may stand like lighthouses amidst the storms of thought?

Nor will I, in any case, tie my life to any system of metaphysics or mystic theology. Mystic Systems come, and may go: a life is true apart from them. If such an aid help one to realise one's life, one's aspiration; so far it is good for one. If it confuse and perturbate one's life, one's ideas, it is clearly ill for one. And one simply excretes it. I may admire: but it does not fit my nature, and I will have no more of it than fits my nature. If mystic theology is ever to form a part of my life, it must be what God shall teach me, not Coventry Patmore, nor another. And it will not be a thing which snaps my nerves like opium. I was never made to serve my Maker by fever-fits—or He would have given me another set of nerves. One of the old Saints of the Desert (since we are upon mysticism) gave as his experience that, while demons could take the shape of angels, you knew the true from the false angel because the former caused in you a sensation of peace and tranquility, the latter of perturbation and agitation. It remains still the best of tests for the individual soul in things spiritual.

What a curious epistle this has become! I think the pen has written for itself, I had so little intention of saying all this when I sat down. Anyway, you will know that I go to Crawley with an intention, and can compendiously find the result of my quest when I return. The System and calmness, or calmness without the System: my abiding instincts before all—What is the System? that is no part of my inquiry. I wish to know points which, answered in the affirmative, settle the question without putting me to the trouble of further novitiate.

Ever yours,
Francis Thompson

Love to Mr. Meynell, and Monica.

During 1891–92 Thompson paid a number of brief visits to the Franciscan monastery at Crawley, located about two hours from London by train. During this time, he had been introduced to the mystical theology of Coventry Patmore by the Meynells, and was at first repelled by it. Later he became Patmore's complete disciple.

35. To Alice Meynell

1 Fernhead Road,
Paddington W.
[September 1892]

Dear Mrs. Meynell,

Your sudden arrival on Tuesday prevented me from answering your letter—the letter from Anglesey—but I resolved nevertheless, as soon as the *Register* permitted, to tell you by note how delighted I was to receive that letter. Indeed, after you left, I felt as if it were night, with a great hole in the heavens where the moon ought to be. What I had intended to forward in answer to your letter I forward now. The concluding words of it, "friend and child," reminded me of some lines written at the time I was composing *Amphicypellon*. They were written hastily, to relieve an outburst of emotion; and, not thinking there was any poetry in them worthy of you, I never showed them you. But when I read those concluding words of your letter, I remembered the lines; and resolved to transcribe them, that you might see you could not have addressed me more according to my wish.

Madam has been worse than I anticipated, and told me something which has left me very unhappy. I fear, indeed, I shall hardly sleep.

Ever your own,
Francis

I hope you are going to have no headaches, "wheel" or otherwise; but to be just happy for a while, now the *Register* is done. And that to-morrow, for once in a way, and Saturday, you will do just what you like and take pleasure in doing: If, indeed, it is possible to you for one day to drop that inveterate habit of thinking so much of other people, that you put yourself away in a corner and forget that you have left yourself there. And since I think you must have had far too much of my company forced upon you during the last fortnight, if I leave you now as much as may be without me you must ascribe it solely to my anxiety for anything which might fatigue you; not to neglect, of which I am incapable, or weariness, which no man—I least—could feel in your companionship.

Friday noon. I intended this to have gone to you last night, but it was too late: so I leave it behind me this afternoon. I had first of all written a note of very different character, in which I told you what Madam had said to me, and asked you, if you could, to reassure me. But I decided not to send it, on a re-reading. Firstly, because I began to doubt whether it might not be a breach of Madam's confidence, in a certain way. Secondly, because, being written in the full rush of feeling after what I had heard, it was so vehemently emotional that I feared you might at once despise and be troubled by it. Yet I confess, after all, I have some doubt whether it had not better have gone. I have suffered so from reticence all my life: and the opening out of hearts and minds, where there is confidence, puts an end to so much secret trouble that would grow monstrous if it were brooded over. I will be back for dinner this evening.

F. T.

> The poem enclosed was *In Her Paths*, written in late 1890. It was published in *Merry England*, July 1893. The following letter is probably the one he says he wrote but did not send.

36. To Alice Meynell

British Museum, Saturday Evening
[September 1892]

Dear Mrs. Meynell,

It is a small matter, and hardly, I suppose, worth taking a second thought about in your mind. Yet as I seem to have offended you, and as to offend you *is* the most grievous of things, you must pardon me if to *me* it is a grave matter. I mean the misunderstanding this afternoon.

I wish then to say that I did nothing except with the design to consult your wishes. When I came in this morning, you told me that I was punctual to my time, but that you must go out; and asked me not to mind. It was clear, therefore, that you remembered our overnight agreement, and that there was no need for me to remind you of it. And it was clear, too, that you understood me to have come early in the morning for the express purpose of keeping my agreement, and that there was no need for me to explain my desire that you would go through A *Portrait* with me. Yet you came back from your shopping, and never signified your willingness to go through it; you saw me finish my letter to Madam, and sit down patiently to wait, yet you still made no sign of readiness. Now, delicacy forbade *me* to ask *you*; because it was you who were conferring the favour, not I. Consequently, once I had made sure that you remembered my request, and knew what I had come for, I felt that I could not delicately, in the absence of any encouragement or signification of willingness from you, press from you a favour which it seemed probable you had repented. If nothing had passed between us since I entered the house, of course it would have been my part to remind you of the overnight agreement. But your own words forestalled that; and so it seemed to me that the only thing I could courteously do was to wait until you signified your readiness to fulfill the agreement which you had already signified your remembrance of. No such signification of readiness came from you before we went down to lunch: and, I repeat, I did not like to ask you, lest I should be pressing on you the fulfillment of a promise you had repented. When we went down to lunch without your having intimated any readiness to commence the task you had agreed to overnight, I felt convinced that you shrank from it for some reason—perhaps sheer boredom—and, to say truth, I felt sharply wounded. For if there is one dread I have perpetually before me it is to presume on your good nature and toleration. When I went upstairs after lunch, my eye fell on the proofs lying in your place. Then, I thought, I understood the matter. You were anxious to get your essays revised, in order to send them to C.P., who had, you told me, telegraphed regarding them. I was very sad that I should have pressed on you my own selfish affair, when, as I now found, your own work was pressing on your hands, while mine could wait indefinitely. So I determined that the only way I could repair the unintended selfishness I had been guilty of, was to take my leave of you under some pretext, and so spare you the task of keeping a promise wrung from you in the kindness of your heart, but which interfered with what you desired to be at work on. Great was my consternation when I did this, and found that you resented it. I meditated whether I should draw back, since I had angered you where I meant only to consult your hidden wishes. But I saw that you were so cold and estranged from me, that the going through the poem would have been a constrained affair, painful for both of us. So I left.

It seems to me that the more I strive to please you and serve you, and to think always what may be your pleasure, not mine, the more I alienate you from me, so far as a lady so sweet can be alienated from anyone. If you understood one thing, I think, you would have judged me better in the past. It is this. I am unhappy when I am out of your sight; and would pass every hour, if I could, in your exquisite presence, only to feel the effluence of your spirit in contact with mine. But *you*, of course, can have no such feeling in reference to me; and would often gladly be without my presence when my love for you prompts it, and your good nature prompts you patiently to bear it. Now my sense of this inspires me with a continual timidity about inflicting my society on you in any way, unless you in some way signify a desire for it. Hence such misunderstandings as that of today.

Let this be sufficient, and let it not come between us. I know how it must tax you to endure me; for you are a friend, a mother; while I, over and above these, am a lover—spiritual as light, and unearthly as the love of one's angelic dreams, if you will—but yet a lover; and even a Seraph enamoured must be a trying guardian-angel to have to do with.

Ahi! soavissima Madonna Alice, avete pietà di me!

Ever yours, most beloved lady,
Francis Thompson

P.S. I send you herewith the best I was able to do in the correction of the blank-verse *Orison-Tryst*. But its weaknesses are too inherent to be really removed—they are in the texture of it.

> Quoted from *Alice Meynell: A Memoir*, by Viola Meynell, pp. 106–9. The manuscript of the original has been mutilated, leaving only the last third intact. The disturbance underlying this letter was probably occasioned by Thompson's relapse into addiction in the fall of 1892. His misery becomes clearer in the following three letters.

37. To Alice Meynell

Monday Evening
[September 1892]

My own dear lady and mother,

How did it come about that what began between us in confidence this afternoon ended, somehow, in constraint and reticence? I could not understand it at the time; I could only feel that, while I was tenderly grateful for your dear kindness, I had somehow fallen out of touch with you after the first moment. And I was miserable to feel it. I have now come to the conclusion that the fault was all on my side. Though I said otherwise at lunch (for I hate parading one's private ills before strangers), I had slept little last night, eaten nothing in the morning, and was able to eat little at lunch. So that I felt utterly spent, and unable to stand the strain of emotion, or to respond to your spirit with the instinctive perception I am accustomed to have for it. I trust you, honour you, and love you more than ever,—O believe me: it was simply that paralysis of the heart and emotions which follows a prolonged strain upon them. Pardon me, and do not let it rest here. Confidence has gone too far not to go farther, or die altogether. Give me an opportunity to-morrow, if possible; at any rate the sooner the better. And I will open to you, if you wish it, my most secret soul; that on my side you may never misunderstand me through distrust or want of knowledge. That I promise you. On your side, be all exactly as you will. It is marvellous to me how I missed grasping your sweet and sympathetic purpose this afternoon; but

I did. Let it not persuade you to believe me anything but your loving child, friend and sympathiser.

Francis

38. To Alice Meynell

Wednesday Night
[September 1892]

Dear Mrs. Meynell,

I, at least, did not on Tuesday night adopt the attitude that you had no reason to be angry with me. On the contrary, I told you that I was very sorry I had lapsed from my word to you. It is a minor matter, but I had not again broken my promise on that Tuesday when I spoke to you. I had broken it the day before, and was bitterly remorseful for having done so. You had lightened my heart and strengthened me immensely in that night's interview: for I thought that you had taken what was indeed the true view of the matter. Namely, that under a weight of suffering of which you had not, nor ever can have, any conception, I had lapsed from my word for a single day; but having got relief from God when my burden was become beyond the strength of human nerves, I had resumed my courage and was going forward again in the path that I had promised you. You had, I thought, taken this true and merciful view; and instead of visiting me with your anger, were going to pray that I might be sustained, and to encourage me by your affection and sympathy. I went to bed, comforted, and praying that God would help me on my side to cooperate with you, and to spare you any addition to your sorrows from me. But this morning I get your terrible letter, and feel that Heaven has indeed crowned the awful trouble which has been accumulating on me for the last month, by withdrawing from me your love and sympathy, which alone gave me courage to struggle against it, and try to keep my soul from the influences which were dragging it downward. God help me, for I feel blinded and paralysed. Before Heaven I tell you, that if you knew all as I know it, you would feel that never man had more claim on you for patience than I have, however hard it may be to extend it to me: and that I am indeed more sinned against than sinning. But I make no further claim on you. I bow to your decision. Henceforth I will only come to your house when business calls me there; and if you are brought into contact with me, it need not be beyond the ordinary formalities of courtesy. I will draw back into the hermit, and leave your lives free from me; and perhaps when the curse of me is removed from the house it will settle back into its ordinary condition. As you will not see me now for (I suppose) a fortnight, it will be all the easier when you come back for us to fall into these new relations, which are the old.

I will send to Palace Court to-morrow the leaderette which Mr. Meynell asked me for. If there is anything else he wants from me, perhaps he will send a note to my lodgings.

Yours sincerely,
Francis Thompson

P.S.—Will you, as a last favour, keep what I send you with this, in memorial of the time before this man's shadow fell across me; when indeed I lived highly, and loved you, God knows, as I still do, as purely as an angel? That may be commoner in your experience of men than in mine: I do not know. They are your letters, which I have worn in front of my heart since you first began to send me any: though two precious ones are lost. I am no longer worthy to wear them, since I have forfeited your love and respect. Will you keep them, "For sake of the dead him whose name they bear"? I am writing on Wilfrid Blunt, and my mind is full of lines of his.

> "Lame, impotent conclusion to youth's dreams
> Vast as all heaven! See, what glory lies
> Entangled here in these base stratagems,
> What virtue done to death! O glorious sighs,
> Sublime beseechings, high cajoleries,
> Fond wraths, brave raptures, all that sometime was
> Our daily bread of gods beneath the skies,
> How are ye ended, in what utter loss!
> Time was, time is, and time is yet to come,
> Till even time itself shall have an end.
> These were eternal—and behold, a tomb.

> Come let us laugh and eat and drink. God send
> What all the world must need one day as we,
> Speedy oblivion, rest for memory."

P.P.S. The postscript is repented of, and I have not returned you the letters. Do not think, dear lady, that I reproach you with your action. Within your knowledge you have acted perfectly justly, as you always do. And perhaps it will prove for the best in the end. Good-bye, if this should reach you in time. Indeed, and indeed, your husband's note only reached me in time. In my despair, I was writing to Coventry Patmore. And if that note had reached him, offering him my unqualified alliance, it would have been the death-knell of all our souls.

> It is evident from this letter, pathetic in its attempt at justification, that Thompson's renewed drug-taking had distressed Alice Meynell to the point of causing her to limit his visits to the Meynell home. Before the letter was sent, however, a note arrived from Wilfrid Meynell asking Thompson to call. Thompson's answer follows. (A review by Thompson of the poetry of Wilfrid Blunt appeared in *Weekly Register*, November 19, 1892.)

39. To Wilfrid Meynell

Thursday Evening
[September 1892]

Dear Mr. Meynell,

I am not fit to come in to-night. I have broken my promise to Mrs. Meynell both yesterday and to-day. She was wrong in thinking that I had broken it on the Tuesday when she spoke to me; nor did I guess that she thought so. I had broken it the day before, for the first, and it might have been the last time; broken by the pressure, night and day, of an extra-natural conflict in which you do not believe because—Englishman-like—it is outside your personal experience, as before that it was outside mine. But that Monday night and on the Tuesday following I found myself completely delivered; as if God saw that the limits of human endurance had been passed. I was full of remorse for what I had done, and resolved never again to add to her own sorrows by giving her such pain on account of me. Then, on the Wednesday morning, came her letter as a crushing blow, breaking me utterly to pieces on the top of all I had gone through. I fell into wild recklessness and carelessness about my soul; and, as I have said, I broke my word to her completely both that day and to-day. Therefore I cannot come in to-night. But be comforted, if you can. Your little note has given me a ray of hope and comfort again; and if you can pardon and overlook what is past, I on my side will take up the task of amendment again. The dreadful conflict against the unseen will of that man at Lymington seems altogether to have passed from me; and if I am only delivered from the thought that she and you have cast me off and turned against me, I can once more regain the mastery of my own self and soul. God and her innocence help her, and God help us who are left behind. If she will write me two lines to say that she pardons me and does not withdraw her affection from me, she shall, please God, hear a good account of me when she returns. I send her, by way of explanation, the letter I wrote last night, but feared to forward to-day.

Yours,
Francis

Wilfrid Meynell's solution to the problem of Thompson's relapse was a retreat from London surroundings to the healthful atmosphere of North Wales. Late in December 1892, Thompson departed for Pantasaph, to take up lodgings in the guest-cottage of a Franciscan monastery. The monks, informed of Thompson's problem, had agreed to look after him.

40. To Wilfrid Meynell (?)

[late December 1892]

. . . Now you'll think I'm in a state of lighthearted exhilarance, which is very improper in me, considering all I have to repent of. Therefore I beg to assure you I'm suffering like old Nick. But when one is in this condition, one must laugh out or weep out. Too much of water hast thou [word erased]; therefore I'll grin through the very biggest horse-collar I can find. Don't think, though, that I repent having come here: if I were in London I would simply take a header into the Thames—only that it's such a damnably dirty place for a poet to drown in. But I'm in a most unconventional state at present; ready to go smash among all conventions like a bull in a chinashop, and can cry with Joe [word illegible] "wot larks!" I have half a mind, by way of final outrage, to make love to what I think the loveliest girl I have ever seen. But I have still some convention hanging about me in a tattered condition; and it may preserve an elementary decency in the bastard offspring of nature and art—

which signs itself
Yours affectionately,
F.T.

> The only text of this letter is an incomplete pencil draft in Notebook BC-10, datable to early spring 1893, at Boston College. It appears to fit the period of withdrawal from addiction he was then undergoing, and was perhaps his first letter from Pantasaph. The girl was Maggie Brien, daughter of his landlady.

41. To Mrs. Elizabeth Blackburn

[December 29, 1892]

. . . I am in a very nice cosey little cottage with good kindly Welsh people—and I love the Welsh provided they are Welsh Welsh. They have the primitive virtues. I have a very pretty and refined girl to wait on me, to whom I speak three and a half words per diem, and a fire all day which is more beautiful and beloved than any woman for whom Eve and her abominable apple are responsible. I am a Zoroastrian, a Magian, a Parsee . . . Please give Mr. Meynell my thanks for his letter and for sending me here. Very cold, intense frost, but dry and endurable with the fire. Glorious mixture of moonlight and sunset from the Calvary which crowns the hill above the monastery last night. Spent Xmas eve in writing verses—a poor thing but mine own . . .

> This fragment is quoted by Mrs. Blackburn in a letter of January 9, 1908, to Wilfrid Meynell. The verses were almost certainly an early eighteen-line draft of *Little Jesus*, now in the Boston College Collection.

42. To Wilfrid Meynell

Pantasaph
Jan. 4th, 1893

Dear Mr. Meynell,

C'en est fait, as regards the opium; though I have only just taken the turning which leads out of the debility consequent on the breaking-off. But I am now able to begin to get about a bit, and take exercise. That is to say, I should be able, but—. Which, next to my wish to tell you that I was safely out of the opium, is the motive of my writing. I can't get out, because snow has fallen, and by a foolish trick before I left London I have ruined my boots. Cowering over the fire at Fernhead Road one night, I let my foot hang too near the bars; and before I noticed it, the tip was burned off. At first I thought it was only the tip of the sole, and so nothing was spoilt but appearances. Since I came here, however, I discover to my dismay that the upper-leather is charred along with the tip of the sole; and it has come away from the sole, split, and begun to peel off, leaving the snow free to get in through the open end of the boot. So that just when I want and long for walking to act as a tonic against my debility, I am compelled to stay in the house. For the snow here is not like London snow, which I cannot face; it is virgin, dry, and pleasant for walking on; while the air is sunny and clear. There is hard frost, but it is a dry cold, and has none of the stupefying effect on me of London fog and frost. In fact, everything is beautiful for the time of the year. There is one other thing I want to know. Am I to ask Father Marianus to stamp such letters or Ms. as I may want to send off? I send this through Madam, as I do not like to ask Father Marianus till I know whether you have arranged for him to do so.

I am very comfortable, thanks to your kindness and forethought. Father Anselm seems to have taken a fancy to me—also he is afraid of my being lonely—and comes to see me nearly every other day. He took me all over the monastery on Monday, and has just left me after a prolonged discussion of all the things which "none of us know anything about," as Marianus says—when he is getting the worse of an argument.

Yours affectionately,
Francis Thompson

Thompson had lodged at 1 Fernhead Road, Paddington, during the latter months of 1892. He had been at Pantasaph perhaps two weeks when this letter was written.

43. To Wilfrid Meynell

Pantasaph
Thursday [January] 1893

Dear Mr. Meynell,

Enclosed is for the *Hobby-Horse*. You will get a note enclosed by me to Mrs. Blackburn before I got her communication. Very much better to-day; indeed I feel pretty well myself again. Just two days within the fortnight I said it would take.

Yours affectionately,
Francis Thompson

Madam has told me your message as to the forwarding of letters, etc.

It has not been possible to identify the enclosure for *The Hobby Horse*. The reference to a "fortnight" dates the letter to the first week of January.

44. To Mrs. Elizabeth Blackburn

[February 1893]

. . . I am very pleasantly domesticated with my agricultural family. One of the girls laughingly spoke of me the other day as "our brother Mr. Thompson." My landlady is a very motherly, kindhearted woman; and the girls are all merry, lighthearted creatures, which is a great godsend to a melancholy man like myself . . . *Your* priest has not yet arrived. A priest came on the day of your letter and I thought at first it might be he. He passed as I was playing "rounders" with two children and a peasant-girl and tearing round the garden like a school-boy . . .

> This fragment is quoted by Mrs. Blackburn in the letter of January 9, 1908, to Wilfrid Meynell. The cottage at which Thompson lodged—called Bishop's House—stood at the monastery gates. There were five girls and one son in the Brien family.

45. To Wilfrid Meynell

Bishop's House, Pantasaph
[April 3, 1893]

Dear Mr. Meynell,

I am sorry I was of so little assistance to you. I got your postcard late on Tuesday; and committed an error of judgment by wasting part of my time on a leaderette which I see has not proved suitable—as I feared might be the case. Away from all papers but the previous week's *Register*, it was difficult for me to find any subject at all; nor of course had I the benefit of your advice regarding the treatment even of the only one which occurred to me.

Hearing from Madam that she was going to Palace Court, I enclosed a little note for her; but she has written again in a fashion which leads me to suppose that she had left before Thursday. It does not matter, as Fr. Anselm has lent me a stamp to write to her. I have left her so long without a letter that I must write. It is a more important matter that Fr. Anselm, hearing from me that she was at P.C., sent the proofs of her *Annals* article there. Would you have the kindness to forward them, if she left before they arrived; as Fr. Anselm would be embarrassed if they were not returned in time.

I have had great discussions with Fr. Anselm à propos of the *Language of Religion*. Mr. Patmore might as well have signed his name: Fr. A. recognised the writer as soon as he came to the bit about the "Divine Lover." Some lineal descendant of poor Canon Toole wrote to him suggesting that the article was un-Christian, and should be cut up in the *Annals*. He rushed to read it in a militant mood; but was surprised to find that he largely agreed with it. I advised him to tell his correspondent so; and I believe he did. He has a little note in this month's *Annals,* going about as far, I think, as it could be expected he would go. But if Mr. Patmore does not remember a certain parable about a rich man, a poor man, and a ewe-lamb, and feel prickings of conscience—he is a hardened poet. My projected article, I may observe, is the ewe-lamb.

I send you two bantlings in verse. I do hope your fatigue this week has not told heavily on you. But where you have all been, and what you have been doing—it is mystery.

Yours affectionately,
F.T.

"Clarence Ford" only just arrived this (Monday) afternoon. Impossible to get the review done and off before to-morrow evening. What *are* you playing battledore-and-shuttlecock across the Channel for?

> At Pantasaph Thompson continued to help with the work of the *Weekly Register* as well as write for *Merry England.* Coventry Patmore's article "The Language of Religion" appeared in *Merry England* for February, March, and April 1893. The "two bantlings in verse" were probably *Little Jesus (Merry England,* May 1893) and *Desiderium Indesideratum (Merry England,* June 1893). Clarence Ford was the author of a biography of Madame de Krudener, reviewed by Thompson in *Merry England,* May 1893.

46. To Wilfrid Meynell

Pantasaph
Monday [June] 1893

Dear Mr. Meynell,

Fr. Cuthbert has sent me through Mrs. Blackburn a message—or quasi-message—to the effect that he is unwell and needs rest; and that perhaps I might be stirred up by Madam to write the leader instead of him this week. Accordingly I am sending you a leader, contrived as best I can in the absence of all papers. You can use it or not as you think fit;—I mean that it must not hinder you from supplying Fr. Cuthbert's place in any better way which you may wish.

You shall have it on Wednesday. Many thanks for your very kind letter. For the review of Mr. Patmore's book I must ask you to wait a week; since I have lent it to Fr. Anselm, and he is gone to Chester for the Consecration ceremonies. Your other requests I will carry out forthwith.

I received the clothes, which were very welcome. The trousers alone bothered me, proving ludicrously wide, and too short. After a strategical survey of them, I shut myself up and went in for three days of daring tailoring operations. As a result, they are now re-formed in a sufficiently tolerable manner, which reflects great credit on my versatile genius; though I pretend not they are of a style which peers might praise, and duchesses adore.

Yours affectionately,
Francis Thompson

Thompson's review of Patmore's *Religio Poetae* appeared in *Merry England*, September 1893.

47. To Coventry Patmore

Pantasaph
June 15, 1893

Dear Sir

. . . The esoteric essays—which I naturally turned to first—could only have come from the writer of the Unknown Eros. One alone I have the gracelessness—not to dispute—but to wish to extend. It is that on the *Precursor* where I quite admit the interpretation but am inclined to stickle for an interpretation which would cover and include your own. Against one reprehensible habit of yours, revealed in this book, I feel forced to utter a protest. In a fragment of a projected article, which has remained a fragment, I had written of "poets born with an instinctive sense of veritable correspondences hidden from the multitude." Then I went on thus;—"In this, too, lies real distinction and fancy. Leigh Hunt, interpreting Coleridge as shallowly as Charmion interpreted the soothsayer, said that fancy detected outward analogies, but imagination inward ones. The truth is that inward resemblance may be as superficial as outward resemblance; and it is then the product of fancy, or fantasy. When the resemblance is more than a resemblance; when it is rooted in the hidden nature of things, its discernment is the product of imagination. This is the real distinction; fancy detects resemblances, imagination identifies." Now if you will return to your own *"Religio Poetae"* you will see of what I accuse you. Masters have privileges, I admit, but I draw the line at looking over their pupils' shoulders various odd leagues away.

To be serious; your little book stands by the stream of current literature like Cleopatra's Needle by the dirt-eating Thames.

I fear, alas! it will not receive the mysterious hieroglyph of the British Artisan.

I remain
yours sincerely
Francis Thompson

The text is taken from an incomplete copy supplied by Harriet Patmore to the Meynells. Thompson and Patmore had not met at this time and were not to do so until October of the following year, when Patmore visited the Pantasaph monastery. Thompson's review of Patmore's *Religio Poetae* appeared in *Merry England*, September 1893. Thompson's "projected article" remained unpublished till it appeared in *Essays II* (1959) entitled "Analogies between God, Nature, Man and the Poet."

48. To Wilfrid Meynell

[June 1893]

. . . I find Lane has already announced the poems in his book list; so I am bound to go through with them; else I would let them go to the devil. I made myself ill with overstudy, & have been obliged to give my head three weeks' entire rest. But I am much better again now. Inwardly I suffer like old Nick; but the blessed mountain air keeps up my body, & for the rest—my Lady Pain and I are *au mieux* . . . The country here is just beginning to get beautiful, & I am feeling the first quickening pulse of spring. Lord it is good for me to be here—very good. The clogged wheels in me are slowly beginning to move . . .

> Quoted from VM II, pp. 44–45. In May the publisher John Lane had contracted to bring out a collection of Thompson's poetry from *Merry England,* with some unpublished pieces. Thompson began preparing the manuscript about mid-May.

49. To Wilfrid Meynell

Bishop's House, Pantasaph
[July 1893]

Dear Mr. Meynell,

Herewith I forward my poems, together with a note for Lane, apologising for any delay after the promise given through you. Would you kindly let me have a postcard to allay my natural anxiety as to whether they arrive safely?

I do not know whether you leave it to the publisher to add the *Contents;* but in case not, I have inserted such a table at the beginning—without numbers of pages, which depend on the printing.

The sestet of your sonnet in *M.E.* is beautiful.

Yours in hurry,
F.T.

> The poems forwarded comprised the manuscript of Thompson's first volume, published by John Lane in November 1893. Wilfrid Meynell's sonnet *Love Thy Neighbor* appeared in *Merry England,* July 1893. The following letter, to the publisher Lane, accompanied the manuscript of *Poems.*

50. To John Lane

Bishop's House, Pantasaph
[July 1893]

My dear Sir,

Herewith I forward to you my poems; and most sincerely apologize for my delay in forwarding them, after the message which I gave Mr. Meynell for you. At the last moment I found it necessary to weed out a portion of my selection, in order to bring it within the limit fixed by you. I hope that, as far as I can judge, it is now reduced to the requisite compass.

Yours sincerely,
Francis Thompson

J. Lane Esq.

51. To Alice Meynell

Pantasaph
[September 1893]

Dear Mrs. Meynell,

I have received the findings of the court-martial over which you presided; to which the under-signed begs to make answer, in form and manner following.

1. To the first indictment he pleadeth guilty, and knows not how he omitted to alter the word, as had been his own intention. He begs, therefore, that for "soilured" may be substituted "stealth-won."

2. In answer to the third indictment, he submits himself to the judgment of the court, and desires that Domus Tua shall be omitted, and the requisite alteration made in the numbering of the poems.

3. In regard to the second indictment, having already fully considered the matter, he refuseth to submit himself to the court, remaineth *en contumace*, and is prepared, in token of his unalterable resolution, to suffer the utmost rigours of the critics.

Now I carry the war into the enemy's country.

I do you to wit [*sic*] that a foul and malicious alteration has been committed on the body of one of King Phoebus' Lieges, in a magazine bearing the style and denomination of *Merry England*. And I hereby warn you, that if the same outrage is extended to the same unoffending poem in my volume, I shall hold you all and severally responsible. Hereunder follow the details of my accusation.

The passage of which I complain appeareth thus in the aforesaid magazine.

"Those fireflies of God to invite,
Burning spirits, which by night
Bear upon their laden wing
To such hearts impregnating,
For flowers that night-wings fertilize."

Then follows a fresh stanza:—

"Mock down the stars' unsteady eyes,
And with a happy, sleepless glance,
Gaze the moon out of countenance."

There should be no fresh stanza, and no stop at all after "fertilize." The pause should come after "impregnating," in the previous line; and then the next lines run on (as in the corrected pages I returned on Thursday):—

"For flowers that night-wings fertilize
Mock down the stars' unsteady eyes etc."

The meaning (which I should have thought perfectly clear) is that flowers which are fertilized by night-insects confront the moon and stars with a glance more sleepless and steady than their own. Surely anyone who knows a forest from a flower-pot is aware, that flowers which are fertilized by night-insects necessarily *open at night*, and emit at night their odours, by which those insects are attracted. The lines so unfortunately altered are, in fact, explanatory of the image which has gone before. But I sometimes wonder whether the best of you Londoners do not regard Nature as a fine piece of the Newlyn school, kindly lent by the Almighty for public exhibition. Few seem to realize that she is alive, has almost as many ways as a woman, and is to be lived with, not merely looked at. People are just as bad here, for that matter. I am sick of being told to go here and go there, because I shall have a "splendid view." I protest against Nature being regarded as on view. If a man told me to take a three-quarter view of the woman I loved, because I should find her a fine composition; I fear I should incline to kick him extremely, and ask whether he thought her five-foot-odd of canvas. Admiration both of a woman and Nature may begin there. But he is a poor lover who ends there. And having companioned Nature in her bed-chamber no less than her presence-room, what I write of her is not lightly to be altered. So please see that the passage in my volume stands as I left it in the pages which I returned to you.

I am delighted to hear from Mrs. Blackburn of the great success of your books. I hope you will fulfil your promise to send me them soon, for I am looking forward to them with great desire.

It was most stupid of me not to have acknowledged Francie's hair. It is beautiful, and excited great admiration among the people I am lodging with.

Having ended by catching a horrible cold, I seem now beginning to mend. The violent alterations of the weather just now from hot to cold, and cold to hot, are very trying. I would it were either hot or cold. Give my love to all who are at Palace Court. Tell Madam, if she is with you, that she has left me without . . .

> The manuscript of this letter is incomplete. Thompson is dis-
> cussing the proofs of *Poems* with Mrs. Meynell. "Your books"
> refers to the two volumes published by Mrs. Meynell in fall
> 1893—one of poems and one of essays.

52. To Alice Meynell

Pantasaph
Friday [September] 1893

Dear Mrs. Meynell,

I need hardly say how gratified I was to receive a letter from you. I return herewith the pages; but I must ask you—or Mr. Meynell— to render me one small assistance. Where I have terminated a word by an accented "-èd," the printers have omitted the accent. I have corrected this to the best of my ability; but I do not know the proper sign. If you would look through the pages, and wherever I have inserted in the margin an accented "-èd," put the proper mode of correction, I should be much obliged to you. They are the best pages of poetry I have had submitted to me. It seems to me that they read better than I had expected—particularly the large additions to *A Poet Breaking Silence*, which were written at a time when I was by no means very fit for poetry, and so caused me some anxiety. I only hope such be the case with regard to an entirely fresh poem of the same series, with respect to which I have the same anxiety. If I had kept the Ms. longer in hand, I should have omitted that poem, and instead added to the poems on children *Ex Ore Infantium*. Your interest in the volume is very dear to me. I cannot say I myself feel any elation about it. I am past the time when such things brought me any elation.

I have not either of your books, and of course should most greatly value them. I have heard from Mrs. Blackburn that they have been very successful, though I myself have seen few of the criticisms on them. I need not say how deeply I rejoice in your success. Any success which this melancholy age is likely to give you must be far under your due.

We had here for some ordinations Pope Hennessy's old adversary, Archbishop Scarisbrick. He rivals Mr. Patmore in his hatred of Gladstone. Entering a house here where there was a portrait of the Premier, he turned its face to the wall. G.O.M., he says, stands for "God's only Mistake." He declares the *Register* to be an organ of no consequence at all. I think it did *not* side with his Mauritian Grace.

Will you excuse me from writing more just now? I am not very well, and am much depressed. I will write further when I am in better spirits. In the Ms. I sent at . . .

> The manuscript of this letter is incomplete. *To a Poet Breaking Silence* was written in August 1890. *Ex Ore Infantium* is better known as *Little Jesus*; it was later included in *New Poems*.

53. To Wilfrid Meynell

Bishop's House, Pantasaph
[September 1893]

Dear Mr. Meynell,

Please forward the books, by all means. I have seen Fr. Marianus in regard to returning them; and he says the best way would be for me to leave them at the Monastery when I have finished with them, and he will see about returning them. He says they constantly have someone going from the Monastery to Holywell.

I am very sorry to hear from Madam that you have something the matter with your eye. I do hope you may get over it successfully. From the handwriting of your note I was afraid you were not well. Like many peoples of nervous organization, myself included, your handwriting varies strongly with your state of health; and I was sure you were nervously wrong in some way.

I have been wondering what criticisms had appeared on Mrs. Meynell. I have seen none, except the *Fortnightly* and the *Chronicle*. Coventry all abroad about her poetry, Le Gallienne all abroad about her prose. But the latter's notice of her poetry showed real perception, and was the best appreciation of it I have seen from an outsider. Coventry was excellent with regard to the side of her prose which he had seized; but rather provoking for seizing it, since he has sent the *Chronicle* off after him on what is a false trail. The side is there; but it is not the prominent side, surely, and certainly not the side most markedly characteristic of her.

Yours affectionately,
Francis Thompson

I am getting on very well, and the climate suits me admirably. Have you seen the passage from Bell Scott's memoires which I enclose, about Rossetti's death-bed? I have not seen the memoirs myself; but between what Bell Scott says about the Rossetti circle, and what the Rossetti circle now say about Bell Scott, it seems to me that, on the whole, the Shelley gang were a rather preferable set. It must be remembered that Swinburne has satirised *The Angel in the House* under the title of *The Person in the House*; but nevertheless I think even the "Cockney corsair," as Severn called Trelawney, would have been a sweeter companion than A.C.S.

> The last page of the manuscript of this letter has been altered by cutting and pasting. Material of undetermined length is missing after the phrase "preferable set."

54. To Wilfrid Meynell

Pantasaph
Monday [September] 1893

Dear Mr. Meynell,

I return the Dedication. The other will follow to-morrow, as it is not so easy. With regard to what I send. The line "weeping unslakened" says what I meant it to say, and I have decided against any alteration. That which burns, you slaken by allaying it. "Weeping unslakened," therefore, is a compact metaphysical way of saying burning tears, whose burning has no allay. In the quatrain which follows, the expression is undoubtedly very condensed. But I consider that the only blameworthy obscurity arises from a printer's error. The meaning, paraphrased, is this. "If the hid and sealed coffer, whose contents are not his own (since he has no power to bring them to light), may proffer their finding to those who loose his seal—here then is this, your finding." The substitution of "losers" for "loosers" of course renders the meaning unintelligible. The use of the word "having" to signify "possession" is a well-known Elizabethan usage. Shakespeare is full of it—the first example which occurs to me is: "Your *having* in beard is simply a younger brother's revenue." My decision on these points is a final one.

I may say that I tried the lines on Madam, who had not seen the dedication. "Weeping unslakened" she interpreted at once, without difficulty. In the next quatrain, she hesitated at "To the losers may proffer." Then I discovered the printer's error; and when I had corrected that, she interpreted the line as readily as the rest. Now, Madam I consider a fair type of the average intelligent but not specially poetical critic. You may lift your eyebrows at this. But reflect, that the lower you rate her intelligence, the less is the necessity for altering what she can understand.

With regard to substituting your full names for the initials, do as you please. But I cannot consent to the withdrawal of *your* name. You have of course the right to refuse to accept the dedication to yourself. But in that case I have the right to withdraw the dedication altogether, as I should certainly do. I should belie both the truth and my own feelings if I represented Mrs. Meynell as the sole person to whom I owe what it has been given me to accomplish in poetry. Suffer this—the sole thing, as unfortunate necessities of exclusion would have it, which links this first, possibly this only volume, with your name—suffer this to stand. I should feel deeply hurt if you refused me this gratification.

Yours affectionately
Francis Thompson

The phrases discussed are all from the dedication to *Poems*. As published, it carried the inscription "To Wilfrid and Alice Meynell."

55. To Wilfrid Meynell

Bishop's House, Pantasaph,
Sept. 14th, 1893

Dear Mr. Meynell,

I forward you two pages with my corrections in response to your criticisms. I must ask you to let Lane have them, and explain why they come to him at this eleventh hour. Because, you see, on Tuesday I sent off the second pages direct to Lane, in order to save time; and said that I had only found one correction to make, which I sent him. Now here come two more, and I have not the face to send them on to him.

With regard to the alterations I now enclose to you. In the *Fallen Yew*, by the correction of two words I hope that I have removed the obscurity, grammatical and otherwise. In *Monica Thought Dying*, I have simply substituted "eleven" for "thirteen." The word "eleven" fits the metre perfectly well without altering the rest of the line; since the final "e" is a natural elision. Mrs. Meynell will know what I mean. Most elisions are artificial and conscious. Such is the elision of the "a" in "seraph," whereby the line in the

Fallen Yew does scan, and so needs no alteration on that score. But there are a few words wherein we make unconscious elision, even in daily conversation. The final "en" after a "v" we always so elide; and consequently it is the exception for a poet to count the final "en" in such words as *heaven, seven,* or *eleven.* All this is simply to guard against your supposing that I have made an oversight in my corrections.

As for "immeditatably," it is in all respects the one and only right word for the line; as regards the exact shade of meaning and feeling, and as regards the rhythmical movement it gives to the line. So it must absolutely and without any question stand—woe's me for the public! But indeed, what is the public doing *dans cette galère?* I believe, it is true, the public *has* an odd kind of prejudice that poems are written for its benefit. It might as well suppose that when a woman loves, she bears children for its benefit; or (in the case of the poem in question) that when a man is hurt, he bleeds for its benefit. *Comme il est drôle, ce bon public!*

A thousand thanks to Mrs. Meynell for the portrait, which I need not say how I value.

Madam has been eating apples, like her mother Eve; and like her mother Eve has been very much upset by them. (Need I caution you that the apples were as literal as a Welsh gardener could grow them?) I have also been a little out of order the last two days; partly out of good company, and partly out of pure cussedness, as the "large utterance" of the American has it. I heard that my father was at Rhyl, and went over on Monday—only to find that he had left the previous Wednesday, after being there for a month. Which things are strange.

Yours affectionately
Francis Thompson

Love to everyone at Palace Court, including Francie.

After missing his father at Rhyl, a seaside resort about twenty miles from Pantasaph, Thompson did not see him until after the publication of *Poems,* when he visited home in October 1894.

56. To Wilfrid Meynell

Bishop's House, Pantasaph,
Tuesday [September 1893]

Dear Mr. Meynell,

I send you the line altered altogether. This must do. The stanza cannot go out: Mrs. Meynell shows something less than her usual judgment in suggesting so. So fine an artist should have perceived that the result would be the inartistic juxtaposition of two stanzas turning on the same rhyme, and even the same rhyming words.

I need hardly say that I see Mrs. Blackburn's postcard for the first time; but I am able to tell you what is at the bottom of it, for I remember she expressed herself hurt that she had not herself received a copy of Mrs. Meynell's last portrait. She spoke of a promise that she should have one. The postcard is in the fire. Dangerous invention, postcards! They are like revolvers, too handy for the vent of momentary spleen. Put it down to apples, put it down to apples!

Yours affectionately,
Francis Thompson

The poem referred to was A *Fallen Yew*; the stanza in question the third last.

57. To Alice Meynell

Pantasaph,
Thursday [September] 1893

Dear Mrs. Meynell,

I send the first installment of the revises.

I will write more shortly, as I want to talk to you about your essays; which I have re-read with deep admiration.

Your affectionate
Francis Thompson

I send some verses—I don't know what they are like. They are almost entirely taken, some from the Office of the Assumption, some from the Canticle, a few images from the heathen mythology. Some very beautiful images are from a hymn of St. Nerses the Armenian, flabbily rendered in *Carmina Mariana*. You will perceive, therefore, the reason of the motto from Cowley . . . they are almost absurdly easy to defend. I have made sure of careful deference to orthodoxy. If Fr. Anselm had been here I would cheerfully have passed the Ms. through his hands; in fact he supplied . . .

> The manuscript of the letter has been altered by cutting and pasting, especially following the word "revises." The verses were *Assumpta Maria*.

58. To Father Adam Wilkinson

[October 1893]

My Dear Father Wilkinson,

I am very pleased to receive your kind letter, but I must ask you to wait awhile for a proper answer. I have been badly bitten in the arm and am not yet able to use my pen properly. Believe me that it is only inability which at present confines me to this ungraciously brief scrawl. In the meantime, I remain,

Always your old schoolfellow,
Francis Thompson

> Quoted from *Ushaw Magazine*, March 1908. Fr. Wilkinson had been a classmate of Thompson's at Ushaw. The bite on the arm was received from the monastery watchdog at Pantasaph in October 1893.

59. To Wilfrid Meynell

Bishop's House, Pantasaph,
Tuesday [October 1893]

Dear Mr. Meynell,

Many thanks for the copies. The book is indeed beautifully got up—excepting the frontpiece, which I agree with you is a failure. It is not lovely in any sense, and the artist has overstepped the limits within which pictorial symbolism can act. To attempt to render a purely literary image such as the "hearted casement" in black & white is a grievous mistake—the result reminds one of nothing but a half obliterated five of hearts. The *Hound of Heaven* is just the poem which a draughtsman who knew the limits of his craft would have avoided. Warmest thanks for your only too generous article in *M.E.*, and for your energetic and kind arrangements with regard to reviewing of the book. I am in every way satisfied with them, and with Lane's liberal arrangement in regard to the business contract.

Mrs. Blackburn has, I believe, told you that I persuaded her to resign her copy in favour of Fr. Anselm. He richly merited it, not only by his continual kindness to me since I have been here, but by his warm interest in the book. Thanks to him, not only has the monastery ordered a copy, but two copies have been ordered by a private family here. Between you & me it will bore them horribly; but sales are sales all the same. The old schoolfellow whose letter you enclosed to me appears also to have ordered a copy in advance. He is a Benedictine, so that the Orders are bulking largely in regard to the volume. The other of my copies goes to Fr. Cuthbert; since of course neither he nor Fr. Anselm can purchase a copy for themselves. The third I have reserved for myself, and to it I have transferred Monnie's poppy, which had previously been attached to the *M.E.* copy of her special poem. I have been unable to fulfil my promise of writing to Mrs. Meynell about her essays. But will tell you that the impression made upon me by the collected work has been even greater than I had anticipated? They gain by being set in their own environment, instead of among the lower work of the N.O. writers. I am hoping for a copy of her poems when the third edition appears.

Will you excuse more from me at present? I have only just received permission to remove the bandages from my arm, and it is still weak in use, as you will perceive from this horrible scrawl. I have had tedious and complicated business with it.

With warmest love to Mrs. Meynell, yourself, and all,

Yours most affectionately
Francis Thompson

I have had my portrait taken; but it will be a week before the proofs are ready.

> Thompson is thanking Meynell for an advance copy of *Poems*, which was published the following month. Meynell's article on Thompson, "A New Poet," appeared in *Merry England*, November 1893, but Thompson probably read a proof of it, since the portrait he mentions appeared as frontispiece in the magazine.

60. To Wilfrid Meynell

[November 1893]

. . . When the first whirl of language is over (was it not a sin of my own former prose when I waxed enthusiastic?) he settles down to appreciation which is at the same time criticism. Will it be believed, however, that after deprecating superlatives I am actually disposed to rank myself higher than Mr. Le Gallienne's final sentence might seem to imply. I absolutely think my poetry is "greater" than any work by a new poet which has appeared *since Rossetti*. Unless, indeed, the greater work to which the critic referred was Mrs. Meynell's. I frankly admit that her poetry has exquisite unclamorous qualities beside which all the fireworks of my own are much less enduring things. Otherwise I will not vail my crest to Henley, or Robert Bridges, or even William Watson. For the rest I have nothing but warm and surprised gratitude for your untiring efforts on my behalf. I am very pleased with all the letters you have sent me, particularly Vincent O'Sullivan's from Oxford. Am I going to found a school there?

The minor versifier has at any rate the asterisks in "A Judgment in Heaven" which he can catch on to. There he can have the latest device in poetry, the whole apparatus procurable at my printer's. I have not forgotten that it was Le Gallienne's admiration for the specimen sent to Lane which finally decided the publication of my book; and I should indeed be sorry to know that I had repaid him by wounding his feelings.

I have read in the *Register* with great surprise that the *Poems* are exhausted. I am even more glad for my publisher's sake than for my own; since, to tell you the truth, I have been haunted by the fear that Lane's generosity had led him to expend more on the book than he would be succeed in recouping. The *St. James* article I am very pleased with. I only deprecate in it the implied comparison to Dante, and the to me bewildering comparison to Matthew Arnold. It is not merely that I have studied no poet less; it is that I should have thought we were in the sharpest contrast. His characteristic fineness lies in that very form and restraint to which I so seldom attain: his characteristic drawback in the lack of that full stream which I am seldom without. The one needs and becomes strict banks—for he could not fill wider ones; the other too readily overflows all banks . . .

> Quoted from separate fragments in EM, pp. 135–36 and VM II, p. 51. Richard Le Gallienne's editorial report to Lane, dated May 3, 1893, reads in part: "Would certainly publish. Rich coloured, oriental things. Remind me very much of Crashaw." Le Gallienne, a friend and frequent guest of the Meynells, had been familiar with Thompson's poetry since publication of the *Ode to the Setting Sun* in 1889.

61. To Alice Meynell

Bishop's House, Pantasaph,
Wednesday [January 1894]

Dear Mrs. Meynell,

Many thanks for your kind New Year's letter. I have deferred answering it until I could succeed in getting the loan of the *Fortnightly*; which I have now done, thanks to the kindness of one of the Friars. I am glad I waited. Had I written upon the evidence of the extract in the *Register*, I should have pronounced Mr. Patmore's article magnificently generous and that, read between the lines, would have meant that I thought Mr. Patmore had let generosity overmaster justice. But the complete article makes quite another impression. I am delighted with it. From first to last it is pre-eminently *just*; and managed to combine fine praise with discriminate and illuminating criticism of defects and limitations. "Illuminating;" for other critics note the symptoms of one's poetic maladies, he diagnoses the seat of the disease. I have got more help and self-knowledge from his article than from anything else which has appeared. Will you convey to him my warmest thanks for an article which cannot but remain a landmark in my life? I feel that my thanks will acquire a grace not their own, by being delivered to him through you.

I only wish, indeed, that I had a copy which I could keep of a paper so memorable.

I need hardly say how glad I should be to see Mr. Meynell and Monnie, if he decided to come up here. I fear, however, the holiday-time must be too far past by now for me to have a chance of seeing dear old Mon.

By the way, Madam seems to have been writing something to you about my supposed frame of mind in regard to Pantasaph; and so far as I can make out she has mostly read my sentiments by her own. "Rather dull," "pretty contented on the whole," seem to be the phrases she has scattered. Now, sometimes I am unwell, and then of course I am dull, as I should be anywhere. But except at such times I am by no means dull, and thrive in the quiet which is death to Madam, when none of the Capuchins happen to visit her for some time. For the last fortnight I have been very much out of order; which perhaps accounts for Madam's impression that I sometimes find the place dull. I am better now, however; and it was never anything but one of the causeless-seeming disturbances to which I am, as you know, intermittently subject.

Your article in the *P.M.G.* I at once perceived the nature of; so you need not have been afraid I should judge it as deliberate work. I do not care much for my own poem in this month's *M.E.*; nor indeed do I think either of the poems in the last two numbers can be ranked among my successes. The only critic who has pronounced upon them to me is Madam; and *her* judgment is too easily prejudiced to be reliable. She was delighted with *Assumpta Maria*—because, it is probable, she thought it pious. She dislikes *Any Saint*—because, it is probable, she thinks it "fishing." As I say, it does not appear to me that either poem comes to much.

Who, by the way, is the critic of some eminence who says that my pretty thoroughly rebuked coinages are "illiterate"?

I am very sorry to hear that Mr. Meynell has been unwell. I hope he is better. Give him and the chicks my best love.

Yours always affectionately
Francis Thompson

Please thank Mr. Meynell for his very kind and thoughtful present to me at Xmas.

> Patmore's review of *Poems* appeared in the *Fortnightly Review*, January 1894. The Thompson poem in "this month's *Merry England*" was *Any Saint*. The other poem he deprecates, be-sides *Assumpta Maria*, is *Elevaverunt Flumina*. Mrs. Blackburn's letter to Meynell about Thompson's attitude runs in part as follows: "As for Francis I hardly know what to say. I wish he would show some kind of human elation at his unprecedented success, but he seems to take it all in a dull, mechanical way, which is distressing. It is two months now since there has been any change in him . . . It is odd to read all the well-merited praise, and then realise how outside the pale of humanity this great genius is, more irresponsible than any child, with a child's fits of temper and want of foresight and control. He isn't doing a stroke of work, and stays in bed the best part of the day, and lately he falls asleep when he comes to see me. No one can do anything with him." (Quoted from EM, pp. 143–44.)

62. To Wilfrid Meynell

Bishop's House, Pantasaph,
Monday [February 1894]

Dear Mr. Meynell,

I enclose the only two short verses I have at hand. I don't know whether either of them will do. Also I send the autograph *Daisy*. Was the subeditor of the St. James's the author of the review in that paper? In case he was, I have enclosed a slip in the poem. If he was not, please take the slip out. I think Traill's article excellent and kind. But the *Athenaeum*—! Call you this dealing favourably with a man? Heaven save me, then, from the unfavourable dealers! If the writer and myself were not so completely unknown to each other, I should have thought it had the note of personal spite. Of course, he is right enough about the *To Monica Thought Dying*; but that and one or two other poems are not sufficient on which to base a charge of making Mr. Patmore a model—a thing of which the remaining poems are, I think, guiltless enough. It would have been well, indeed, for the restraint and sanity of the poems, if I *had* submitted somewhat to the influence of Mr. Patmore's example. As for Watson's review, it is not, like Symonds's, [*sic*] unfair; it is simply one-sided, and sometimes purblind even from his own standpoint.

Many thanks for your kindness in so promptly forwarding me everything. Say all that you think ought to be said to Miss Tynan—I beg her pardon, Mrs. Hinkson—for her kindness in the *Bookman*. By no means say what I say to you; that the article is in substance a réchauffée of things said in the dailies and by Mr. Patmore in the *Fortnightly*. Nevertheless it is warm and appreciative, and I am grateful to her for her friendliness.

The sale of the book is indeed astonishing. Let us hope that the league of the weeklies will not materially damp it.

Will answer Monnie. Best love to yourself and all.

Yours always,
Francis Thompson

P.S. Ask Mrs. Meynell if I may keep Mr. Patmore's letter?

"Traill's article" was a review of *Poems* in *Nineteenth Century*, February 1894. The *Athenaeum* review, February 3, 1894, was by Arthur Symons, who said in part: "If Crashaw, Shelley, Donne, Marvell, Patmore and some other poets had not existed, Francis Thompson would be a poet of remarkable novelty . . . his work, with all its splendours, has the impress of no individuality; it is a splendour of rags and patches." Katharine Tynan's review was in the *Bookman*, January 1894. *Poems* sold some two thousand copies in its first six months.

63. To Monica Meynell

Bishop's House, Pantasaph
[February 15, 1894]

Dearest Monica,

I was so glad to have a letter from you. I was beginning to think you had forgotten me, and getting horribly jealous of Father Marianus because you wrote to him and told him you would keep his portrait among your dearest treasures, or something of the sort. Then your mother made me half expect I was going to see you here, and you did not turn up. I hear you are nearly as tall as your mother now. If you go on at this rate, next time I see you you will have to lift me up in your arms to kiss you. I don't think I could kiss you with any dignity under those circumstances. I should say: "Let me down, Miss Meynell, if you please. I'm getting too old to be kissed." Is your hair getting curlier in proportion? And do you still put your thumb in your mouth?

You must have missed your skating this winter. And it was too cold to swim, so I don't know what you have doing with yourself. Going to school, and getting dreadfully clever, I suppose. I have learned something, too—I have learned to play *Reverse*. Come here, and I will beat you two games out of three. This place is too far from the sea, so *I* never got a bathe all the summer—and it was such lovely weather for bathing, I wished I were a duck, with nothing on but feathers. Or perhaps a swan—that would be more poetical.

I return your father the letter from the *Review of Reviews*. I hope he doesn't want the proof of my portrait back; because a girl at my lodgings has gone off with it. I'm sure I don't know why; for she does not like me, and keeps out of my way as much as possible. But the ways of girls are unsearchable, like the ways of Providence.

What nice letters you are getting to write now! Do let me have another soon.

With best love to your father, your mother, and all the "kids".

Always, my Sweet,
your poet
Francis Thompson

The original is missing; this is taken from a letter-book of Thompson's letters to Monica kept by the Meynells. The "girl at my lodgings" was Maggie Brien.

64. To Wilfrid and Alice Meynell

Bishop's House, Pantasaph,
Wednesday [April 1894]

Dearest Wilfrid & Alice,

As you are together, in my thoughts, so let me join you together in this note. I cannot express to you what deep happiness your visit gave me; how dear it was to see your faces again. I think "the leaves fell from the day" indeed, when your train went out of the station; and I never heard the birds with such bad voices.

I send you herewith the poem I have been at work on. It is very long, as you will see; as long, I think, as Wordsworth's great Ode. That would not matter—

"so were I equal with him in renown."

But as it is—!

My fear is that thought in it has strangled poetic impulse. However of all that you are better judges than I.

Does the dear singer still refuse me her songs?

My health is better again, though unfortunately more fluctuant than I could wish. Love to all the chicks. I particularly wanted to tell you when you left to give my love to Evvie as well as Monnie; but I forgot. With very best to yourselves, dear ones,

Yours ever,
Francis Thompson

Early in April 1894, Wilfrid and Alice Meynell paid Thompson a visit at Pantasaph, and this letter was written shortly after their departure. The salutation marks the first time during their six-year acquaintance that Thompson addressed the Meynells in correspondence by first names. A letter of Alice Meynell's, written in answer to the above, make it clear that the poem sent was *From the Night of Forebeing* (his line estimate was inaccurate: Wordsworth's *Intimations* is just over 200 lines, while *Forebeing* runs to 368).

65. To Alice Meynell

Bishop's House, Pantasaph,
Saturday [summer 1894]

Madonna soavissima,

Just a line to say how delighted I have been with your Pall Mall article on Pantasaph. It is entirely in your old sensitive subtly-perfumed style; which, to say truth, I have been half afraid you might be losing amidst the drudgery of *Autolycus* and such gear. How it touches me to hear the well-remembered, unique voice once again, "piercing-sweet" as ever! What gratification it has given at the monastery perhaps another than I may tell you, or may have told you. I hope it is the prelude to a fresh welling-forth of the old waters.

I have still several poems to finish. Weather here has turned stormy & cold, curtailing my exercise. Dearest love to Wilfrid, & the chicks. Will answer his letter soon. Always & always yours,

Francis Thompson

And you will not send me your poems, dear lady?

> Quoted from a copy preserved by Mrs. Sowerby. Alice Meynell's article on Pantasaph was "At Monastery Gates." "The Wares of Autolycus" was a feature in the *Gazette* to which Alice Meynell regularly contributed.

66. To Father H. K. Mann

[summer 1894]

My Dear Father Mann,

I have not only to thank you for your kind letter and recollection, but also for procuring me the pleasure of the best review of me which has appeared. The interest of my old college and school-fellows in my success has been very grateful to me. You may rely upon it that I see very clearly what is justified in such adverse criticism as has appeared on me, and shall not be backward to utilise it in working out my own ideals. Would you have the kindness to forward the enclosed letter to my Newcastle reviewer, whose address I do not know. Please, therefore, forward it direct if you know his address: if not, his brother. Excuse this all too brief note, but I am crowded with correspondents, who all require answering as soon as possible.

With all affectionate remembrances,
Believe me, Yours sincerely,
Francis Thompson

A review of *Poems* appeared in the *Ushaw Magazine*, March 1894. The Newcastle reviewer was J. L. Garvin whose lengthy commentary on *Poems* appeared in the *Newcastle Chronicle*, February 15, 1894. Garvin later became an intimate at Palace Court and a friend of Thompson's.

67. To Alice Meynell

Bishop's House, Pantasaph,
Monday [October 1894]

Dear Lady,

I thank you for your kind letter—though it observed an impenitent silence on the subject of your songs unsent. (That last phrase has a ring of the only Lewis). I have had a charming visit from Mr. Patmore. He bore himself towards me with a nobility and magnanimity which are not of this age's stature. I am going to write an article on his poetry, *à propos* of the issue of the new collective edition; and yourself, Wilfrid, and he, will have to decide between you to which of the monthlies it had better be offered. By the way, he repeated to me two or three short poems addressd to yourself. They are exquisite, and more worthy of you than anything which a *deus minorum gentium* like myself has been able to do. I hope there may be sufficient astral influence in your eyes to evolve a series of such songs—in every way worthy, it seems to me, of his genius. You would then have a triple tiara indeed—crowned by yourself, by me, and highest-crowned by him. Poetry will be the poorer if he does not do it.

He seems to have left just in time to escape most dismal weather.

A thunderstorm broke over us the very day he went; and now it is a day of dense fog and steady rain. Consequently I have very poor and unhappy brains for writing.

I will answer Monnie as soon as I have made up my mind whether anything less than a tablecloth will suffice for her request. It virtually means writing about a hundred lines on the two sides of one sheet. I think I shall try the wrong side of a wall-paper.

Love to Wilfrid and the children, and heaven keep from you "wheels" and all such things.

Always your affectionate
Francis Thompson

> "The only Lewis" was Lewis Morris, whose volume *Songs Unsung* was just then published. The visit to Pantasaph by Patmore marked the first meeting between the two poets and was the start of an important friendship. "Wheels" refers to headaches.

68. To Alice Meynell

[October 1894]

My Dear Lady,

. . . the long poem was written only as an exercise in blank verse; indeed, as you will see, I have transferred to it whole passages from my prose articles. So it is solely for your judgment on the metre that I send it. It is my first serious attempt to handle that form, and it is not likely that I have succeeded all at once; especially as I have not confined myself to the strict limits of the metre, but have laid my hand at one clash among all the licences with which the Elizabethans build up their harmonies. The question is whether individual passages succeed sufficiently to justify the belief that I might reach mastery with practice, or whether I fail in such a fashion as to suggest native inaptitude for the metre.

Madam thinks the poem a failure. Being a mistress of numerous metre, she counts all her feet; though her chosen method is the dactyllic, since she uses her fingers for the purpose. It is well known that by this profound and exhaustive method of practical study, you may qualify yourself to sit in judgment on Shakespeare's metre, if he should submit his Ms. to you from the Shades.

I confess my practice is so slovenly that if anyone should assure me that my lines had eleven syllables apiece, I should be obliged to allow that I had never counted them. We poor devils who write by ear have a long way to go before we attain to the scientific company of poets like Madam, who has her verses at her fingers' ends.

F.T.

Quoted from EM, p. 177. The poem sent was *An Anthem of Earth*; for some further remarks on it by Thompson, see letter 116. The poem appeared first in *Merry England*, November 1897, indicating that the Meynells read and put it into print almost immediately. Alice Meynell later called it Thompson's "most magnificent ode," putting it at least on a par with *The Hound of Heaven*, though there have since been many who disagree with that estimate. In December, Thompson returned to London for a visit, during which he prepared *Sister Songs* for publication.

69. To the Editor, the *Westminster Gazette*

[spring 1895]

. . . My business is as one of the—I suppose I should say shameful —seven pilloried by your critic, to give my private witness for Mr. Le Gallienne. The *gravamen* of the charge against him is not that he praised too effusively; it is the far more heinous accusation of log-rolling—in other words, of praising in return for favours received, or favours which it was understood were to come. Here then, are the facts, in my own case. When my book appeared it was reviewed by Mr. Le Gallienne in terms no less generous than those used by him recently in the *Weekly Sun*. When his first review appeared Mr. Le Gallienne and myself were totally unacquainted and unconnected. Before the second, printed in the *Weekly Sun*, we had met once casually. And this is the whole extent of my personal acquaintance or communication with one who is accused of praising me because he is my friend. Nor does the meanness anonymously attributed to Mr. Le Gallienne end there.

He is accused of praising me not only as a friend but as one whom I praise in return. Allow me then to say that I have never before or since his review of my poems written a line about him in any quarter . . .

> Quoted from EM, pp. 141–42. Though obviously sincere, Thompson is not quite correct when he says he was "unconnected" with Le Gallienne before the first review; Le Gallienne had been a friend and house guest of the Meynells. EM says this letter was never sent, but see the following letter.

70. To John Lane

Ivy Cottage, Pantasaph,
Saturday [April 1895]

Dear Mr. Lane,

Your letter comes as a great surprise to me. When I left London, some copies of the poem were being privately printed at the Westminster Press, in order that they might be used for working from, to save the Ms. from possible destruction. It was understood that one of these printed copies should be forwarded to me to make my revision from, as soon as the printing at the Westminster Press was completed. With this understanding, I did not take the Ms. with me, when I came here; and ever since I returned I have been waiting for a copy of my own poem, and have not received it. Apparently everyone concerned has been provided with a copy, except the unimportant author. I was wondering what was the reason of the delay; and lo! I get a letter from you charging it all on my shoulders! If I had been accorded the elementary courtesy of a copy of my poem to revise, the revision would have been in your hands long since. I do not lay the blame on you: it is evidently Wilfrid Meynell who has been at fault. If you cannot send me a copy of the poem yourself, then rout up Meynell, and make sure that a copy goes to me *at once*. When once I have the poem to revise, I will send the revision *direct to you*, with the least possible delay; so that there may be no more hitches through trusting to the broken reed of Palace Court. But unless you look after it yourself, letters will procure a very slow and uncertain response from Wilfrid Meynell.

All that I have at present is some advance pages of the *First Part*. But the *Second Part* also needs alterations; slight, and quickly made, but made they *must* be—or I will not let the poem go to the press. So, I repeat, I must have a copy at once of the complete poem. I am very sorry for your delay; but I think you will see I am not responsible for it. The author is the one person about whom no-one seems to have troubled; and as a natural consequence, at the last moment you have the author blocking the way. It is not your fault, nor mine; but for heaven's sake in future do not depend on Palace Court sending me anything, if you wish for expedition and the avoidance of misunderstanding. Anything you can send me direct yourself, send me, and you will find I am not such a thorn in the flesh of the publisher as you have no doubt been thinking me. In this instance you had of course to depend on Palace Court; and you must not suppose that I am putting the blame on your much-burdened shoulders.

I wrote the promised letter on behalf of Le Gallienne to the *Westminster Gazette*; but so far as I know it was not inserted. Would you tell Le Gallienne this?

I am afraid I have been a little peppery; but the pepperiness was not on your account. So pray pardon it to a naturally astonished author, and believe me with warmest remembrances of your kindness when I was in London,

Yours sincerely,
Francis Thompson

Thompson had returned to Pantasaph early in February. The Westminster Press, which printed *Merry England* and *The Weekly Register*, was owned by Wilfrid Meynell. The "letter on behalf of Le Gallienne" was a protest against the charges of log-rolling that appeared in some of the commentary on *Poems*; a surviving portion of it appears above as letter 69. Thompson left Bishop's House and moved to nearby Ivy Cottage in October 1894.

71. To John Lane

Ivy Cottage, Pantasaph,
Wednesday [May 1895]

Dear Mr. Lane,

I send you herewith the advance pages which I have of the *First Part* of my poem; on which I have made all the alterations I want. By the same post I have sent instructions to Meynell as to three corrections which I desire him to make for me in the *Second Part*, of which, as I told you, I have no copy. He will thus be able to let you have that Part at once, without sending it to me for correction; since under pressure of present necessity I will be content with those changes which I have dictated to him from memory, and will forego further alterations in the Second Part. So the whole Poem is now ready for you as far as I am concerned.

Some of my corrections in the pages I send you have reference merely to printers' errors, which have very likely been corrected in the bound copies of the Poem. But your printers will be able to see when this is the case. The other alterations, though few, are radical and important; amounting to entire rewriting of some lines and passages.

I am very sorry to have been the involuntary cause of so much vexatious delay to you.

I see from Le Gallienne's notice in the *Realm* that Lionel Johnson's poems are out—though he has chosen the worser part, and not kept to the Bodley Head.

With kindest regards,

Yours very sincerely,
Francis Thompson

It is a striking fact, as reported here, that Thompson is revising, *from memory*, a long poem he had written five years before and which he had not reread for over four months.

72. To Wilfrid Meynell

Ivy Cottage, Pantasaph,
Wednesday [June 1895]

Dear Wilfrid,

Let it be "Sister-Songs," as you suggest. But keep "An Offering to Two Sisters" where it now is—on the title-page. Mind you, though, that it *is* "An Offering to" etc.; and not "Inscribed to," as *you* write it. The latter would cause confusion, since the *Inscription* at the close of the poem is *not* to the two sisters, but to their two parents.

Sister-Songs was my own first alteration of the title, but was dropped I hardly recollect why. The weather here is splendid—none too soon, for up to May it was villainous.

Madam sends her love.

I see that Vernon has something about me in the *New Review.* What is it like, if you have seen it?

With best love to all; in haste,

Yours always,
Francis Thompson

Sister Songs, written in 1890, was published by John Lane in June 1895. An edition privately printed by Wilfrid Meynell about the same time bore the title *Songs Wing to Wing.* Its original title, *Amphicypellon,* is discussed by Thompson in letter 20.

73. To John Lane

Ivy Cottage, Pantasaph,
Tuesday [June 1895]

Dear Mr. Lane,

I have to ask your pardon for my delay in replying to you; but I have not been, and am not well. I duly received the advance copy of my book, with the *format* of which I am satisfied. There are two errors of punctuation (one an unfortunate error) and a dropped capital at the beginning of a line, which ought to be corrected before you go to press with any further edition.

I am surprised to hear you say that you have no agreement with me about the book. An agreement was forwarded me to sign on May 25: I signed and sent it to you on the day that I received it; which I presume would be May 26. I have the duplicate of that agreement, and I enclose you the letter which I received with it. But as there is only one point in which I see any material difference between the two agreements, I sign the one you have now sent me, rather than put you to further delay. That one point is, that the other agreement allowed me six gratis copies; this allows me none beyond the one you have already sent me. Now, I have no personal occasion for so many as 6; but I should have liked two more copies or at any rate one more, which I desire to send to Mr. Patmore with a personal inscription in my own writing. I leave this matter, however, to what you consider fair and courteous.

What you say about the probable sale of the book does not take me by surprise. I am not a business man, but my own judgment was against the public printing of the poem until I had a more assured position as a writer; though the Meynells, and I understood you, thought otherwise. Consequently I had already considered the advisability of following it by a collection of new poems, which I have already commenced to revise for that purpose. I am happy to find that your opinion coincides with mine.

I have just seen Le Gallienne's notice. He hits the central defect of the Second Part very accurately. I shall desire to put the new volume in your hands as soon as possible: but there is much revision to be done, and my health at present allows me but fitful ability to work at it.

Yours very sincerely,
Francis Thompson

There is no indication of the nature of Thompson's illness at this time, though it was probably nothing more than his usual dyspepsia and colds.

74. To Coventry Patmore

Ivy Cottage, Pantasaph
[July 1895]

Dear Mr. Patmore,

If you are not irreclaimably disgusted with me, it will be rather owing to your forbearance than my deservings; for you have every right to be. I did actually write a letter to you at Easter: but a temporary difficulty about such a mundane matter as stamps delayed its dispatch until it became obsolete; and since then I have been full of good intentions with their common accompaniment of non-performance. I have, indeed, been suffering severely in health; so that only the occasional and—under the circumstances —absolutely painful impulse of verse has had power enough to rouse me from my inertia. Today I feel a temporary lifting sufficient for me to drag myself to writing; though you will see from this very shaky hand that I do not exaggerate my nervous prostration. I received A.M.'s portrait with deep feelings of gratitude for your thoughtful kindness. It is curious that the very evening before you sent it off I had been talking about Sargent's drawing, and wishing inwardly that I had a copy of it—not then knowing that it was to appear in the *P.M. Budget*. Since then I have received and read your book—read it not once but often. I want much to talk to you about it; but I fear I must wait till a day when my head is clearer. I will only now say generally that it is the profoundest prose of yours I have yet read. It is only by comparing you with yourself that I can mark my sense of it; for no other modern writer furnishes any standard of measurement. Where all is deep, the *Aurea Dicta* appears to me the deepest. It is pure wisdom; the other sections being, in differing proportions, mingled with the lesser profundity—or rather the profundity in a lesser kind—of knowledge. I have read no such collection of aphorisms. There is enough to build the reputation of sages seven times seven. I marked the saying which took me most; then found I had marked three quarters of them, and went back and reselected amongst my selections; and finally wondered why I should mark any, when each, in turn, seemed the most worthy of marking. Do you notice, by the way, that in one of them you have slipped into a very beautiful heroic line?—

"Meeting unequal claims with equal duty."

If that had been cited to me, I should have said: "Shakespeare, of course, but I do not remember it. Where does it come?"

I shall either send you with this, or later, a small poem of my own; not for its literary merit, but because, without such a disclaimer, I fear you would think I had been the first to find your book "d—d good to steal from." As a matter of fact it was written soon after Easter, and was suggested by passages in the liturgies of Holy Saturday, some of which—at rather appalling length—I have quoted at the head of its two parts. That was done for the sake of those who might cavil at its doctrines. Indeed—perhaps with superfluous caution—I intended much of it to be sealed; but your book has mainly broken the seals I had put upon it. There is quite enough in it yours, without the additional presumption that I had hastened to make immediate use of your last book. As far as others are concerned, it must rest under that imputation, to which the frequent coincidence in the selection of symbolism—as an example, the basing of a whole passage on the symbolic meaning of the *West*—very naturally leads. To yourself such coincidence is explicable, it will not be to outsiders.

I have many things which I have been storing up to say and ask you, but they must wait for another day and a less deadened brain. From or of A.M. I have heard nothing since I left London. How is your own health? You spoke of it as restored to its normal condition: I hope with all my heart it remains so. But your preface rather saddened me; it seemed to have been written *de profundis*.

My own ill-destined volume has appeared, and even Lane has evidently realized beforehand that it ought not to have appeared. I have seen a review in the *Chronicle*—by Le Gallienne, I presume. By no means enthusiastic, and mainly just in its non-enthusiasm. I am apathetic about the book, as a bad business which I cannot mend, and wash my hands of.

Kindly remember me to Mrs. and Miss Patmore, and to Piffy, and believe me,

Yours always,
Francis Thompson

I cannot get the poem copied in time to send with this. So I send you what is at least lighter reading.

> The poem suggested by the liturgies of Holy Saturday was *Orient Ode*, published first in *New Poems* (May 1897). Patmore answered this letter in a note of July 11, saying in part about *Sister Songs:* "Thank you much for your book and its precious inscription. I quite agree with you about its publication at this time, for which you are not responsible. It is abounding in 'fine things' and 'striking' but it is not what a poem by you ought to be, and what many of your other poems were—*single* fine things."

75. To Wilfrid Meynell

Ivy Cottage, Pantasaph,
Wednesday [July 1895]

Dear Wilfrid,

I hope Fr. Cuthbert will be writing to-day to tell you; but in case anything should delay his doing so, I write to relieve your perplexities myself. I can obtain lodgings on the same terms as at present, with the people that used to have me before I went to Ivy Cottage. Consequently you need not be called on for pre-payment. It will be much better in every way than going to the other place, which Fr. Cuthbert at first supposed the only thing possible, not knowing that my old landlady had any room for a lodger in her present house. I shall be with people that I know and like, and who know and like me, and will not want to get rid of me on account of my erratic ways. They are used to them of old, and like me well enough not to mind them. I shall have a bed-room and sitting-room,— and there will be no necessity, as I say, for you to make any difference in your present system of payment. Madam knows the people I speak of—the Briens—and I daresay you remember my being with them. And no doubt she can explain to you anything you want to know about the matter. But as Cuthbert's placid and slow-moving spirit takes some time to fetch about between cross-winds, I thought best to write in case he should delay writing till to-morrow—and things are getting rather close for delays.

Madam will have told you that I am not well and that I want some medicine, which I told her to ask you to get for me. I am waiting for it anxiously, though it is too soon for it to have reached me yet. I am suffering from a complaint for which my father prescribed at Storrington, and you sent me the requisite homoeopathic medicine from London. It cured me then, and I hope it may do now, if you will be kind enough to get it for me. I gave the name of it to Madam. I am a little better just now, but very weak and fluctuant.

Kindest love to Mrs. Meynell and the children.

Yours ever,
F.T.

Thompson left Ivy Cottage and moved to Creccas Cottage, located over the hill just behind the monastery, in July 1895. He had earlier lodged with the Briens at Bishop's House.

76. To Wilfrid Meynell

[August 1895]

. . . I should much like to see further notices of my book if you would not find it too much trouble. Lane has sent me only Le Gallienne's in the *Star*. From another source I have had the *Daily Chronicle, St. James* and *Manchester Guardian*. Lane speaks of reviews in the *Realm, Saturday* and *Athenaeum*. If the two latter are by Symons, as he says, I do not want to see them. He is the only critic of mine I think downright unfair . . . Coventry has sent me a poem of Mrs. Meynell's from the P.M.G.—"Why Wilt Thou Chide?" No woman ever wrote a thing like that: and but one man—Coventry himself.

Quoted from EM, pp. 145–46. The book referred to was *Sister Songs*, of which Le Gallienne said in part: "Passion, in its ideal sense, has seldom found such an ecstatic, such a magnificently prodigal expression." Other critics, though finding much to admire, were decidedly less enthusiastic about the poem as a whole. "P.M.G." was the *Pall Mall Gazette*.

77. To Coventry Patmore

Creccas Cottage, Pantasaph,
Sunday [August 1895]

Dear Mr. Patmore,

I was very disappointed at the sudden frustration of your visit, to which I had been so much looking forward; and still more sorry that its frustration should have come from ill-health. You are the only man with whom I can talk at all: with all others it is a matter of playing an intermittent chord or so, as an accompaniment to *their* talk. Real interchange of mind is impossible, when you know that the most casual dropping of one of your inward thoughts would produce as profound a silence as if you had enunciated a maxim in Chinese. It is a welcome relief with one man to have the seal off your lips. Still more, yours is the conversation of a man who has trodden before me the way which for years I trod alone and often desperate, seeing no guiding parallel among modern poets to my aims and experience. I hope at least the bad effects of your journey have not continued after your return to Lymington.

I send you the poem you ask for; though, to say truth, with more than diffidence. I have no great expectation of its amounting to much poetically, on account of my ill-health at the time it was written. So pray understand that I shall be in no way surprised or put out if you do not judge it worthy of me. I think you know that I esteem it more honour to be condemned by an austere than approved by a lax judgment.

It is by no means on the high theme of your book, as you will see, and only traverses it incidentally, and in details. I do not care to desecrate by weak handling the highest themes, until I find myself past the transitional stage in poetry, and secure that what I do will at least be integral.

Believe me,
Always yours,
Francis Thompson

The poem sent was *Orient Ode*. Patmore answered in a letter of August 28, which reads in part: "Two readings leave your poem only obscure in parts, but not, perhaps, more obscure than prophecy should be. I see with joy, how much we are upon the same lines, but our visions could not be true were they quite the same; and no one can really see anything but his own vision. In the manner of your verse you are gaining in simplicity—which is a great thing. But I will speak of that more fully by and bye. In the matter I think you outstrip me. I am too concrete and intelligible."

78. To Coventry Patmore

Creccas Cottage, Pantasaph,
Monday [September 1895]

Dear Mr. Patmore,

Many thanks for your kind pains with the poem. I shall defer writing more particularly about it today, for there are one or two points I want to discuss at some length. I send you now a little thing which I think I should flinch from A.M. seeing. She would be indignant at the "mighty cruelties." I think you will not. Like Cromwell, I take it, you would disdain that your painter should omit a wart.

I have received the book you forwarded—a worthless Yankee "epic" on Columbus, inscribed by the author to Francis Thompson Esq., care of Coventry Patmore Esq., with kind regards to both." By some enclosed "Notices" I see that he has sent his book to Newman and Aubrey De Vere. In our case the economical fellow has apparently tried to kill two poets with one stone—a very heavy one.

Yours always,
Francis Thompson

The "little thing" sent by Thompson was *A Captain of Song*, which bore the inscription: "On a portrait of Coventry Patmore by J. S. Sargent, R.A." Patmore responded on September 27, 1895: "Your 'Captain of Song' is a very grand poem, and quite free, though colossal, from any partial and violent emphasis. I am not, however, that Dantesque being, which you and Sargent make me out to be; but that is no defect in the poem or the picture, *as* a poem and a picture . . . I do not think that A.M. would disapprove. I have not hidden from her the 'mighty cruelties'. They have often drawn tears from her eyes."

79. To Coventry Patmore

[late September 1895]

Dear Mr. Patmore,

The poem, even if I am to take your high and valued praises quite literally, has a defect of which you must be conscious, though you have courteously refrained from noticing it. It echoes your own manner largely, in the metre, and even in some of the diction—the latter a thing of which, I think, I have seldom before rendered myself guilty.

Now it is possible in rare cases—e.g. Keats' "Hyperion"—for an echo to take on body enough to survive as literature. But even should my poem so survive it must rest under the drawback of being no more distinctive Thompson than "Hyperion" is distinctive Keats.

With regard to the other poem, I want to allude particularly to your invaluable correction of my misuse of the Western symbolism. On re-examination, the whole passage discloses a confusion of thought naturally causing a confusion of symbolism. My attention was called to the point about Egyptian worship by a footnote in Dr. Robert Clarke's "Story of a Conversion," in *Merry England*. I at once perceived its symbolic significance, and asked myself how it came that we reckoned our points of the compass facing north. The only explanation I could surmise was that it was a relic of Set-worship among our Saxon ancestors. Do you mean that *historically* men have prayed in three distinct periods to W., E., and N.? . . .

Always yours,
Francis Thompson

Quoted from EM, p. 193. In an earlier letter, Patmore had explained: "The world has worshipped turning to the West, to the East, and to the North. The 'New Eve' is the South, and, when we 'turn thither, all things will be renewed, and God will turn our captivity as Rivers in the South,' and we shall know Him in the flesh 'from sea to sea.'" Dr. Clarke's "The Story of a Conversion" ran serially in *Merry England* during 1890–94, appearing intermittently.

80. To Wilfrid Meynell

Creccas Cottage, Pantasaph,
Tuesday [late September 1895]

Dear Wilfrid,

I hope you reached home and got through Thursday without being too much knocked up. May I remind you that I am owing poor Fr. Raphael (whose father is dead) some tobacco; also that sonnets and such like commodities will by no means flow without smoke. And (though *that* is less pressing) perhaps I might remind you at the same time about the *Lux in Tenebris* ode. As I said when you were here, it was (when I was in London) in the same box as my other poems, but enclosed in a large envelope—and had, I think, a letter along with it in the envelope. However, the poem is not a matter of immediate hurry; but the tobacco is devoutly to be desired.

Give my love to Mrs. Meynell and the chicks; tell Monica that I will not hurry more than I can help over the *Poppy*; love to Madam, and kind remembrances to Madame Von Teuffel.

Yours ever, dear Wilfrid,
Francis Thompson

From this letter it appears that Wilfrid Meynell had visited Pantasaph shortly before. *Lux in Tenebris* was the first title for *From the Night of Forebeing*.

81. To Coventry Patmore

Creccas Cottage, Pantasaph,
Wednesday [October 1895]

Dear Mr. Patmore,

I have been intending to write to you since your letter regarding the symbolism of the points of the compass; but ill-health and depression have delayed me. A violent paroxysm of the A.M.–malady burst on me at the time I wrote A *Captain of Song* (hence the tone of that poem); such as I have not known since the days, three years ago, when I put my passion under my feet. It has only recently dropped from me, and left me feeling broken and much older. Indeed, one woman here told me that my beard was showing more white streaks, and my manner growing sterner. Your own experience, I think, will make you pardon my negligence.

I think your *Saturday* letter very felicitously put. But alas! small are the chances of any government acting on it. I fear the "compliment to journalism" points too surely to Edwin Arnold. And when you say that Mrs. Meynell's sex will keep the minor poets silent, you forget the swarm of feminine poets who are also more or less journalists, and the journalists who are their lovers or admirers.

I have not received the *Selections*. A.M. has only once in my life sent me any book of hers—her *Essays*—and I expect it is the only one I ever shall receive from her. Women—and this sweet Lady and fine genius is "no more but even a woman"—have a fatal ease in "getting used" to devotion. It soon comes to seem no such mighty merit on your part; since after all it is not your doing—you cannot help it. I should indeed like to see the book. The selections in themselves must possess a peculiar interest for me; and the Preface I am most eager to read.

You rather mistook the purport of my inquiry in regard to the symbolic question. I wanted to know whether there had been any actual progressive development among the nations with regard to the quarters in which they worshipped—as an historic fact, apart from symbolic meaning. But this is such a minor matter, and the concluding hint of your letter contains so much of value to me, that I am not sorry you misapprehended me. Of course I am quite aware that it is impossible to answer openly—indeed impossible to ask openly—deeper matters in a letter. But that is not requisite in my case. It is enough that my gaze should be set in the necessary direction; the rest may safely be left to the practised fixity of my looking. Indicative language, such as you employed in your letter, you may safely trust me to understand. With regard to what you say about the symbolism of the North, I had substantially discerned it for myself. Indeed it formed part of a little essay which

I had projected, arising out of a footnote to an essay already written. It will be none the worse for the corroboration of your remarks: there is always something in your way of stating even what is already to me a *res visa*, which adds sight to my seeing. The quotation from the Psalms is new and grateful to me. But I was aware of the thing to which it points. Shakespeare speaks of—

> "All the grisly legions which troop
> Under the lordly mon
> "The lordly monarch of the north;"

(I was confusing it with a passage in Comus); and Butler remarks—

> "Cardan believed great states depend
> Upon the tip o' th' Bear's tail's end."

Set was given by the Egyptians the lordship of temporal powers; and to him the Bear was sacred. And of course I am aware of the esoteric meaning of this and of Cardan's saying. Indeed this was what I intended by my observation, that I surmised our Northern aspect in reckoning the compass to be a relic of Set-worship among our Teuton ancestors; though of course I was aware that Set, by that name, was an Egyptian deity. Also I am familiar with the principle of dual significance in this and mythological imagery generally. Indeed, without the knowledge of this principle, both Scripture and the mythologies are full of baffling contradictions. When I began seriously to consider mythologies comparatively, I cut myself with the broken reed on which all the "scientific" students fall back—this significance belongs to an earlier, that to a later period of development. But having eyes, which "scientific" students have not, I soon saw that facts gave me the lie in all directions. And when I came to make a comprehensive study of the Hebrew prophets, with the Eastern mythologies in mind, I speedily discerned the systematic use of the dual significance, and difficulty vanished.

I encountered one of the local ghosts the other day, for the first time in my now considerable residence here. I will tell you of him when I am in better spirits. It is a suicidal day, warm and wet, with a filthy standing fog.

Always yours,
Francis Thompson

Patmore had discussed the symbolism of the compass in a letter to Thompson of October 14. Patmore's letter to the *Saturday Review* suggested Alice Meynell for the vacant post of poet laureate. *Selections* (from Patmore's prose, edited by Mrs. Meynell) was published in early October. The Pantasaph ghost was a subject of continued interest in the area during 1895–96; the sight of it, Thompson reported, "charged his body like a battery so that he felt thunderstorms in his hair." See letter 85 for more on the ghost.

82. To Wilfrid Meynell

Pantasaph
[fall 1895]

. . . Am overflowing with a sudden access of literary impulse. I think I could write a book in three months, if thoughts came down in such an endless avalanche as they are doing at present. But the collecting and recasting of my later poems for Lane blocks the way for the next month, so that I can only write an essay in an odd hour or two when I lie awake in bed . . .

Quoted from EM, p. 184. The "literary impulse" stayed with him, producing many of the verses, such as *The Mistress of Vision* and *The Cloud's Swan Song*, that later appeared in *New Poems*.

83. To Wilfrid Meynell

Creccas Cottage
Dec. 24/95

Dear Wilfrid,

I write to wish you and all your dear ones a very happy Christmas. And I send you herewith two poems, as to which I desire your judgment and Mrs. Meynell's whether they should go into my book. One is an old poem which you have not seen. The other is a poem printed in *Merry England*, half of which I have re-written, substituting entirely fresh matter. Please return them to me when you let me know your judgment, for I have no other copies.

The task of completing my volume has expanded, through much rewriting. Since I shall not publish another volume of poetry for two or three years, I wish to close up every rivet I can. When I have got it out of hand, I shall turn my undivided attention to completing my other projects, and breaking open the doors of the Reviews; for your back will soon have enough to do to support those who are dear to you, and I must not be on it. But first I wished to finish this task, on which may have to rest my future claim to memory; since I feel no security that I shall live to see a third volume. What labour could do on it I have done; and it contains many new poems.

My landlady is very anxious to get her money. I know that she is poor, having now a house not big enough to take in any lodgers besides myself, and can ill afford to wait over the two months.

I hope you are all well, though I know that Christmas is always a difficult time for you. My health is very fluctuant, as always during winter; but it might be worse, and we have snow now, which is a relief to me from fogs and storms. With best love to Mrs. Meynell, yourself, and all the children.

Always yours, dear Wilfrid,
Francis Thompson

> He is discussing the projected contents of *New Poems*; the poem revised from *Merry England* was *Ode to the Setting Sun*. *New Poems* was actually his "third volume"; he is here discounting *Sister Songs*, his second book.

84. To Wilfrid Meynell

Creccas Cottage,
Tuesday [December 31, 1895]

Dear Wilfrid,

Many thanks for cheque and for your kind letter. Have given the receipt to Fr. Anselm, to keep for Fr. Cuthbert till he returns.

If Cuthbert has been in the habit of forwarding the receipts to you, please let me know, and I will tell Anselm to send it on to you.

Have sent two "Occs." to *P.M.*; one accepted, do not know about the other.

I wish every happiness and prosperity to you and yours for the New Year.

Always yours,
Francis Thompson

P.S. Just got dear Monnie's letter. Tell her I am delighted to hear from her, and that I will answer her as soon as I can. But to-day there are four more *inevitable* letters waiting to be written—and I am afraid one of them won't get written. I am glad to hear that she, at any rate, had an "awfully jolly" Christmas. Mine was a very gloomy one. I did not get your letter, and I did get another full of bad news. I dined at Miss Langdon's, and the two girls, big and little, were very kind to me, but I found it hard work to keep a bright face for them. Fr. Raphael says that Monnie is taller now than the big one, and *she* is taller than I am. She very nearly got kissed on Xmas Day before I remembered she was not Monnie,—something in her frank boyish way reminded me so much of Mon.

> Neither of the two "occs." (occasionals) sent to the *Pall Mall* was published. "Miss Langdon" was a Pantasaph neighbor, not otherwise identified.

85. To Alice Meynell

[early 1896]

. . . Is it true that you are going to collect your contributions to the papers during the past few years? I sincerely hope so . . . There was a Dr. Head, a member of the Savile Club, over here last autumn with Everard Feilding, who spoke with great enthusiasm of your "Autolycus". He quoted a bit relating, I think, to Angelica Kaufmann, who spent a large number of years in "taking the plainness off paper." The phrase delighted him, as it did me who had not seen it . . . I passed a pleasant night with the two. We were sleeping in a haunted house to interview a ghost; but as he was a racing-man, he probably found our conversation too literary to put off his incognito . . .

> Quoted from EM, p. 188. A volume of Alice Meynell's essays, *The Colour of Life*, was published in 1896. In a letter written in 1908 to Wilfrid Meynell, Feilding recalled the ghost-chasing incident: "We camped a few nights in a derelict mansion, rejoicing in the appropriately ominous name of Pickpocket Hall, in hopes of interviewing the spectre. Needless to say, we failed." (EM, p. 187.)

86. To Wilfrid Meynell

[February 1896]

. . . My landlady is urgent with me to remind you about her bill; since she says it has been sent in a fortnight, and there will soon be three months' account due instead of two.

Anselm has lent me three *Registers*, from which I learn for the first time about this wretched Purcell. I sympathize strongly with you over it, and do not think in your place I could have kept my language so temperate. The executors cannot take blame enough to themselves. Their conduct was astounding, to my mind, in its culpable negligence. Anselm had a business letter from a priest, in the close of which he spoke about the petty tyrannies he had to endure during his life from various ecclesiastics; "one of whom is now getting his deserts in the public press!" Is it not disgusting? It is the old Catholic gang, it seems to me—the "Cousins"—who are having their mean revenge on the dead man they hated and feared while he was alive.

That reminds me I never acknowledged my receipt of your book. I care less for the serious part—with exceptions such as the beautiful and truly poetic passage on the coming of Spring—than for the lighter portions such as the conversation at the dinner-table; which seems to me to show an admirable power of deft and feathery satire that I have seen in nothing of the kind since Dizzy. I heard that Herbertus Dei Gratia et favore Apostolicae Sedis etc. said it ought never to have been published. There was a little hit at him, which accounts for the opinion. Except in the use of proper names, I do not see that it goes further than Dizzy went. But our Cousins are not used to having their sacred persons satirized. And yet *Mostly Fools* should have familiarized them with the process, too.

I hope I may get a little more into trim by the end of the week. Except for the exhaustion of yesterday's walk, I seem certainly brighter to-day than since this wretched mischief wore me down.

With best love to Mrs. Meynell and Monnie and all the darlings,

Always yours affectionately,
Francis Thompson

> The first portion of the manuscript of this letter, of undetermined length, is missing. E. S. Purcell was the author of a rather critical biography of Cardinal Manning, published early in 1896. Meynell's book was *The Cousins*. "Herbertus," etc., was Cardinal Vaughan. *Mostly Fools* was a novel by E. Randolph.

87. To Wilfrid Meynell

Creccas Cottage, Pantasaph,
Thursday [mid-March 1896]

Dear Wilfrid,

Heartiest thanks for the cheque, which I have been delayed in getting changed at the Monastery. It is done at last, thank goodness, and I send you the receipt.

I am very sorry to hear your intelligence about Lane, which confirms my worst fears; and no less sorry to hear you are all so ill.

As for what you ask, it is a very trivial matter, which so far as I am personally concerned has long since passed from my mind. What I think I may and had better write about it, I will write to the Lady herself, as soon as my book is off my hands.

I am really better, though I shall not all in a hurry recover thorough health. The weather here is frightfully trying, as I daresay it is with you.

Tell Mon I am keeping her birthday in mind, though at present I need every hour of health I can get for work.

Dearest love to Mrs. Meynell, yourself, and the "kids" as Monnie would say.

Always yours,
Francis Thompson

I don't know whether Madam is with you. If so, tell her I am sending her Shakespeare *via* Anselm. I have all sorts and conditions of correspondence unanswered—worse luck.

A priest of these regions questioned me about the success of my last book. I told him I was going to turn myself to prose. He expressed strong approval of what he evidently regarded as a turning to less low and shady ways than those I had so long persisted in following (he knew me as a boy); and suggested that I should write stories for *Tit Bits*. Clearly he would begin to think me a fellow of some moderate talent and eminence, if I could get the classic stamp of *Tit Bits* set upon my work; to say nothing of the far more remunerative career it would open to me. He was soberly serious and encouraging in the advice.

> Thompson and Meynell fell out with the publisher John Lane over the payment of royalties and Lane's connection with *The Yellow Book*. The third volume of Thompson's poems, then in preparation, was taken from Lane and brought out through Constable. *Tit Bits* was a weekly catch-all magazine of the popular type.

88. To Coventry Patmore

Creccas Cottage,
Tuesday [March 1896]

Dear Mr. Patmore,

I regret exceedingly my delay in answering your letters; but I have been very unwell since the New Year with one of my worst and most prolonged attacks of acute dyspepsia, accompanied by intermittent vomiting; from which I am now only partially recovered.

My meaning about V.B. was that he had come to grief *financially*, and, according to my information at that time, had disappeared from all his friends. Since then, I have heard of W.M. being in communication with him; but whether he now visits at Palace Court I have no means of knowing. In any case, surely the fact that, as you tell me, he had announced himself engaged before this crash came, prevents any occasion for uneasiness with regard to him. Surely no woman can believe in the constancy and exclusiveness of his devotion after that. And I am sorry to hear of your resolution to break off all communication with A.M., which I cannot think will make for your happiness; and I wish you might find it possible to recede from it. It appears to me that what you saw at Palace Court, interpreted by what you mention of her demeanour, may bear another construction than what you put upon it. V.B. would be quite capable of adopting that demeanour out of personal and petty spite towards yourself, relying on her gentleness and timidity to prevent a public snubbing, which I do not think she is capable of administering to any man. And so she might well be embarrassed and frightened. It is impossible to believe that she had altered towards yourself, after that poem of hers, which you sent me, her expressions in the preface to the *Selections*, and what I saw and told you of her evident feeling about you in the last days of my own stay in London. I am sorry to think that the outpouring of my own bitter mood possibly stimulated yours; when I should rather do what I can to mitigate the darkness of your life.

I have just been reading a passage of yours on the advantages of paucity of material for producing effect. How true it is! I think it is an art and a knowledge which comes more natively to poets than to other men. One learns it, for example, in the manipulation of casual knowledge for purposes of imagery. I remember Anselm's expression of comical surprise at a passage in *Her Portrait* where I had employed the terms of Canon Law relating to ecclesiastical property. "I was floored," he said. " 'Why,' I said to myself, 'here's a whole passage of *De Contractibus* in poetry'!" His surprise was increased when I remarked that I had never read any work on the subject. "I would have sworn you had read that very book," he declared. "I could show you the page on which it comes. All the terms on that page are employed, and with accurate knowledge." I laughed, and said I got the terms where anyone could get them— from English history. It would seem a simple matter to you; to him it seemed miraculous. Equal, but more legitimate, was the surprise of another person at finding "a whole passage of Anna Kingsford in poetry." It was a passage describing the earth's *aura*, really remarkably like a passage on the same subject in a book of Dr. Anna Kingsford's, which I had not at the time read. Of course

I got the knowledge neither from books nor oral teaching, but purely from contemplation; and great was that person's scepticism at being assured that contemplation, if exactly followed, was a more infallible teacher of science than any book or any "scientist."

I must cease my long-delayed letter, for I feel a return of my sickness. I forward you the papers, which greatly interested me. What a pity that you could not have upheld the dignity of the Laureateship in the eyes of Europe! This absurd appointment might have been pointedly contrived to give the office its death-blow. What man of mark will take it when Austin is gathered to the kindred shades of Nahum Tate and Whitehead and Pye?

Always yours,
Francis Thompson

I received an American letter lately, from which it seems that the *Angel in the House* is being read in the Catholic reading-circles of remoter America. The *Unknown Eros*, I fear, is too strong meat for these babes.

> The Thompson passage describing the earth's aura occurs in lines 7–34 of the *Proemion* to *An Anthem of Earth*. Alfred Austin succeeded Tennyson as poet laureate in 1896.

89. To Wilfrid Meynell

Creccas Cottage, Pantasaph,
Friday [April 1896]

Dear Wilfrid,

My landlady has spoken to me about the bill for my lodgings, which it seems has been running for thirteen weeks, and amounts (at 15/6 a week) to 10.1.6. She is very uneasy about it, and says she can wait no longer. In fact, it comes to paying or going. As you know, I am not in the habit of interfering with matters which you transact through Cuthbert. But being spoken to personally about it, and placed in a very difficult and unpleasant position—and Cuthbert absent; I have no choice but to write personally and represent matters to you.

I send you a small contribution towards it, which I have just received. I little expected to be paid by a Catholic magazine for poetry, and sent them bad verses enough; regarding it as a mere compliment for their article on me, which they had taken the trouble to bring to my notice.

I have got so forward with the revision of my poems, that I have been able to lay it aside for a bit, in order to work at a prose article. Unfortunately, even if it be accepted, it must take some time for the result to declare itself; so that it is of no use to meet the present emergency.

I shall be disappointed if my new volume does not make a success. I have great hopes when I look at the poems as a collection.

I have not been at all well for some little while, but am pulling round again now. I am sorry to write you such a troublesome letter; but there is no help for it, for the necessity is pressing. With love to all,

Always yours,
Francis Thompson

The Catholic World (New York) published Thompson's poem *Love and the Child* in June 1896.

90. To Coventry Patmore

Creccas Cottage,
Pantasaph,
Thursday [summer 1896]

Dear Mr. Patmore,

I do not know what you have been thinking about me—very harsh thoughts, I fear. But I have had a very harsh time of it, between illness and anxiety. And now, when I write, it is only to declare finally my inability to visit Lymington as things stand at present. I wish indeed I could be with you; but it will not be. My financial affairs have come to something like a crisis. Lane, as I have long feared, is proving himself a broken reed, and his promises of payment most unreliable and dilatory in performance. And unless I wish by the end of next month to find myself in the same straits which I have just come through, I must try to get in some immediate money. So I am tied down here to the imperative writing of pot-boilers. If I went out of Pantasaph just now, I doubt whether I should get back to it. It would be delightful to be sitting with you in your study, instead of solitary and anxious grinding of dust for the uncertain British consumer, who objects to the adulteration of his dust with flour. But there is no folding of the arms to rest for me at this juncture; and that pleasure, which the fates seem to combine against, I must forego.

I have been very unwell, and it is a hard fight for health now. I thought at the time I received your postcard I was going to have rheumatic fever. I have still pains in my knee-joints, but I doubt whether it is not rather weakness than rheumatism—absorption of the synovial fluid producing grating of the membranes. I know not whether doctors recognize such a thing, but it seems to me a possible cause of pain.

Cust and his staff have retired from the *Pall Mall*. I fear this will affect Palace Court ultimately, if it has not done already. I see no prospect of things growing anything but steadily blacker for literature. There is a Philistine reaction all round, and the drawing shadow of war is sending a chill of monetary depression before it. There will be a big smash before long—I have steadily believed it for years—it started in that gigantic swindle the American market. The whole thing is propped up on unreal money, and at the mere rumour of cannon the whole fraudulent cloud will dissolve.

This is not cheerful, but I am in heavy physical depression—heavier than my affairs in themselves are sufficient to account for. Thank you for the cutting. I am glad that I have been the means of causing a large number of people to talk about Crashaw, and some perhaps even to read him, if they can find a person to lend him for nothing. It would be temerarious to guess how many critics had ever opened a "metaphysical poet" before it became necessary to praise them in order to show the critic's knowledge and my want of originality. Not that I charge this upon the Liverpool man; but some of the Lancashire reviewers have been particularly omniscient in this line.

I wish things may right themselves a little, and that they may ultimately allow me a visit I so heartily desire. But I have fairly had my back against the wall for the last few weeks. The financial difficulty opened upon me just concurrently with your invitation, and put me into suspense as to my immediate position at the same time that I was beaten down by one stroke of illness after another.

Always yours,
Francis Thompson

Harry Cust resigned as editor of the *Pall Mall Gazette* in the spring of 1896; both Wilfrid and Alice Meynell had contributed regularly to the magazine and they continued under the new editor.

91. To Wilfrid Meynell

Creccas Cottage, Pantasaph,
May 2nd/96

Dear Wilfrid,

I shall be forwarding my book in a few days, when I will answer Mrs. Meynell's letter; for the kindness and sympathy of which, in the meantime, I thank her warmly. I enclose herewith my landlady's bill. Also the Guardian (Fr. Sebastian) advanced me a sovereign for my journey to Ashton, which I must ask you to repay him. As I managed to lose the return half of my ticket, and had to get another, it did not more than carry me through, with my expenses at the other end. Likewise I had to get a new pair of boots to go in, the ones I had being quite impossible; but though I forward you the bill for these, I should hope this latter item may be able to stand over for a while, unlike the other two.

I never saw my father again. I cannot speak about it at present; my stepmother made it very bitter for me. It has been nothing but ill-health and sorrow lately—but I must not trouble you with these things.

I saw my sister, looking the merest girl still, and sweeter than ever. She did not look a day older than ten years ago. She said I looked very changed and worn, older than my portrait. Everybody made the same flattering remark.

I hear that there is an article concerning me in the *Edinburgh*

Review. I should be very glad if you will—or can—send me the *Edinburgh*. It would do me good; I never since I knew you felt so low-hearted and empty of all belief in myself. I could find in my heart to pitch my book into the fire; and I shall be thoroughly glad to get it off to you, for my heart sinks at the sight or thought of it. The one remaining poem which had stuck in my gizzard at the last I succeeded in polishing off last night, sitting up all night to do it; and I must start on the Preface as soon as this letter is off. Of course I will return the *Edinburgh* if you send it and wish so. I hear something about Mrs. Meynell bringing out a collection of her articles: is it true? I hope so. I have had a poem sent me for my opinion by a poetical butcher (!) who is an admirer of my poems. Ludicrous, because uneducated; or else there is some raw material in him. I do hope you are all well again.

Yours always,
Francis Thompson

> Thompson's father died, rather suddenly, on April 9, 1896. Hastily summoned home to Ashton at the last moment, Thompson arrived too late. On the return journey he stopped off at the Manchester convent of his sister Mary (Mother Austin). The *Edinburgh Review* published a highly laudatory review of Thompson's poetry in its April 1896 issue.

92. To Wilfrid Meynell

Creccas Cottage,
Monday [May 11, 1896]

Dear Wilfrid,

I am still waiting in hopes for the *Edinburgh*. You do not communicate with me in the *Register*. No-one here gets it, unless Madam or someone sends it to Fr. Anselm; and Anselm is away for his health. So there is no getting any copy of it.

Herewith I send the book. By all means try another publisher. But I would suggest you should sound another, and see whether he is likely to take it, and on decent terms, before you break with Lane. It would be imprudent, I think, to throw Lane over before you know whether you have another to fall back on. If the result of your sounding be anything like satisfactory, then take the step of throwing Lane over. It is becoming almost a stigma to publish with him. Everard Feilding asked me whether I knew he was the publisher of "a certain kind of literature." Moreover I think he would want the book cut down. Now, if Alice and you, *after you have read it in proof*, say "this is bad poetry," I will cut out half the book; but not half a line to please a publisher's whim for little books and big margins. I was cabinned and confined over my first book; with my spurs won, I should be at liberty to make this book comprehensive. It will be a book as large as the *Unknown Eros*; for if the *Unknown Eros* has about twenty more poems, none of them is as long as some half dozen of mine. Treated in the sumptuous style, it would make a book about the size of Rossetti's first volume; but there is no reason why it should be got up more than just well and simply. It is not as long as it looks; for there is much waste space, through each poem being written separately. This would disappear in printing; since in so considerable a volume it would be absurd to adopt the practise of beginning each poem on a separate page. Actually, there are about fifty-seven poems, long and short. I believe this will be my last volume of poetry—in any case my last for some years—and I am determined to make it complete, that I may feel all my work worth anything is on record for posterity, if I die. If the book would sell rapidly, like my first, I could divide it; since the publisher would accept another volume. But I know it will not; and I must get it all through now, for no publisher will be in a hurry to take another from me. It is my poetic last will and testament; I have been preparing it for three years, and I will not make it less complete for mere publisher's reasons.

I must ask you and Alice to defer your reading of it till you have it in proof. It is utterly strange to you, will need judging from other standpoints than my work you are used to; you will perhaps think well to recommend important omissions: and such recommendations would carry no weight if you had read it in Ms. After you have read it in proof, they would have my attentive ear, so long as they are based purely on defect of poetry. You have often recast a judgment made on my Ms.; not often, I think, after you had seen my work in print.

I except from this request the Preface, Dedication, & Contents; which you are at liberty to comment on *instanter*. The Preface is only half as long as it looks; having been cut down in revision so as to touch only what strictly required a word of explanation.

Alas! my father's death touched me not at all financially. There was nothing to leave, my sister told me. If there had been, my step-mother would have seen that none of it came to me. Lane talks nonsense about the public and "light lyrics." The public ever loved what it could read with one eye shut; but my first book did not succeed through "light lyrics." There is a reaction against poetry, mysticism, and everything not Philistine—that is the truth of it; and Lane's greedy fatuity is largely responsible for it. He wanted to repeat his success with Mrs. Meynell and myself at least twice a year: the public felt the thing was becoming an artificial fraud, and threw over true and false together—even as a Yankee-made Mahatma was sufficient to send all mysticism once more into disrepute. I have sacrificed something to the levity of the critics. I have put a whole section of the lightest poems I ever wrote after the first terribly trying section, to soothe the critics' gums. If they are decent to the measure of their slight aim, that is all I care for; they aimed little at poetry. That they are true to girl-nature I have a woman's certificate, beside the fact that I studied them—with one exception—from an actual original. And they are "simple" enough, I hope, to fulfil their function of a light lining to the heavy cloud of the first section. Again, I have put a batch of four "simple" poems at the opening of the Miscellaneous section, to catch the critical eye; though their importance is not such as to give them a place so prominent. So that I have done what artifice could do to lighten a very stern, sober, and difficult volume. It is more varied in range than my former work; and by my arrangement I have done my best to emphasize & press into service this, the solitary redeeming fact from the popular standpoint.

From the higher standpoint, I have gained, I think, in art and chastity of style; but have greatly lost in fire and glow. It is time that I was silent. This book carries me quite as far as my dwindling strength will allow; and if I wrote further in poetry, I should write down my own fame.

Please be careful with it; for I have no other complete copy of a large number of the poems. Let me know when Mrs. Meynell returns, that I may fulfil my promise of writing to her.

Hoping to see the *Edinburgh*,

Always yours, dear Wilfrid
Francis Thompson

With the letter he forwarded the complete manuscript of *New Poems*. Regarding his father's estate, he was misinformed. Dr. Thompson left a gross sum, in property, insurance, and cash of £1,500. The poems "true to girl-nature" comprised the sequence *The Narrow Vessel*; the "exception" was *Love Declared*, a first version of which was written at Storrington in 1889.

93. To Wilfrid Meynell

Creccas Cottage, Pantasaph,
Wednesday [May 1896]

My dear Wilfrid,

I have heard nothing from Lane. I cannot agree to your proposal about the play. I withdraw from Lane because of the class of literature with which he has identified his name; and to take my poems from him on that account, and at the same time publish another book with him, would be a singular act of inconsistency. You are in no way responsible. I instructed you to offer my book to another publisher, and you have no power to act otherwise. My withdrawal is in no sense an act of hostility to Lane. I cannot associate myself longer with publications of which I disapprove. And I consider that he does not advertise and push poetry as he did to begin with. But if the second reason did not exist, the first would be sufficient motive for me to persist in my resolution.

You are at liberty to show this to Lane; and to let him understand that I am personally responsible for the step, and have no intention of receding from or modifying it. I must decline to publish anything further with him whatever.

The original letter has been altered by cutting and pasting after the word "inconsistency," and again in the last sentence. The "class of literature" objected to was *The Yellow Book* and *The Savoy.*

94. To Wilfrid Meynell

Creccas Cottage,
Sunday [May 1896]

Dear Wilfrid,

Will you give one of the enclosed letters to Mrs. Meynell, and forward the other to Monica? I am sorry to hear that poor Viola has got the mumps, and Sylvia has had them. I had them once, and they made such havoc of me as I shall remember. But luckily this is one of the cases where the sex feminine is a shield, and the male sex a penalty. We have got better weather again, and so my health has shown some improvement these last few days. I hope the society of one of your life-long idols has done you good. I should imagine he must be a singularly fascinating companion, if there is any judging temperament from writing.

Always yours, dear Wilfrid,
Francis Thompson

"Sylvia" was Madeline Meynell. The identity of this particular "life-long idol" is not known. The letter he enclosed for Monica follows.

95. To Monica Meynell

Creccas Cottage, Pantasaph,
Tuesday [May 18, 1896]

Dearest Monnie,

I sent you yesterday the long-awaited *Poppy.* I have taken care not to spoil the inside with paint, as I did the outside; and so you can take it out and frame it without trouble. All I have done is to put at the top a copy of your poppy, as it is, pressed and dried, at the top of the poem in my own volume. As for the little pencil-sketch inside, you can give that to Evvie; and tell him to draw what I *intended* to draw, if anyone had ever taught me drawing. He could give me points and a beating, though he is untaught himself.

I am very glad to hear of an admirer, and such an admirer as Mr. Meredith; for I am depressed and sick-hearted. I sent your father my new book at the beginning of last week.

The pansy is a beauty, and the yellow poppy delightful. I am glad to hear you are enjoying yourself so much. We have had more than a week of lovely weather here; but it changed to cold yesterday, and I have got neuralgia in consequence. Your friend Fr. Anselm is away from here, and not likely to be back before the end of the month at the earliest. There is nothing to tell you about, for life is very quiet in Pantasaph. I send you the inscription you asked, to put in *Sister-Songs*. Has not Sylvia got a copy too? Please let me know. I wish I had the portrait of her which appeared in the *Album*, to put in my *Sister-Songs*.

With kindest love to your mother and yourself,

Your loving,
Francis

> Monica was paying a visit to the home of novelist George Meredith, near Dorking, when this letter was written. Thompson's personal copy of *Poems*, with the original poppy "pressed and dried" is still preserved by Mrs. Sowerby.

96. To Monica Meynell

Creccas Cottage, Pantasaph,
Sunday [May 1896]

Dearest Monnie,

Thank you for your charming letter. You are quite on your travels—first Dorking, and then Clevedon. We have fine weather here again, and I hope the same is the case with you. I am sorry to hear about Sylvia and Viola: I had the mumps once, and I never want them again. How did you escape? You must not think I have sent you anything precious. The only thing serious [?] is just a plain copy of the *Poppy*. As for the drawing, you could make as good a one for yourself.

Your letter has been sent on to Fr. Anselm, who is still away; and I don't know when he is coming back. What do you do with yourself all day? Are there any children at Clevedon for your companions? Have you a garden there as you had at Dorking? The hail here has made havoc with all gardens that were exposed to it. The beds in front of the Monastery guest-house were all planted with tulips, and it just beheaded them. The brother gardener was carrying tulip-heads away by the tray-full afterwards. Now they are beds of bare stalks. But the fields are still very pretty, covered with large dog-daisies. I like the French name better, *marguerites*; they are far too delightful to have such an ugly name as dog-daisies, being just like small white crysanthemums. The hawthorn still keeps on the hedges, and there is a great deal of beautiful laburnum about, which does not seem to have suffered; so that the country looks lovely enough. But the fruit is all ruined; and there is very little here at the best of times.

Somersetshire, I think, is the cider-country; so you ought to have any quantity of apple-blossom, and there is nothing I love better. Here it is all stripped by the hail.

> with dearest love, my Sweet,
> Always yours
> Francis

The original is missing; this is taken from a letter-book kept by the Meynells.

97. To Wilfrid Meynell

> Creccas Cottage, Pantasaph,
> Wednesday [May 21, 1896]

Dear Wilfrid,

Many thanks for the *Edinburgh*, which has indeed pleased me. I did not expect such an enthusiastic review of my work, and particularly of my last book, from a periodical so conservative and slow-moving as the *Edinburgh*.

I am very gratified by what you say about Meredith. You know, I think, that I hold him the most unquestionable genius among living novelists. I have read five of his novels; *Harry Richmond, Evan Harrington, Richard Feverel, Diana of the Crossways, One of Our Conquerors*. Nothing beyond this.

I have had a most characteristic letter from Monnie, and have just answered it.

I cannot give your message to Fr. Anselm, for he is not likely to be back for some weeks, so I am told. He seems to be on a roving tour for the benefit of his health.

Would you kindly send me a few stamps. I get my supplies from Anselm without difficulty; but since he is gone I notice that the authorities begin to look black when I have to ask them to stamp several letters in succession, as I have had to do this last week. There are still several letters which must be written now I am clearing off my unanswered correspondence, and I do not like to ask them to stamp any more.

So I should be very much obliged if you would send me a few till Anselm comes back. Half a dozen would be enough. There is one letter to my stepmother, one to my sister, to the Bishop of Shrewsbury, Mrs. Meynell, Coventry Patmore, and Hayes. I think that is all which are pressing.

> With love and thanks,
> Always yours affectionately,
> Francis Thompson

The weather here has been lovely for more than a week, but it is now bitter cold and hail.

The *Edinburgh* article called Thompson "a great poet"; the phrase "my last book" refers to *Sister Songs*. The Bishop of Shrewsbury was the former Canon John Carroll, an Ashton friend of the Thompsons'.

98. To Alice Meynell

Creccas Cottage, Pantasaph
[early June 1896]

Dear Mrs. Meynell,

I shall be very happy to accept your kind invitation. I will leave on Friday, if I hear from you that you will be ready to receive me by that date.

Your book was a delightful surprise; for I had no idea that it was on the verge of publication. I think it in every way worthy of you. The opening essay, *Winds of the World, Cloud, Eleanora Duse,* these are my chief favourites at present. *Winds of the World* and *Cloud* are a wonderful and exquisite blending of the observation of the artist and the poet.

I am relieved that you are able honestly to admire the first section of my book. I felt distressingly dubious about it. The whole book I look back to as a bad dream, so unexampled in my previous experience was the labour I bestowed on it. Indeed during the last six months, over and above the rewriting upon rewriting of the poems which were ready to hand, I must have written about thirty new poems, long and short; for there were not above twenty or so when I began on the book. I hardly wrote more than thirty in the whole five years preceding my first book; so that it was an unprecedented strain for me.

More about your book I shall be able to say when I see you.

I have had a letter from Monnie, which has been seeking me in Holywell, Greenfield, and Birmingham. She had addressed it to Holywell, leaving out Pantasaph! And the epistle concluded— "Please excuse the writing, for I am writing this *on the floor!*"

With best love to Wilfrid

Always yours,
Francis Thompson

This suggested sojourn in London was primarily intended for discussions of the manuscript of *New Poems*. In the five years preceding his first volume Thompson actually wrote about fifty poems.

Wilfrid Meynell about 1890

The entrance to the Meynell home at 47 Palace Court, Bayswater, London

Thompson to Wilfrid Meynell, February 1889

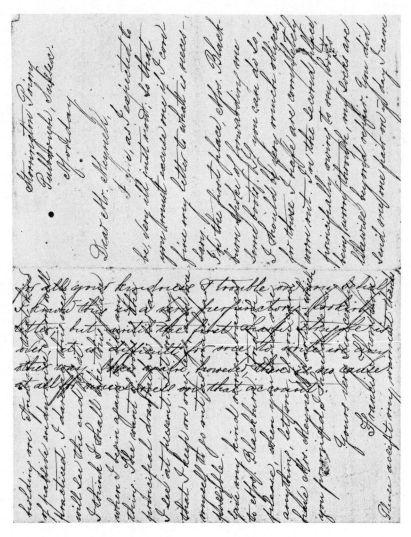

No. 1 Fernhead Road,
London, a Thompson
lodging during 1892

Alice Meynell about 1890

Creccas Cottage, Pantasaph

Coventry Patmore

Mrs. Meynell

T15

4

1

Bishop's House).
Pantasaph.
Monday.

Dear Mr. Meynell,
    I enclose the only two
short verses I have at hand.
I don't know whether either
of them will do. Also I
send ye autograph *Daisy.*
Was ye subeditor of ye
St. James's ye author of ye
review in that paper? In
case he was, I have en-
closed a slip in the
poem. If he was not, please
take ye slip out.

1

I think Fraill's article
excellent and kind.
But ye Athenaeum —— !
Call you this dealing favourably with a man? Heaven
save me, then, from the
unfavourable dealers! If
ye writer & myself were
not so completely unknown
to each other, I should
have thought it had ye
note of personal spite.
Of course, he is right
enough about ye *To
Monica Thought Dying;*
but that and one or

2

two other poems are
not ~~enough~~ sufficient on which
to base a charge of
making Mr. Patmore
a model — a thing
of which ŷ remaining
poems are, I think, fruitless
enough. It would
have been well, indeed,
for ŷ restraint and
sanity of ŷ poems,
if I had submitted
somewhat to the in-
fluence of Mr. Patmore's
example. As for Wat-

3

son's review, it is not,
like Symonds's, unfair; it
is simply one-sided, and
sometimes purblind even
from his own standpoint.
Many thanks for
your kindness in so
promptly forwarding me
everything. Say all that
you think ought to be
said to Miss Syman
— I beg her pardon,
Mrs. Hinkson — for
her kindness in the
Bookman. By no means
say what I say to
you; that ŷ article

4

is in substance a
réchauffée of things
said in ỹ dailies
and by Mr. Patmore
in ỹ Fortnightly.
Nevertheless it is warm
and appreciative,
and I am grateful
to her for her friend-
liness.
The sale of ỹ book is
indeed astonishing. Let
us hope that ỹ league
of ỹ weeklies will not
materially damp it.

5

Will answer Monnie.
Best love to yourself
and all.
    Yours always,
        Francis Thompson.
P. S. Ask Mrs. Meynell
if I may keep Mr.
Patmore's letter.

6

Breccas Cottage
Pantasaph
Thursday

Dear Mr. Patmore,

I do not know what you have been thinking about me — very harsh thoughts, I fear. But I have had a very harsh time of it, between illness and anxiety. And now, when I write, it is only to declare finally my inability to visit Lymington as things stand at present. I wish indeed I could be with you; but it will not be. My financial affairs have come to something like a crisis. Lane, as I have long feared, is proving

1

himself a broken reed, and his promises of payment most unreliable and dilatory in performance. And unless I wish by the end of next month to find myself in the same straits which I have just come through, I must try to get in some immediate money. So I am tied down here to the imperative writing of pot-boilers. If I went out of Pantasaph just now, I doubt whether I should get back to it. It would be delightful to be sitting with you in your library study, instead of solitary and anxious grinding of dust for the uncertain British consumer, who objects to the adulteration of his dust with flour. But there is no folding of the

T41

2

arms to rest for me at this juncture;
and that pleasure, which the fates seem
to combine against, I must forego.

I have been very unwell, and
it is a hard fight for health now. I
thought at the time I received your
postcard I was going to have rheumatic fever. I have still pains in
my knee-joints, but I doubt whether
it is not rather weakness than rheumatism — absorption of the synovial
fluid producing gratity of the membranes.
I know not whether doctors recognise
such a thing, but it seems to me a
possible cause of pain.

Eust and his staff have retired
from the Pall Mall. I fear this
will affect Palace Court ultimately,
1 if it has not done already. I see
no prospect of things growing anything

3

but steadily blacker for literature.
There is a Philistine reaction all
round, and the drawing shadow of
war is sending a chill of monetary
depression before it. There will be
a big smash before long — I have
steadily believed in it for years —
and I should not be surprised if
it started in that gigantic swindle
the American market. The whole
thing is propped up on unreal money,
and at the mere rumour of cannon
the whole fraudulent cloud will
dissolve.

This is not cheerful, but I am in
heavy physical depression — heavier
than my affairs in themselves are
sufficient to account for. Thank
you for the cutting. I am glad
that I have been the means of
causing a large number of people

4

to talk about Crashaw, and some
perhaps even to read him, if they
can find a person to lend him for
nothing. It would be temerarious to
at guess how many critics had eke
opened a "metaphysical poet" before
it became necessary to praise them
in order to show the critic's knowledge and my want of originality.
Not that I charge this upon the
Liverpool man; but some of the
Lancashire reviewers have been
particularly omniscient in
this line.
  I wish things may right
themselves a little, and that
they may ultimately allow me a
visit I so heartily desire. But I
have fairly had my back against
the wall for the last few weeks.

5

The financial difficulty opened
upon me just concurrently with
your invitation, and put me into
suspense as to my immediate position at the same time that I
was beaten down by one stroke
of illness after another.
        Always yours,
        Francis Thompson.

T H I

6

Francis Thompson in 1898

28 Elgin Avenue
Sunday

Dear Wilfrid,

I have been very unwell all ye week-end; and to-day it came to a climax. I was confined to bed all day, and touched nothing but a cup of tea till eleven to-night. I got relief about nine p.m., but too late to get it to you, though I made ye attempt.

I am sorry, both because I should have liked to dissipate your loneliness, & because I wanted myself to see you. I want ye loan of Patmore's two vols. of poems, & (if you have ye thing) of a Spenser (ye complete poems); both for articles;

two articles on Coventry — & naturally I want to do them as well as may be in brief time & at brief notice, being moreover in very poor health.

Are you staying over Monday? If so, I will come in — for ye, if possible, & I trust to manage it, knowing no present obstacle which may not be set aside. But I fear you may be off again to-morrow evening.

Sorry to miss ye Duchess's message, whatever it be — nothing of profound necessity, I hope. Much sorrier to miss you, if Monday be o'er-late, as I dread.

Yours with warmest love,
F. T.

Entrance to No. 31 Elgin Avenue,
Paddington, a Thompson lodging
during 1891

Wilfrid Meynell, about the age of 90, in the garden
at Greatham

99. To Wilfrid Meynell

Creccas Cottage
Thursday [June 11, 1896]

Dear Wilfrid,

I will be with you on Monday. I suppose my landlady will expect me to pay my bill before I leave, so I am sending it herewith.

Do you know that Miss K. Douglas King is—with the exception of Winifred Lucas—the only one of your female friends I ever desired particularly to meet? I have a vivid interest in her—more so than in Miss Lucas, whose peculiar cast of somewhat chilly intellect makes her more interesting as a book than as a person. She is a poet now, undoubtedly; but I very much question whether she will be a poet when youth has subsided. The thin side of her verse is the emotional side; and it is precisely this which is affected by the passing of youth. Her intellect even now has a meagre emotional body—its ribs show through her poetry. If this thing she does in the green wood, what will she do in the dry? Miss King, on the other hand, has the temperament of genius heaped up and running over. I read through all her *M.E.* stories some months ago; and was startled by their individual and impressive note. I admired them strongly—not, I think, for that which she would desire to be admired in them. I think she would claim admiration for their realism. I admire them for their idealism. In all the chief characters there is something which never was in any such character. And that something is Miss King. This, for which most would reprobate her, I admire. It is the light which never was on sea or land. And the proof of this essential character in these outwardly "realistic" sketches, is that her distinctive note comes out just as strongly in the last of her *M.E.* stories, which is frankly ideal. Her weak point is a feminine tendency to pile up the agony, heaping one acutely emotional touch upon another, until the accumulated effect is overstrung. Some French novelists gain pathos by accumulated touches. But then the touches are carefully minor and unimpressive singly; so that the pathos gains on you imperceptibly as a mist, and you are unaware of it until it grips you by the throat. Where the artist's tendency is to work by poignant detail, there should be reserve and selection in quantity. And she is given in passages to out-bursts of whirling words in which she trenches on the province of the "emotional" female novelist. One vast Marie Corelli is enough for that; Miss King can afford to forego such inartistic arts. In that last story of which I speak—the story of a violinist who suddenly becomes deaf—she shows a transition; the close of the tale being marked by a truly effective reserve, without losing anything of her real emotional power. There is a very striking and attractive in-dividuality disclosed through all the stories; and this is a higher and rarer thing to me than any amount of plodding "realism." If it is of any value to her, pray convey to her my sincere admiration of her true gift. I have seen incidentally that she has published a book. I hope it has been a success—but I doubt these dull critics when they are not given a "lead."

Anselm has come back. I think he hoped that Mrs. Meynell would send him her book—but do not say I told you so. I said she probably did not know where it would find him.

> Always yours,
> Francis Thompson

> Thompson's remarks on Katherine Douglas King were probably prompted by a letter of Meynell's informing him that the young woman was then a guest at his house. Thompson met Katie at Palace Court the day of his arrival in London, be-ginning a friendship which quickly blossomed into romance lasting, rather uneasily, for some four years. In 1900 Katie married a Protestant clergyman, Edmund Godfrey Burr, and died in childbirth on March 26, 1901. What Thompson says about her literary abilities is an exaggerated personal response, for her stories in *Merry England*, and her four novels, reveal only a work-a-day talent, sentimental and very much the stereo-type of the day.

100. To Coventry Patmore

> Creccas Cottage, Pantasaph
> [June 1896]

Dear Mr. Patmore,

Have you seen A.M.'s new book? It has just reached me. I can see already that there are some exquisite and entirely worthy things in it. But at present I cannot enjoy them in peace. My whole soul is burning over the last essay in the book; and I must needs write to someone and ease myself of protest. She is upholding the undeniable thesis that much—most—of the expression we assign to the eye is due to the eyelid. But that contents her not. She must needs deny any power of expression to the eye itself. The eye is only bright as a glass bead is bright. When Lockhart says that the eyes of Burns "literally glowed" when the poet spoke with feeling or interest, he is illuded. "No eye literally glows; but some eyes are polished a little more, and reflect. . . . But set within the meanings of impetuous eyelids the lucidity of the dark eyes seemed broken, moved, directed into fiery shafts." A poet, with eyes of observation, and damned science can falsify her seeing even to this! Time was when I put to myself the same question; and it led me to study closely and long the action of the eyes apart from the lids. The result confirmed to me the uniform assertion of the poets. The actual eyes, under the play of feeling, are constantly changing like a shoaling sea. Their luminosity waxes, wanes, gradually, suddenly —in which latter case they sparkle, flash, or glow. Their quality alters; even, in some eyes, their colour. Your own are remarkably changeful. Their colour lightens or darkens. In this latter point I am supported by the independent remark of a very acute observer. Nor is it the lids. I watched, only the other day, the light rise and shine in the downcast eyes of a child, where the lids were motionless except for the slight and regular twinkle which is constant and automatic in the lids at all times. A.M. has against her not only universal impression, but the *consensus* of the poets; behind her, deduction from "scientific knowledge." That is her weakness: she is proud of her "science," (because it is unusual in a woman), and accords it too unquestioning an homage. She would see better if she respected science less. Though scientists in camp stand together against me, I would not challenge the *consensus* of the poets. It is the blood, she reasons, which is eloquent; the cheeks may speak, but not the eyes. Dangers of science for a poet, who should see and not rationalize! There is the blood behind the blood, the invisible blood, the true vital fluid, the *liquor vitae*. There, if you must have an agent before you will credit a phenomenon, there is the agent, everywhere present, not least in the eyes. And the reinforcing of

this invisible vital fluid through the nerves I take to be very parallel
to the reinforcing of the visible blood through the arteries. Yes,
this sparkle, this flash, this glow, is the true blushing of the eyes;
they blush in light. As to the links which may intervene between
the cause and the phenomenon, that is a matter of mechanism: I
have never till now considered it. My present notion is that the
sudden jet of *liquor vitae* from the nerves, intensifying and ac-
celerating its current through the particles of the eye, must cause
actual increased vibration in those particles, thence flash and
sparkle; as when a jet of gas is passed through water—a rough and
inaccurate comparison. Whether this is so, or whether there are
other considerations which do not dawn on me, I care not greatly.
Nor can one altogether leave out of one's thoughts that this *liquor
vitae* is itself, so to speak, light *in petto*. Now, this she is not to
blame that she does not know; but she is to blame for sophisticating
her poet's discernment of phenomena by *a priori* deductions from
the basis of material science. "You only *think* you see it. It cannot
be, because etc." When a poet begins to talk like that, he is falsi-
fying the precious gift of the natural eyes which he has in common
with the child. Many a bit of true seeing I have had to learn again,
through science having sophisticated my eye, inward or outward.
And many a bit I have preserved, to the avoidance of a world of
trouble, by concerning myself no more than any child about the
teachings of science. Especially is this the case with regard to light.
I never lost the child's instinctive rightness of outlook upon light,
because I flung the scientific theories aside as so much baffling distortion of perspective. "Here is cart for horse," I felt rather than
saw, and would nothing with them. But I am vexed at a poet
carrying materialism in this way into the Holy Places of the body.

I hope you may be in better health than when I last heard from
you. I have profited somewhat by some weeks of fine weather; but
I fear it is rather in the nature of a respite than anything else.

There are some fine things in what I have had time to read of
the book, as I have said. One on rushes and reeds; and one on
Cloud, in bits of which she has unconsciously interpreted something of the myth of Hermes, in its bearing on the poet in his
parallelism with the cloud. She has no explicit consciousness of the
relationship, which enhances her discernment in seeing the in-

dividual resemblance. The book is dedicated to you. And just a fortnight ago I sent to London a volume of poems—the product of the last three years—which I had also (knowing nothing then of her intention, or even that she had a book on the point of appearing) taken the liberty of dedicating to you. It should have been my second book; if W.M. had not frustrated my careful waiting by committing me to the publication of my last ill-starred volume— which has sold only 349 copies in twelve months. This will certainly be my last volume for at any rate a few years, possibly altogether, unless my bodily decline is stayed. I am making an endeavour to get another publisher, considering Lane both unsafe and unsavoury.

Always yours,
Francis Thompson

Tuesday. I have come to London for a month. A.M.'s book, like all her writings, grows upon one the oftener one reads it. I hope I may see you before I leave here. Am already engaged to go to George Meredith's for a day, while a girl I have met here wants me to visit her; which is pretty fair for the very evening one reaches town.

> Thompson appears to have entertained a lifelong preoccupation with the spiritual and emotional power of eyes. His first published prose ("Paganism Old and New," in the June 1888 *Merry England*) was largely devoted to a demonstration of the way in which modern poets used women's eyes as an indication of spiritual beauty. *Sister Songs* was the "last ill-starred volume," but Thompson's report of its sale is incorrect: royalty statements show that in its first six months it sold 349 copies in England, an additional 250 in the United States. The postscript was added after his arrival in London on June 15. The "girl I have met here" was Katie King.

101. To Harriet Patmore

47 Palace Court,
Saturday [late June 1896]

Dear Mrs. Patmore,

Having a quiet minute before starting to dine at Boxhill, I write to thank you for the kindness which made my visit to Lymington so pleasant. We had a very speedy journey back and were placed (at Brockenhurst) in charge of a country child going to service in London. There was considerable danger that I should have to stay behind at Waterloo to look after her—being weak hearted about children—but luckily her mistress turned up at the last moment. Tell Mr. Patmore I will answer his letter when I come back. Mrs. Meynell wants to accompany me on my first [error for "next"] visit to you if possible.

With kindest regards to Miss Patmore
Believe me, Yours sincerely,
Francis Thompson

> This letter is available only in a copy made by Harriet Patmore. George Meredith's home was at Box Hill.

102. To Wilfrid Meynell

Monastery, Pantasaph
[July 28, 1896]

Got safe back. Not up to much, but will write in a day or two. Quite cold after the South. Love to all.

F.T.

> Thompson left London for the return to Pantasaph on July 27; the date of this postcard is July 28.

103. To Coventry Patmore

Creccas Cottage, Pantasaph,
Saturday [mid-August 1896]

Dear Mr. Patmore,

I am rather better today than I have been since my return, so I sit down to write to you. I have been very unwell, and often obliged to keep my bed the greater part of the day. My head has been the great trouble, threatening congestion or something of the kind; the blood rushing to it in an alarming way at night, and keeping me awake far into the dawn. Then the next day it is stupefied and will let me do nothing. However, I think I am coming round by degrees.

Day has slipped day, with the hope each day that I might be better able to write the next, until I am dismayed to discover the lapse of time. There was no offence at all in the matter you mention. You have been most generously kind to me; and I can truly say that I never yet fell from any friend who did not first fall from me. I thank you for the great honour you have done me by your offer to come up and look after me if I needed nursing. Fortunately it has not come to that yet. I thought you would understand from my postcard to Mrs. Patmore that if I delayed writing it was owing to illness; but as I say, I was not aware how time had drifted on since.

I am sincerely sorry to hear about your interruption of relations with A.M. Being entirely in ignorance of things, of course I cannot judge what cause she has given for it. I heard nothing until the beginning of the week, when I got a letter from Wilfrid, and discovered that he was away from home. I had written to her, forgetting she would be at Meredith's (as I suppose from your letter is the case) and of course I have had no answer from her yet.

I have not seen Meredith's article—I am so completely cut off from the outside world. Until this week, the only persons besides yourself who had shown any recollection of my existence were two ladies, mother and daughter, whose acquaintance I only made during my recent London visit. They surprised and touched me very much by both writing very charming and delicate letters of regret at my sudden departure. That was a very absurd and annoying situation in which I was placed by W.M.'s curious methods of handling me. He never let me know that my visit was about to terminate until the actual morning I was to leave for Lymington. The result was that I found myself in the ridiculous position of having made a formal engagement by letter for the next week, only two days before my final departure from London. Luckily both women knew my position, and if anyone suffered in their opinion it was not I. I should like to have been able to judge how far Meredith's article was taken from yours. It is an extraordinary bold proceeding if it is.

Constable has accepted my book, on the same terms as Lane, but with the promise to advertize it fully. I am glad to be out of Lane's hands, because I came to the conclusion two years ago that he was financially unsound. Moreover he was guilty of some sharp practice with me last year, and I vowed to myself I would give him a lesson that not every poet was safe game for that. He has leisure to reflect now that his "smartness" has been a poor speculation.

I must ask you to excuse an abrupt termination of this letter. I have got a sudden attack of sickness, and find myself unable to go on.

Always yours,
Francis Thompson

In a letter of July 29, Patmore had offered to care for Thompson at Pantasaph, thinking the illness worse than it actually was. When Thompson failed to reply, he repeated the offer on August 10. A postscript to the second offer reads: "Have you read G.M.'s review? It is stolen from beginning to end from my last article, which, he has persuaded her, is calculated to injure her!" The "two ladies" were Katie King and her mother. A final sentence in the letter has been scratched over and is illegible.

104. To Wilfrid Meynell

Pantasaph
[August 1896]

Dear Wilfrid,

I have been unwell this last week, or I would have answered your kind letter before. I have been troubled by a return of the sickness and flooding of blood to the brain, which had left me in London. Thank you for all your trouble on my behalf, and I am glad it has been successful. Thanks also for the clothes. The arrangement with Constable seems to me all that could be wished. The only detail which I do not understand, is what you mean by payment of royalties in advance. I am glad to be in the hands of a stable publisher, whose ability to carry out his terms is in no doubt. In regard to Lane, you can feel I am entirely behind you. If you had not proposed a change of publishers, I should have proposed it myself. Ever since his trickiness when he played us off against each other at the time of the agreements, I have been finally resolved on a change the expediency of which was already in my mind.

What am I to do in regard to the 16/9 still owing on my land-lady's last bill? She has pressed me for it two or three times.

I have received an extraordinary letter from Coventry, to which I only refer in so far as it concerns myself. He asserts, as he did at Lymington, that Mrs. Meynell is offended with me. And this time he gives a reason. I am not going to repeat it. Repeating of private letters or private talk only makes mischief, and does more harm than good. I recognize in it a wonderful distortion of a very simple thing. The distortion is his; but the thing must have come from someone—it passes my wits to think who. Only her own assurance could make me believe it was Mrs. Meynell; still less do I believe that it represents her feelings, so alien is it to her calm good sense. Therefore I simply set it aside; and only mention the matter to ask you both to treat anything coming from Coventry about myself as I treat anything about you—disregard it. It would take reams to dis-cuss the misunderstandings which would otherwise sprout up. Not that he wilfully misrepresents things. But athwart the rolling clouds of his dark moods everything looms distorted and disproportioned. I have whirling moods enough to understand and sympathize with this; but I will not notice anything which comes to me through such a heated medium. A little common sense is the best remedy —and I at least mean to have it. If Mrs. Meynell is really offended with me (and she has managed most successfully to disguise it) it must be for some better reason, or she will have to find one. I will not trouble to notice asserted "offences" based apparently on simple and inoffensive things, in whatever grandiloquent language Cov-entry may trick them. I simply do not believe a word of it, or else there is strange change in her nature. But it is nonsense; and with the warning to set aside any parallel things you may hear about me, I leave the matter.

Do you know at all when Constable proposes to bring out my book? Have the notices of Mrs. Meynell's book begun to come in yet? I have seen Meredith's article, and one in the *Chronicle*.

Always yours,
Francis Thompson

No hint of this particular "misunderstanding" has survived; Patmore's "extraordinary" letter is also lost.

105. To Wilfrid Meynell

Creccas Cottage, Pantasaph,
Monday [September 15] 1896

Dear Wilfrid,

I return the agreement, with my approval, having thoroughly mastered its contents. I got drenched through on my way home, and have been unwell with a bad cold; but am now better. I did not get *En Route;* they had sent Doubleday's parcel on to you the very day I returned. I hope you got home without any further colds. We have had nothing but wet weather here all the time. The correction of the type-written Ms. is almost finished; and it will be ready to-morrow or the day after. Love to Mrs. Meynell and all the children.

Always yours,
Francis Thompson

Hayes has written to ask me to visit him on the 22nd. Please let me have a line at once to know whether I may go. It is a long-promised visit, so I do not want to disappoint him; and I need to answer without delay.

> The manuscript of *New Poems* had been typewritten for the printer and sent to Thompson for final editing. His asking Meynell for permission to visit Alfred Hayes (who lived in Birmingham) was really a request for the fare.

106. To Wilfrid Meynell

Pantasaph
Friday [September 27, 1896]

Dear Wilfrid,

I never supposed you purposely left me in the lurch; but what cannot be, cannot be, and where there is not money at hand to send, it cannot be sent. So I supposed this to be the reason of your silence; being under the firm impression that I had told you in my first letter that Hayes wanted me on the 22nd. I am sorry if it is through such an undreamed omission that the misunderstanding has arisen. I am going to-morrow.

I have sent the corrected poems to Doubleday; with alterations which I hope will approve themselves to him, and which no doubt he will let you know.

I sounded Coventry about the projected Quarterly, since Doubleday seemed to want him. He says it will probably succeed; that he would have been glad to help, and would have put his heart into it; if he had heart enough left for anything. From which I conclude that he might be coaxed into writing, if he thought Mrs. Meynell wanted it. It remains for some more official person than I to approach him—preferably Mrs. Meynell herself. But whoever does it, do not emphasize Meredith's connection with the project. If Coventry thought it was *his* scheme, he would like enough recoil in pique. I said nothing about Meredith. Doubleday asked Meredith to write, who is his personal friend; that is enough explanation of Meredith's share in the business, without mentioning his connection with the project. If Meredith could be decently murdered, Coventry would do it; and he persists in attributing his own sentiments to me—who am thinking about far other things than Meredith; a charming fellow and a novelist of genius, but who does not personally concern me in any way.

The two bills I send you arise from the fact that you did not completely pay the last bill; hence they kept it in hand until you payed the balance in the present bill.

Always yours,
Francis Thompson

The visit to Alfred Hayes took place between September 28 and October 10. The reference to "the projected Quarterly" is the only surviving record of what appears to have been a project by Constable involving Patmore, Meredith, Mrs. Meynell, Thompson, and other leading names of the period, but it came to nothing. Arthur Doubleday headed the Constable firm.

107. To Coventry Patmore

Creccas Cottage,
Wednesday [November 1896]

Dear Mr. Patmore,

I know not what you have thought of me. I have been oscillating between proofs and illness—not serious; but crippling one's faculties while it lasts; partly the result of unhealthy weather. There is some kind of influenza about, so that I have to be careful. I am temporarily quit of proofs, and in rather better health to-night; so I sit down to answer you. I got both your letters. The first was enclosed with the magazine, where you probably forgot having placed it. The article amused me; though it is a disingenuous attempt to belittle under the guise of judiciality. I think A.M. has been back from Boxhill for some time; but I hear little. The *Academy* has come out under new management; and to the first number—an excellent starting-number—she contributes a review of Kipling's *Seven Seas*. I hear nothing more of the new Quarterly. I have just had a little college-magazine sent me from a Californian "University," containing a review of my first volume. It is a capital specimen, in touches, of youthful assumption. The writer concedes me sustained sweep enough for "merely lyric poetry." The poetry of great names from Pindar to Patmore; whereby Spenser of the *Epithalamion* is greater than Spenser of the *Faerie Queene*, Wordsworth than Tasso or Camoens! He has found out that my poor little *Daisy* is a Swinburnian poem, and would not have been written but for *Felise* (which I believe I have not read) and *An Interlude* (of which I remember but the name). But being Swinburne, they must needs be the antithesis of my simple poem, in spirit, method, and metre. Young America further credits me with reminiscences of Browning (Browning!) and Sidney Lanier—an American I had never heard of when my book was published. And it says that my music is "thin" beside the "wonderful cadences" of Rossetti. Yes, it actually says that; and quotes the *Stream's Secret* as a specimen of the "wonderful cadences". To this pass have we come in matters metrical. It is kindly meant enough, or they would not have sent it me. The man's remark on my "mysticism"—"Most of us have come to know an ampler and wholesomer world than this,"—is a delightful piece of hoary youthful experience, for which I forgive him much. I wish I were able to write you a brighter and more interesting letter than this; but my brain is dry and nerveless, so that several things I had thought of beforehand have gone clean out of it.

Rightly or wrongly, I like A *Captain of Song* in its printed dress; but it is very sombre and painful. I do not know when the book will be out, but I imagine as fast as it can be got ready now. It is far from what you have a right to expect from me, or I from myself; but ill-health has sorely trammelled me, making it what I could, not what I would, or might have done if my body were at all equal to the calls of my mind.

I hope you are not unwell—cheerful I know I cannot expect you to be. Nor have you the resource of being sometimes able to escape pain for an hour or so in literature, as I do now and again manage.

Believe me,
Always yours,
Francis Thompson

Meredith wanted to see my proofs. I politely evaded the request, which he did not make personally, but through W.M. It had got so late; indeed, that it has been just as much as I could manage to get through them in tolerable time.

> The "little college magazine" was *The Sequoia* (October 1896) published by Stanford University. It contained an article on Thompson by one "Alfonso G. Newcomer." A *Captain of Song* first appeared in the *Athenaeum*, December 5, 1896, and was republished in *New Poems*.

108 To Arthur Doubleday

Creccas Cottage, Pantasaph,
Thursday [November 1896]

My Dear Doubleday,

I regret that I cannot consent to the omission of the translations. If anything is left out, it must be the section *Ultima*, not the translations. I said at Pantasaph that I would keep these, whatever I left out. They were held over from my first book and I will not hold them over again. I regard the "Heard on the Mountain" as a feat in diction and metre; and in this respect Coventry Patmore agrees with me. But I do not at all mind leaving out the section *Ultima* . . . Page 20 is my fault, for bad marking. Page 15 is your printers' fault, who can understand nothing between "to-night," and "tonight." Whereas I want it "to night,"—two separate words. Otherwise the line is nonsense.

I want to have Revises of the whole book, lest any other corrections should fail of being properly made.

I have not yet had proofs of the dedicatory poem or the *Contents*, but I suppose they will be sent me together.

> A portion of this letter was printed in EM, p. 306; the remainder (after the second "Ultima") exists only in a mutilated manuscript.

109. To Harriet Patmore

Creccas Cottage, Pantasaph,
Monday Nov. 30/96

Dear Mrs. Patmore,

I am shocked and overcome to hear of your—and my—bereavement. There has passed away the greatest genius of the century, and from me a friend whose like I shall not see again; one so close to my own soul that the distance of years between us was hardly felt, nor could the distance of miles separate us. I had a letter from him but last Monday, and was hoping that I might shortly see him again. Now my hope is turned suddenly into mourning. The irrevocableness of such a grief is mocked by many words; these few words least wrong it. My friend is dead, and I had but one such friend.

Yours, in all sympathy of sorrow,
Francis Thompson

> Coventry Patmore died suddenly on November 26, 1896. Thompson's characterization of him as "the greatest genius of

the century" must be read in the emotions of the moment, but it is true that Thompson afterward continued to think of his friend in such terms.

110. To Wilfrid Meynell

Creccas Cottage, Pantasaph
[early December 1896]

Dear Wilfrid,

I send you my lodging-account for the last two months.

Of nothing can I write just now. You know what friends we had been these last two years. And I heard from him but the Monday before his death. There is no more to say, because there is too much more to say.

Yours always
Francis Thompson

I have just got your letter, so I reopen mine. I feel a natural delicacy in pressing you about the matter; but since it is now the beginning of December, I would like to know something definite as to whether I am to visit London. There are one or two things I was reserving, in the expectation of shortly seeing you; but if that is not to be, then I ought to consult you about them by letter. I confess I should like to see you, dear Wilfrid, for I feel very heavy-hearted about the loss of one of the brave few who were bound to me by closer than common ties.

I am fearful about the *Athenaeum* project. I told Coventry I had altered the sub-title to prevent identification, lest the poem should offend his friends; and since he did not dispute it, I conclude he took my view that it might give displeasure. To dwell on the harsher side of his character just now, has an ungracious air.

> The *Athenaeum* project concerned publication of *A Captain of Song*; see following letter and note.

111. To Wilfrid Meynell

[early December 1896]

... I am sorry I could not wire the correction in time. I did not see your letter till too late on Thursday to do anything. I would rather have had the phrase altered, and hope Mrs. Meynell may have taken on herself to do so, since it only affected the poem temporarily. In my book I shall retain the original phrase, which Coventry would have objected to have altered in permanent record. He accepted and justified my use of the phrase, in a poem drawing only an aspect of his character. But where it was connected with him as a funeral poem, I would certainly have wished it replaced by something else. About all things I trust soon to have personal talk with you.

Always yours affectionately,
Francis Thompson

Ms. incomplete. The *Athenaeum* published *A Captain of Song* as an obituary poem to Patmore on December 5. The Meynells had suggested that Thompson make a temporary change in the lines "Ye shall mark well / The mighty cruelties which arm and mar / That countenance of control." Shortly after writing this letter Thompson left Pantasaph for good and took up residence in London.

112. To Wilfrid Meynell

2, Whitehall Gardens, London, S.W.,
Thursday [December 17, 1896]

Dear Wilfrid,

I reached here all right last night, and found that they had put off dinner till eight o'clock, so that I was in plenty of time. I have done a perhaps rash thing—promised Doubleday to come to him again when they return after Xmas. I forgot that you cannot be without your dress-clothes continuously—particularly at a time when you are likely often to have occasion for them. They dress for dinner here, so that I shall have to use them daily.

Mrs. Doubleday is very kind; and she is a simply exquisite pianist. Doubleday and I fraternized over music. He is of course at his work to-day, but there are some people coming to dinner to-night, I believe. It seems quiet and nice enough so far; I am left to my own devices during the day, which is just what I like. Best love to Mrs. Meynell, the children, and yourself.

Always yours,
Francis Thompson

On his return to London Thompson was, for about a week, the house guest of his new publisher, Arthur Doubleday.

113. To Wilfrid Meynell

2, Whitehall Gardens, London, S.W.,
Wednesday [December 23, 1896]

Dear Wilfrid,

I shall be with you about dinner-time to-morrow (Friday). The column was indeed interesting. I got the *Academies* from Hind, and also the request for an article on De Quincey, which shall receive due attention.

Love to all
Always affectionately yours,
Francis Thompson

The article on De Quincey appeared in the *Academy* (of which Charles Lewis Hind was editor) for January 9, 1897.

114. To Charles Lewis Hind

16 Elgin Avenue W.,
Monday [April 1897]

My dear Hind,

I was taken very ill last week, and was totally unable to get in my work for the *Academy*. Having pulled round, I send you herewith the *Wordsworth*, and trust to let you have the *Fiona McLeod* in the course of tomorrow, or at any rate by Wednesday morning at the latest.

With regard to your request for articles on Shelley, Browning, and Tennyson; I am sorry that, after careful consideration, I must ask you to hand them over to someone else. Considering the importance—the great importance—of the writers I am asked to treat, I do not feel that I could do justice either to my subject or my own reputation within the limit (of 1,000 words) proposed. In the case of such minor men as Landor, or even possibly Macaulay, I should not object to the limitation—biographical details being omitted. But I simply cannot pledge my name to a disposal of Tennyson or Browning in about two columns. It would be a mere clumsy spoiling of material which I might to greater advantage use elsewhere. I could only undertake it on the terms that the length of the article should be determined by the organic exigencies of my treatment alone. Of course I have never dreamed of anything beyond five columns as what you could reasonably allow me for important articles. If some have extended to more, it has been the result of mis-calculation, and I should have quite acquiesced in your cutting such excessive articles down. And when I speak of five columns as the outside limit I could have expected, I by no means mean that I should pad out the article to that amount, at all costs. The probability is, that with biographical details omitted, it would naturally conclude itself in less, more often than not. And I certainly should not dream of adding a column or a line, for the sake of adding a column or a line. But though two columns would be a feasible limit in the case of lesser men; for writers such as the three you mention, I could not, with regard for my reputation, undertake it. So, with regret at having to differ from you, I will ask you to place the articles elsewhere.

Yours very sincerely,
Francis Thompson

Thompson's review of Wordsworth appeared in the *Academy*, April 10, 1897; that of Fiona McLeod in the issue of April 17. The articles on Tennyson, Browning, and Shelley, running about 2,000 words each, appeared in the issues of April 17, May 8, and May 22.

115. To Wilfrid Whitten

16 Elgin Avenue,
Friday Night [late April 1897]

Dear Whitten,

Do let Hind know the *Browning* has gone in, if you can. I would send him a telegram myself, if I knew where.

Yours,
F.T.

Have been bad with sick headache; am upset now, but better.

Wilfrid Whitten was an assistant editor of the *Academy*.

116. To William Archer

May 31, 1897

My Dear Archer,

I surmised from the beginning, from internal evidence, that it was to you I owed the kind article on my new book in the *Chronicle*. Now my belief is confirmed by my publisher, and I hasten to thank you, with an emotion which I have very little power to express. Four years ago your article would not have drawn from me this acknowledgement. I had then no enemies: I had a good "lead off", and to praise me was the fashion. Independence was shown by attack; and the common critic, who loves to be, like the god of battles, with the big battalions, followed in the wake of praise, according to his sheep-like nature; carefully saying over again what his brethren-sheep had said before him. To-day all is changed. My chief supporter (Coventry Patmore) is dead; the few who really admired me are no longer in a position to make their voices heard; while I have enemies on every hand, raised by the mere fact of my first success . . . And this moment you have chosen to strike by my side with a whole-heartedness you have not before displayed. Nay, if I do not read ill between the lines, you have been gentler to my faults than you would otherwise have been, because you saw that they would find abundant censors; while my merits there would be "none to love, and very few to praise,"—besides yourself.

In all this there is a courage, an independence, a chivalry, for which I thank you indeed much; but for which I admire you yet more. It is a brave act, when the cry is against me, and to support needs more independence than formerly to oppose. And I am the prouder of it because I am so all but unknown to you that no one can say (as they are accustomed to say) that you have supported me out of private friendship. If I have not hitherto known you, I feel that now I *do* know you—at least I know "the better part of you," your spirit. I have no hope that my book and name, that sinking ship which the many are deserting, will survive the organized attack on me. But at least you have made a gallant last stand for me, and I shall not be smothered out of existence without a struggle. I never knew until late years how powerfully people's views (theological, philosophical or otherwise) influenced their attitude toward contemporary poetry. But I found that my friend, Patmore, depreciated writers solely or chiefly because he hated their philosophy. I have found that George Meredith's admiration for my work falls off as he recognizes the opposition between my philosophy and his. He may allege other reasons, but I am convinced that is the basic reason. Yet I myself can admire *his* poetry, though I am in fundamental antagonism to his philosophy. And so with others. Beauty is beauty, though it may be inspired in defense of what I hold to be more or less untrue.

As to the substance of your article: I am very pleased to find you upholding the *Anthem of Earth*, which a former supporter has described as more like highly figurative prose than poetry. It is not surprising, since he holds my namesake Jimmy (of *The Seasons*) to be a master of blank verse. You are quite right as to the derivation of the form in many passages. It is from the later Shakespeare. Unlike most critics, I have always considered Shakespeare's late blank verse to be his greatest and most characteristic. But it needs an understanding, as well as an ear, to appreciate it; while the more smoothly *linear* versification of his earlier periods can be followed by the ear alone. I deliberately took it as a model; thinking that my lifelong study would enable me to do what critics have pronounced impossible, what even Coleridge confessed he had tried to do and failed—i.e. catch the rhythm of Shakespeare's verse. I have not merely read it constantly, but I have analysed its principles. When I was a child of seven, standing in my nightgown before the fire, and chattering to my mother, I remember her pulling me up for using a certain word. "That is not used nowadays," she said; "that is one of Shakespeare's words." "It is, Mamma?" I said, staring at her doubtfully. "But I didn't know it was one of Shakespeare's words!" "That is just it," she answered. "You have read Shakespeare so much that you are beginning to talk Shakespeare without knowing it. You must take care, or people will think you odd." She was a prophetess. Now everybody is thinking me "odd," and that I do on purpose what is often as unconscious as that childish Elizabethanism uttered in my little nightgown before the fire.

Will you pardon me for so long and egotistic a letter? The main thing is, that I thank you most warmly for an article the insight of which is rendered the more remarkable by your lack of any personal sympathy with my views; and the courage of which, at this juncture, is beyond all praise . . .

Thanking you again with all my heart,

I remain,
Yours very sincerely,
Francis Thompson

Quoted from *William Archer*, by C. Archer, pp. 221–23. Thompson exaggerates the critical reaction to *New Poems*, published this month. Individual reviewers were occasionally violent, but none of them denied him a high place among the leading poets of the time, and some continued to rank him with the great poets of the language. Archer's answer to this letter is quoted in EM, p. 242.

117. To Charles Lewis Hind

16 Elgin Avenue, W.,
Wednesday [June 1897]

My dear Hind,

I cannot manage the articles till the end of the week; having a poem to finish for the *Chronicle*, and but a day or two for it. But having done that, I shall be free. If you cannot wait till then, you must give it to someone else; but if you can, by the end of the week I shall be able to attend to your wishes. I regret the delay, which yet I cannot help.

Yours sincerely,
F. Thompson

The poem for the *Chronicle* was *Ode for the Diamond Jubilee of Queen Victoria*, published on June 27, 1897.

118. To Alfred Hayes

16 Elgin Avenue W.,
Tuesday [summer 1897]

Dear Hayes,

How long it seems since I have written to you! In truth I have been going through all kinds of fresh experiences: I have not been at all well, and it has been as much as I could do to keep myself afloat in my new position. I am settled down in London, and am in the full grind of journalism. Except journalism, journalism, (chiefly in the *Academy*, to which I am now a regular contributor), I have done nothing for months. I send you herewith my new book. It has gone rather better as regards reviews than I expected, seeing the organized violence with which it was assailed on its first appearance. But how it is going as regards sales I do not know. I know it sold about 350 copies in the first week; and since then I have not had the curiosity to inquire. I expect little, and therefore I hope I shall not be disappointed.

I instructed my publishers to send a copy to Brightwell. Whether he has received it, or whether any notice has appeared in the *Daily Post*, I do not know.

I met Norman Gale, for a too brief moment, at my publishers in January or thereabouts. I was charmed with him. Alas, I am farther off from you than ever; and unless I make a fortune (which I see no chance of) it is not likely I can visit you again for an unknown time to come. And I entertain such a happy recollection of you, your dear wife, and your charming children! Let us pray for the un-expected—which always happens, you know!

Always yours, dear Hayes,
Francis Thompson

I am very busy, or I would write at more length to you. Believe me, that I do not forget you ever.

> *New Poems* was reviewed by Brightwell in the *Morning Post* on July 15, 1897; the review was mixed but Thompson was acknowledged as a true poet. The same paper, on December

30, 1897, picked *New Poems* as the best volume of verse published that year.

119. To Charles Lewis Hind

[November 2, 1897]

My Dear Hind,

I will do as you wish about the Crashaw. I think you are right, but in the absence of any notification I kept to the stipulated length of two columns.

I received the letter you forwarded from Arthur Waugh; but the book which should have accompanied it has not been sent me. Will you please see what has become of it, and have it forwarded at once. I am afraid it may have got mixed up with the books for review; and it is a book I value, sent me as a gift by Waugh, in recognition of my last "Excursion." Please let the matter be looked into without delay.

I am glad to hear that Wells has given you well-deserved recognition in the Saturday.

Yours sincerely,
Francis Thompson

P.S. For fear of any confusion, I may add that Waugh's book is a volume of "Political Pamphlets" belonging to the same "Library" as the volume noticed in my last "Excursion."

> An essay on Richard Crashaw by Thompson appeared in *Academy*, November 20, 1897. The gift book sent by Waugh is not identified.

120. To Unknown

16 Elgin Avenue, London W.,
Nov. 5, 1897

Dear Madam,

Continual occupation and intermittent ill-health, which allow me in these days little leisure to read for my own pleasure, have as yet not suffered me more than to glance at your poems; though in the *Ode to Morning* I find passages of true poetry, and hope ultimately to acquaint myself with the whole. Too often I find myself followed with the malice of writers personally unknown to me: needs must I, therefore, feel it a precious counterpoise and encouragement to have also the undreamed praise of strangers. I assure you that your sympathy, unknown as you are to me, comes home to my heart. My only regret is that your distant kindness and understanding should reach and pass from me like a far-off wind, which is and is not; that I have no more than a transitory link with the generous stranger who sends me her enheartening message. For a poet finds enmity and envy, and the shadow of his own human despondency, too near and all-pervading: the sympathy of his sympathisers seldom reaches him, but remains unknown. Remember this; and do not think I am or can be indifferent to my far-separated friend—for surely friend I may call you in the spirit, since we have interchanged our thoughts, an immaterial converse. From my soul I thank you; and regret the impossibility of making acquaintance with one who has given me a very true pleasure and consolation.

> Yours sincerely,
> Francis Thompson

This letter, found among Thompson's papers, and probably never sent, presents him in an unaccustomed mood—that of replying to an admirer—and the stiffness of his remarks is revealing and rather pathetic. The lady involved remains unknown.

121. To William Hyde

> 47 Palace Court
> [fall 1897]

Dear Mr. Hyde,

I regret to have delayed my answer to your letter so long. Firstly, I was occupied by unavoidable business; secondly, when I was free to consider your notes, it took me some time really to master them, and consider my plan in relation to them. In the first place I do not design a consecutive narrative of any kind. I do not design to treat either topography or the life of London, for both of which I am utterly unqualified. My design is to give impressions of London, for such as present themselves to a wanderer through its streets. I intend to divide the book into parts which—by way of provisional title—I might describe as Fair London and Terrible London. For Fair London the plates you have already done will supply sufficient material in the way of illustration. The other part will consist of studies of London under its darker aspects—weird, sordid and gloomy—being drawn from its appearance rather than its life. Under this section would come some of the plates already done; and I have marked others among your notes, any of which would fall into my ideas. Since the darker aspect of London is particularly evident to a houseless wanderer, it is my idea to include in this section a description of the aspect of London from midnight to early dawn—for which my own experiences furnish me with material. I intend to take my wanderer through the Strand, Covent Garden, Trafalgar Square, perhaps a part of Piccadilly, the Embankment, Blackfriars Bridge, etc., bringing him round to Fleet Street opposite St. Paul's at dawn; and to describe the night effects and the effects of gradual dawn in the streets.

You can see for yourself that some of your suggested drawings would be embraced in this, perhaps some of those already done—for example, "Coffee Stall, early morning;" the "houseless wanderer sleeping in the streets" and even the "factory at night," since I have in mind such a factory across Westminster. Also, as regards the general section, I have in my mind a bridge near a railway station, with long shafts of electric lights, mingled with other lights, utilitarian, and a river; which suggests sufficiently your goods depot with electric light effects. In the same section I should dwell on such a neighborhood as New Cut. Your suggestion as to this or Clare Market will therefore be certain to come à propos, whether by night or day; though I think night exhibits such neighborhoods most impressively and characteristically.

And I intend to describe a night fire; and the effects of vistas of lamps in such a neighborhood as Pall Mall. Locality, you will see, is unimportant. It is *effect* I wish to dwell on; the *character*—of horror, sombreness, weirdness, or beauty—of various scenes. My own mind turns especially towards the gloomier majesties and suggestiveness of London, because I have seen it most peculiarly under those circumstances . . .

> Ms. incomplete. In March 1897 Thompson contracted with Constable to supply the text for an illustrated book on London; William Hyde was to be the illustrator. The project was announced in the *Academy* in April, but a year later Thompson still had written nothing. The book was eventually published with text by Alice Meynell and drawings by Hyde.

122. To Arthur Doubleday

16 Elgin Avenue,
Wednesday, Jan 10/98

My Dear Doubleday,

One letter to you I lost before I could address it; and now I have to write in great hurry, at a distance from pen and ink. Very warmest thanks for your prompt and kind response, which has given me most welcome immediate relief. I have not yet received the Tom O' Bedlam, but it is still early days. It will be hapless fortune if you have lost your copy, for I am quite without one, and unable to remember the poem, which I greatly valued, in common with all my friends. But if so—Kismet. I am most unlucky about the loss of poems, principally owing to the way in which things go astray at Palace Court. Meynell has grown more careless of late years than he used to be while I was unknown and unpublished. So that I am become fearful of letting anything go to Palace Court without I have another copy of it.

As for further work from me—if you mean poetry—I have material for a thin volume whenever, and if ever, you desire to deal again in my wares. It includes the *Pastoral*, and (hypothetically) the *Tom O' Bedlam*. Some revision would first be necessary; so that if ever you desired it, it would be well for you to give me a six months' notice. A happy fit might carry me through in three; but if the Muse were unwilling, it might take six months—with my journalistic preoccupation. Revision is harder than first composition.

It demands a ghost, a resurrection, of the original inspiration; and the ghost is too often slow to rise to one's summons.

I was not run over, only knocked down; sustaining several scalp wounds and concussion. The wounds are now practically healed; and I hope that I have no cerebral consequences to fear. It has been very unlucky, throwing back my affairs just when they were in a better train than they had been since I settled in London.

I knew you were in the country, and was rejoiced to hear from young Meredith that you were much improved by the change. Kindest remembrances to Mrs. Doubleday. I hope the all-accomplished Skittles keeps you company in your rural home, and that her health is benefited by the change. There are no seductive but dangerous gardens for her to get lost in there, I hope, and certainly there are no reckless hansoms to run over her. With renewed thanks for your kindness and friendship,

Yours ever sincerely,
Francis Thompson

Ah! if you knew the contrast with Lane! If you knew the barefaced rascality—but I don't trust my pencil to speak of it. If I see you again, as I hope to do, I will a tale unfold that will make you feel he ought to be drummed out of the ranks of publishers, and have the Bodley Head hacked from the front of his establishment. If Mrs. Meynell's books were not at his mercy, I would have insisted in strong measures being taken against him. But that ties my hands. He is a scoundrel of the first water; and a clumsy scoundrel, if he had a cool man of business to deal with him. But there! I lose my temper when I think of him.

Tuesday. This letter also has been delayed in dispatch. I have been struggling against time and sickness to finish work, and now I have a brief respite to attend to the forwarding of the letter. I have got your enclosure, for which many thanks. I could not stop to write this letter over again, for I feel so unwell, with sickness and vomiting. So pray excuse more at present.

> *Tom O'Bedlam's Song* appeared in the *Dome*, May 1, 1898. Thompson was knocked down by a hansom cab on the evening of November 25, 1898, while crossing High Holborn; he was treated in the Homeopathic Hospital, Queen's Square. Soon

afterward he kept a dinner date at the home of Everard Feilding, who later remembered that Thompson "appeared an hour late, with his head tied up in an appalling bandage." (EM, p. 187.) The new volume of poetry was worked on for some time but never came to fruition. The condemnation of John Lane is a personal exaggeration, occasioned by a disagreement over royalty payments. Lane was kindly remembered by many other writers (cf. *Napthali* by C. L. Hind).

123. To Monica Meynell

[January 1898]

Dear Monnie

I am simply too unwell and done up to go to Crabbett Park tomorrow, as I should very much have liked to do. I was up till 6 o'clock this morning, writing, and am not well altogether. I have much work to do also; but would have set that aside at all costs, rather than disappoint your father and Blunt, if I did not feel too upset to face company. Had it been last Saturday I would have gone; since then I gave myself a holiday, which I badly needed, and I have to make up for it now. Work put off falls the heavier on you afterwards, and that is my case now.

I return the ticket, and am very sorry. But I expect I shall see you about Monday or Tuesday—Tuesday, I think; for my sudden cataract of work is trailing off into slackness of work, as usual (always either too much or too little), and so I shall soon be level with the arrears which have so worried me—together with the legacy of ill-health from the most disastrous winter (as regards its physical effect) I have known since I left the streets.

With kindest love to your father and yourself, my dearest,

Yours ever
F. Thompson

The original is missing; this is taken from a letter-book kept by the Meynells. Crabbett Park was Wilfrid Blunt's Sussex estate before he acquired Newbuildings.

124. To Charles Lewis Hind

16 Elgin Avenue W.,
Saturday [late March 1898]

My dear Hind,

I have been very unwell for the last two or three weeks, or your urgent request should have been better attended to. The *Dunlop* article was finished on Monday week, when I got your letter from Henley, and consequently had partly to rewrite it. And unluckily an attack of sickness which confined me to bed prevented my getting it in yesterday, although it was actually done. But I trust I am now much better all round, and shall be able to give the *Academy* proper attention. It is cutting my own throat for me to neglect it, and you may be sure I should not wilfully keep you waiting as I have done the last two or three weeks. I trust I have met Henley's wishes in the article as it now stands. I had no notion, to begin with, that there was so much to-do over the book; and so I had treated it slightly. I will call in on Monday, in case you have anything you might wish to say in regard to it.

With much regrets for my delay (but really I have been having a pretty beastly time of it),

Yours sincerely,
Francis Thompson

Thompson's review of *Robert Burns and Mrs. Dunlop* appeared in the *Academy*, April 23, 1898.

125. To Mary Thompson

[March 1898]

. . . Thereon forthwith followed the severe and most unhappy cab accident. I have had a year of disasters. You will notice a new address at the head of this letter. I have been burned out of my former lodgings. The curtain caught fire just after I had got into bed, and I upset the lamp in trying to extinguish it. My hands were badly blistered, and I sustained a dreadful shock, besides having to walk the streets all night. The room was quite burned out . . .

Quoted from VM II, p. 115. The new address was 39 Goldney
Road, just around the corner from 16 Elgin Avenue. Since this
fragment was found among his papers, it most probably was
never sent.

126. To Charles Lewis Hind

[? 1899]

Dear Hind,

I regret exceedingly to find that the Mempes was disposed of
along with an accumulation of back review books, nor can I get it
back, for it was sold almost at once. I am very sorry it should
have happened; because it should not and would not have been sold,
had it not gone among others when I was in a hurry, and my mind
occupied only with the work I had in hand. Of course, under such
circumstances I hold myself responsible for replacing it as soon as
I can. Or if you cannot wait, I would suggest you get the book, and
dock it out of my extra money. For instance, this week ten shillings
will fall due to me, over and above what is necessary for lodgings
and personal expense (two 2½ cols. makes 10s over the two pounds
for my lodgings); if you dock that, in the usual course probably a
week or two will yield another 10s extra. I propose this as the only
way which occurs to me.

The only alternative is for me to pick oakum (if they do that in
debtors' gaols). And I have not the talents for oakum-picking.
Though I enjoyed the distinguished tuition of a burglar, who had
gone through many trials—and houses—in the pursuit of this little-
known art, I showed such mediocre capacity that the Master did
not encourage me to persevere. Besides, seeing how over-crowded
the profession is, it would be a pity for me to take the oakum out
of another man's fingers.

Seriously, I am very upset that this should have happened. I can
think of nothing but what I have suggested.

Yours sincerely,
F. Thompson

Hind, in *Napthali*, explained his monetary arrangements with
Thompson: "I . . . eased him from money complexities by

sending his landlady a modest cheque each week and handing him a few shillings on account when he brought in a review." It was not as casual as that, however, for during most of his journalistic period Thompson usually earned sums above what was needed for his board and lodgings, especially after 1900.

127. To Charles Lewis Hind

Wednesday [? 1899]

Dear Hind,

I could not quite finish the article last night, and found myself taken ill to-day with a violent cold, so that I was unable to write a line. You will have it first thing to-morrow, and I am very sorry I have failed to-day. I have had no touch so bad since my pleurisy last winter; though why it came on me so suddenly after being merely unwell yesterday I cannot tell. Perhaps it was sitting up last night in a fireless room. It was like ague-fits of violent shivering, which have passed as suddenly as they came, leaving me feeling weak but capable of writing again. I hope that early sleep to-night will set me right. I am most sorry to have failed you, but there was no sign of such an attack yesterday.

Yours in haste,
F.T.

128. To Charles Lewis Hind

39 Goldney Road, Harrow Road,
Sunday Night [? 1899]

Dear Hind,

Since I was betrayed so unfortunately into putting a hasty definition into clumsy words, I beg to be allowed to define my intended meaning—to define my definition, in fact. I called you, I believe, "a man of the world with a taste for letters." I would be nearer my meaning if I had called you a man of action with a love for letters—and art. Wilfred Blunt, Wyndham, etc., are examples of the class. I might even say Henley. It is true that you, no more than Henley, have ever been a man of action like Blunt or Wyndham. Some more inclusive term is needed. The essential thing is, that *life* occupies the principal place in your regard—not life as it should be lived, the ideal of life in other words—but actual everyday life, "life as she *is* lived." This is foremost, letters or art second. Raleigh and a host of the great Elizabethans belonged to the same school. "Man of action first" is perhaps the nearest I can get to it. "Man of the world" is bungling, because it bears so many significations. Anyway, now, I hope, you have some idea of my meaning. It was an antithesis between the pure thinker and recluse, on one hand; the man interested in action for its own sake, yet with a foothold in letters, on the other.

—Yours ever,
F.T.

129. To Unknown

28 Elgin Avenue,
Saturday [late May 1900]

Dear Sir,

I regret that—in pressure of work and some ill-health—Miss Power Cobbe's letter, which you forwarded me, has not received the immediate attention which it deserved. I regret that my review should strike her in the light in which it apparently does—as, it would seem, a personal attack. I should be sorry to be guilty of anything of the kind, as I most certainly was without intention of the kind. But I cannot see that my review exceeded the limits of impartial criticism. Miss Power Cobbe seems to imply that I in some way found Miss Shore's poems "morally objectionable". I am unaware of any sentence which could create such an impression. For the rest, I was necessarily unaware of Miss Shore's personal circumstances. I was not even aware of its being her first book of poems. When a book comes before a reviewer for criticism, he cannot be expected to know or take account of personal matters— of anything outside the book itself. Many things might plead that he should be very gentle with the author, but he has no knowledge of them. The book is an impersonal thing to him; and the author who publishes a book becomes impersonal, and must expect to be treated as a mere name at the head of so many printed pages. This may be unpleasant, but it is the inevitable consequence of publication. The reviewer has only the book before him. He can only judge it impartially on its internal merits, praising in accordance with its power, blaming in proportion to its failure. If the failure be considerable, this may be a very painful process to the author; but the reviewer has no choice, and the author courted this ordeal, imimplicitly submitted himself to it, by venturing authorship. The critic can but register his impressions, coldly impartial by his very function. Did he abstain from the blame he thought just because (for example) of the writer's sex, it would be equivalent to abdicating criticism where women are concerned, extending the privileges of the drawing-room to the reviewing-column. But women of literary power would be the first to protest against the insincerity of "letting them off" because of their sex. I could point to some recent reviews of acknowledged female writers, to show that criticism at least as searching as mine is now habitually incurred and faced by women. It is on the reviewer's conscience to avoid personal attack, to criticise the book and the book only, to touch nothing of the writer but his literary quality. And this law, I think and hope, I have not exceeded. That an adverse review should give pain, is an unhappy necessity. But it *is* a necessity, from which the reviewer cannot draw back—though he would gladly shirk the ungracious and ungrateful task. But the truth, as he sees it, has to be said;—even about a woman's book. And to censure the book is not to censure the writer. It seems to me (with all respect) that Miss Power Cobbe (for whom I cannot fail to share the honour which her career has earned) loses sight somewhat of this point.

If, in conclusion, I have in any way gone beyond the limit of purely impersonal criticism, it is to me a thing as regrettable as unintentional. But I cannot yet perceive that I have done so.

Yours sincerely,
Francis Thompson

Thompson's review of Arabella Shore's poems appeared in the *Academy*, May 12, 1900. This letter was probably written at Hind's request, to be typed and forwarded; the handwritten copy was found among Thompson's papers. His move to new lodgings at 28 Elgin Avenue, where he was to remain for five years, took place shortly before the writing of this letter.

130. To Wilfrid Meynell

[late June 1900]

. . . a week in arrears, and without means to pay; I must go, it is the only right thing . . . So tomorrow night I shall come in to see you for the last time . . . Perhaps Mrs. Meynell would do me the undeserved kindness to keep my own copy of the first edition of my first book, with all its mementos of her and the dear ones. I dare not risk its shipwreck by taking it with me. Last, not least, there are some poems which K. King sent me (addressed to herself) when I was preparing a fresh volume, asking me to include them. The terrible blow of the New Year put an end to that project. I wish you would return them to her. I have not the heart . . . O Wilfrid, I do think they are rather, *rather* beautiful. I may be quite wrong, but it does seem to me that they are good. I did not guess they were so good as they *seem*. I never had the courage to look at them when my projected volume became hopeless, fearing they were poor, until now, when I was obliged to do so. If I am right it is a crime they cannot be published. O my genius, young and *ripening*, you would swear—when I wrote them; and now! What has it all come to? All chance of fulfilling my destiny over; and I *did* (up to February) still believe in my destiny. I want you to be grandfather to these orphaned poems, dear father-brother, now I am gone; and launch them on the world when their time comes. For them a box will be lodgement enough: *they* do not cost £4 a month, and fail wretchedly in the earning of it. I am an expensive taste, the most ruinous taste you ever had, my poor Wilfrid! I should like to know what you think of them before I go. Katie cannot mind your seeing them now; since my silence must have ended when I gave the purposed volume to you, my agent, and confidant of all my poetry, my dearest! . . . I ask you to do me the last favor of reading them by 8 tomorrow evening, about which time I shall come to say my sad goodbye. If you don't think much of them tell me the wholesome truth. If otherwise, you will give me a pleasure. O Wilfrid, it is strange, but this—yes, *terrible* step I am about to take, which has caused me miserable struggle throughout the week, is lightened with an inundating joy by the new-found hope that here, in these poems, is treasure—or at least some measure of beauty that I did not know of. If it be not so, well, I would sooner know the severe truth: it will not kill me when I am fronting such harsher trouble; above all, the parting from you and my more than second mother, the lady of my first all-crowning poetry; which is like parting from life itself. My own dear friend, till I see you, Ah, not yet goodbye!

> Quoted from *La Vie et l'Oeuvre d'un Poète* by Pierre Danchin, A. G. Nizet, Paris, 1959 (pp. 103–4), who saw the original. Mention of recent articles in unquoted portions of the letter, according to Danchin, dates it to late June, after the 23rd. Thompson's despondency was probably occasioned by the rejection of a new volume of poetry, by the approaching marriage of Katie King (June 26, 1900), and by his surrender to opium (indications are that he relapsed about the beginning of 1900). He was kept from a return to the streets by Wilfrid Meynell, and the mood eventually passed.

131. To Wilfrid Meynell

28 Elgin Avenue,
Sunday [July 19, 1900]

Dear Wilfrid,

I designed to call in on Wednesday, but was sick with a horrible journey on the underground. Yesterday again I intended, and again was sick and exhausted for like reason. Today, though better, I am still not well. I hope I may manage to-morrow. I have been full of worry, depression, and unconquerable forboding. The other day, as I was walking outside my lodgings, steeped in ominous thoughts, a tiny child began to sing beside me in her baby voice, over and over repeated,—

> "O danger, O danger,
> O danger is coming near!"

My heart sank, and I almost trembled with fear. There was every reason for sinking of heart, outside my own gloomy affairs. My prophecies of foreign complications in the East, and universal war, are drawing nearer and nearer to fulfilment. Small-pox has broken out in West Kensington, & at that time (I have no later news) was spreading rapidly. Disaster was, and is, drawing downwards over the whole horizon. And I feel my private fate involved in it. I am oppressed with fatality.

We had Carnival hereabouts on Thursday and Friday, and I tried to dissipate my gloom. I missed the procession both evenings, though on Thursday it passed under our window. The shops here being prematurely shut, I explored towards Westbourne Grove for paper to write, catching only glimpses of the procession *en route*. The Grove was impassable, and I only got my want by turning up Bishop's Road. When I got back, slowly, through the scarce-penetrable crowd, all traces of the procession had disappeared. I stayed out for an hour or two, watching the humours of the thronging multitude. But it was sad gala-making. This toil-imbruted people knew not how to be gay with humanity or spontaneity. The sole sport (even *that* an improvement upon previous decivilised methods) was for girls to dab you in the face with a peacock's feather every score of yards; then display their flying backs, or discharge at you over their shoulders Parthian laughter and gazes ("glances" were too intermittent, too meagre a term for such concentrated and deliberate storm of—shall I say eye-balls? veritable section-fire, unfaltering, continuous) according to their nature.

Only the children made amends for their elders, and won me to participation in their play. It were a stern heart that could grudge them their delighted pranks! I cheerfully submitted my neck to be tickled, or my cheek *effleuré*, by the feathery weapons of the kids; even though it imminently perilled that "volute redundance"— my moustache, which I had been putting (to use a pretty conceited figure) through a course of waxen *papillotes*. "Que mon moustache soit flétri mais que les kids soient diablement s'enjouies!" Mot gigantesque (I quote the French writer who will one day display his peculiar knowledge of things English and of Me) mot gigantesque du célèbre poète *Jim Thomson*, qui naquit dans la ville Écossaise de Manchester; l'auteur du *Castle of Night*, *City of Dreadful Indolence*, et de *Daisy Miller*—poème tout à fait Wordsworthien, sure une jeune Américaine, qui fut cause qu'il se tua subitement d'un coup de pistolet. Il est enseveli dans l'Abbaye de Vestminster; où la peuple entière (fait choquant, mais vraiment Anglais) a chanté sa chanson d'ivrogne, *Crossing the Bar*. (Le *bar*, c'est la porte du *gin-palace*, où les écrivains Anglais, même les plus presbytèriens, comme *Jim Thomson*, s'énivrent du *soda-brandy*, des *Scotch-wiskys*, et des *bitters-gins*; tout en fumants du *black-shag*, dans des *long-clays-churchvardens*). La Reine elle-même d'Angleterre aima beaucoup cette chanson si peu féminine, si dégoutante pour les dames Françaises. Que les Anglais sont bien impayables!

Alas! I forgot you do not read French, so that this remarkable and authentic quotation is altogether lost on you—unless (which I beg as an experiment on my French) you get Mrs. Meynell to translate it. It is not an exaggeration of what even clever Frenchmen can write on foreign matters. There is a passage (cancelled— and small wonder!) in Stendhal's account of Byron at Venice, which for consistent and wonderful inaccuracy, in its own way, runs it close. Enough that I had pleasure in my kids. One charming child of 13 or 15 had a veritable *impromptu* game of "tick" with me. Instead of making an assault and retreating, as with others, under the encouragement of my softened look (when I saw it *was* a child) she returned to the attack twice or thrice—flying and hovering round me, till at last she allowed me to "tick" her; and then, feeling my hand among her bright tresses, with feigned fright but dancing eyes turned back on me, fled in earnest to the shelter of her two sisters (one "grown-up," the other smaller than herself) who were amusedly watching the game. I fell in love with her at sight, for she was delightful: of antelope-lightness, fair complexion and long glittering hair; eyes wherein the innocent mischief could not hide their native gentleness, nor the night that crystalline luminosity which suggested their clear ice-blue. This is trivial; but you see I retain my old slavery to childhood; though this is the first time I knew that I retained anything of my own old attraction for children, which I thought I had quite lost, having got too old and black of visage. Any way, not even the chicks tempted me forth among the crowd on Friday.

Wednesday

My work has been too much delayed by ill health to call in as I hoped. And to-night I have got an article back which I hoped done with,—addition requested. I did it Hind's beastly way, and am found fault with in consequence. He has much cry, and I have little wool to reward my brother. I can hardly get to you before Friday. To say truth, I am ashamed to meet any one at your house till I have reformed my trousers and boots. I am pretty hardened to what people think of me or my clothes; but I am shamed that my friends should have shame of me. I must get some light shoes, which will last (in this weather) till I can manage to get boots. Then I have the trousers you gave me, kept in reserve, but needing alteration before I can wear them without derision. I hope I may manage that by Friday. Oh, that I were a *man* again! I must, I cannot help but go if things do not soon turn. Were it not for the power my love of you gives you over me, it is not the fear of consequences would have kept me back. This time, it would be mercifully short. I have neither the latent stubbornness of constitution, nor the latent belief in a destiny, which made it so tough a strife before. The very streets weigh upon me. These horrible streets, with their gangrenous multitudes, blackening ever into lower mortifications of humanity! The brute men; these lads who have almost lost the faculty of human speech, who howl & growl like animals, or use a tongue which is itself a cancerous disintegration of speech: these girls whose practice is a putrid ulceration of love, venting foul and purulent discharge—for their very utterance is hideous blasphemy against the sacrosanctity of lovers' language! Nothing but the vocabulary of the hospital, images of corruption and fleshly ruin, can express the objects offered to eye and ear in these loathsome streets. The air is fulsome with its surcharge of tainted humanity. We lament the smoke of London:—it were nothing without the fumes of congregated evil, the herded effluence from millions of festering souls. At times I am merely sick with it.

But all this baby-wail is useless, and worthy of the baby I am become. Good-bye, dear Wilfrid, till I see you; which I will manage on Friday, whatever comes, short of actual illness.

Yours ever,
F.T.

You will see I missed a page—so strong is the habit of writing one side.

No date appears on the original, but VM II, p. 163, gives it as July 19, 1900, probably from the envelope. The latter part of the letter, beginning "the very streets weigh upon me . . ." was used also as part of the autobiographical article he was writing at this time. The article was completed but never published and the manuscript has been lost.

132. To Wilfrid Meynell

28 Elgin Avenue,
Thursday [September 11, 1900]

Dearest Wilfrid,

Though I sat up till five last night, I did not finish copying the Ms., and resuming this evening, under the belief that I might finish in half an hour, I find it is eleven o'clock now I have completed it. I will call in to-morrow evening, prompt.

Yours ever affectionate,
F. Thompson

The original letter is preserved in an envelope postmarked with the above date at Maida Hill (Paddington).

133. To Wilfrid Meynell

[fall 1900]

. . . with some quite different standard, [?demanding] loftier qualities, because proportioned to more exalted aims. You have (unhappily,—and the fault no doubt is Katie's and her mother's, led astray by personal fondness) predetermined that the series was a second edition of my poems to Mrs. Meynell; having for . . .

The poems were, in fact, a kind of poetic diary; or rather a poetic substitute for letters. They were more akin to Shakespeare's sonnets than to the *Vita Nuova* or *Love in Dian's Lap* (so far as you can liken them). Better still, you might compare them with *A Narrow Vessel*, which has the same (or a similar) character of casual poetic diary. They were strictly incidental expressions of personal and subjective feeling, nowise idealisations of a woman (save indirectly). They were little safety-valves through which my momentary self escaped, not attempted eulogies of her. (To this there is one exception, the long terminal *Nocturns*, where precisely I recognize real failure). To bring them into relation with *Love in Dian's Lap* is to prejudge failure; because their standard is so alien, so much lower, and more casual and subjective in kind. I do not think they have much left for a second reading, which is a partial defect, cutting them off in substantial character from the best of my work . . .

. . . of their nature and poetic species—above all, if you come to read them in print, you may revise your present view that they are failures. With the exception which I have noted, I am not myself able to feel that they are unsuccessful in their preconceived kind. So far, I feel impelled to dissent from your judgment, for once. *Absence*, in particular, seems to me to be what I meant it to be. But I may, of course, be wrong, and you right. My special distrust of your judgment arises from your comparison of it with Mrs. Meynell's poem from which it is so different, which belongs to an altogether more difficult and exalted order of poetry. Anyway, I have done what I wanted . . .

> The manuscript of this letter, at Lilly Library, Indiana University, is incomplete. It originally consisted of at least two sheets, both of which have been cut. Thompson is referring to his poetic sequence *De Amicitia*, containing about a dozen poems, written to Katie King but never published as a whole. Only after Thompson's death were some of them published as separate pieces. *Love in Dian's Lap* and *A Narrow Vessel* were similar sequences, the first to Alice Meynell and the second to Maggie Brien.

134. To Wilfrid Meynell

28 Elgin Avenue,
Sunday [October 1900]

Dear Wilfrid,

I have been very unwell all the week-end; and to-day it came to a climax. I was confined to bed all day, and touched nothing but a cup of tea till eleven to-night. I got relief about nine p.m., but too late to get to you, though I made the attempt.

I am sorry, both because I should have liked to dissipate your loneliness, & because I wanted myself to see you. I want the loan of Patmore's two vols. of poems, & (if you have the thing) of a Spenser (the complete poems); both for articles.

Two articles on Coventry—& naturally I want to do them as well as may be in brief time & at brief notice, being moreover in very poor health.

Are you staying over Monday? If so, I will come in—for 7, if possible, & I trust to manage it, knowing no present obstacle which may not be set aside. But I fear you may be off again to-morrow evening.

Sorry to miss the Duchess's message, whatever it be—nothing of profound necessity, I hope. Much sorrier to miss you, if Monday be o'er-late, as I dread.

Yours with warmest love,
F.T.

> Reviews of a Patmore biography (see note to next letter) appeared in the *Academy* for November 3 and November 24, 1900. The Duchess of Sutherland was a friend of the Meynells'.

135. To Wilfrid Whitten

Friday Night [mid-November 1900]

My dear Whitten,

I intend to see you, if you should be at the Office to-morrow morning; but for fear I should miss doing so, I send this letter, to make certain explanations.

Firstly; I came up to the Office today at three, knowing I had missed Hind, in the hope of catching you, & finding out whether the 2nd Patmore middle I brought with me was yet of any use, after missing this week. Finding you not likely to be in, I asked for an advance of 10/; was told Hind had said such things were in future to be referred to him. It is most reasonable, since I can imagine it may cause difficulty in the accounts: moreover it is the province of the Editor to decide what moneys shall be allowed. It was an irregular privilege, which I willingly submit to have abolished, and will henceforth submit all such requests to Hind personally. But Andrews offered to lend me the sum on his own responsibility, & let me settle the matter with Hind. Unluckily I accepted the offer, & am now very sorry. It may make trouble for him, & was not a necessity, but only a convenience, for me; since my sole reason for calling in was to see you, as I have mentioned. And perhaps Hind's reason for prohibiting it was that he had resolved not to use the Patmore middle, being so late. The 10/ is nevertheless covered by other work I have in hand. But it now strikes me perhaps Hind does not wish me to do that other work, either. I ought to have thought he might have serious reason for the step, not merely the wish to keep the reins in his own hands, as I hastily supposed. Altogether I am most vexed I took Andrews' good-natured offer. I only hope the blame will be duly laid on me, not on him. But I was in no state for clear reflection, being so giddy from weakness that I tottered in your doorway.

That brings me to my second point of explanation—why I did not see Hind this morning. Since I saw him last week I have been continuously ill, and try as I would, I could not get the article done before noon to-day, still less by Tuesday, when I suppose he expected it (for he named no date in his kind post-card). I made a final effort to get it done last night after dinner (having been ill all day), so that I might bring it to him this morning. For I did not want to appear before him without the article, after having missed the proper time. At least I wanted to have it done when I *did* see him. But though I worked till five this morning, it was still unfinished, when I was taken so sick I had to go to bed. I had no sleep, and when I got up to try to finish it, I found myself so ill I could not touch food for an hour, much less write. And then I had to wind my stomach up with brandy, before I could get food down. After that I was obliged to rest till the food took effect, and I could begin to write. It was then twelve, and it was two before I completed what remained to be done. Then, as I have said, I went off on the chance to find out from you whether the article was now of any use. So I think you will see it was through nothing preventible on my part that I missed seeing Hind this morning.

If you are at the Office to-morrow morning, I shall be there as soon as you are—by ten—or not at all. Do not therefore await me. If I am not there by then, it will mean I am too ill to come. But unless I am as ill as I was this morning (& I hope I shall not be after a night's sleep) I shall certainly be there.

Pardon me if this is not so clear as I could wish. I have touched nothing to-day but part of an egg and one piece of toast, I have had no sleep, and I have been writing for two hours this morning, and seven hours together last night before I was taken sick. And I am exhausted. Unless I find some remedy, you will be spared the trouble of getting rid of your contributor. I have no reserve of strength to spare, and flesh and blood cannot stand this continual throwing up of the little food I manage to take. I never had such continuously acute dyspepsia. The drain on my strength has been going on now for near three weeks, with rarely a day but I vomit up at night whatever I may have taken during the day. And gradually my stomach gets so weak that I cannot eat, without some special stimulus, which I will only use in case of pressing necessity for work, as this morning—since it forfeits its power for good if you make a habit of it. Therefore pray pardon me, since I am naturally depressed, and as little master of myself as of my power for work—which this wretched condition altogether ruins.

Yours sincerely, dear Whitten,
Francis Thompson

The reference to the "2nd Patmore middle" indicates the second section (*Academy*, November 24, 1900) of Thompson's two-part review of Basil Champney's *Memoirs and Correspondence of Coventry Patmore*.

136. To Wilfrid Meynell

28 Elgin Avenue,
Monday Dec. 24, 1900

Dear Wilfrid,

I have summoned up pluck to send my little play (which Mrs. Meynell and you have seen) to W. Archer, asking him whether it afforded any encouragement to serious study of writing for the stage. His answer is unfavourable—though he cautiously refrains from a precise negative.

This sets my mind at rest on that matter. None the less, I wanted to read you one or two bits from my chucked-up *Saul* when I called in; since they seemed to me better than I knew—good enough at least to ask external opinion upon. And being a frankly closet-play, it is beyond the range of Archer.

I never yet missed my Xmas wishes to you, and it seems uglily ominous if I should do now. On Saturday I relied to see you, and again to-day. But I have been working desperately at a poem for the *Academy*. I sat up on Friday to get it in by Saturday morning (to no useful purpose) made myself sick, got little sleep, was sick next day, and only got the thing finally copied out late on Saturday night, having been upset most of the day. Last night I was fool enough (unwarned) to sit up writing letters; as a result I am upset to-day. When I met Whitten this morning, he looked uneasy, repeatedly advised me to "get something." I explained I already had "got" some tea (with my breakfast). "Yes, but—get something more," he said; and alleged that I was looking shrunk with cold. It was only lack of sleep, with the nervous prostration and sensitiveness to weather it always produces. But (following its usual course) it has gone on to sickness, and I cannot come in unless it should pass off. If it doesn't, I must call on you after mass to-morrow, when I shall have had a night's rest, and shall be restored. I don't want you to see me like this. You won't believe what I am going to say about my health, unless you see me as I thought you would see me. It is all the fault of a hard week. I am not yet in physical condition to stand a long poem, especially a forced poem, a *tour de force*, under a narrow time-limit.

Since my last note to you I have been very ill with dyspepsia. Never so ill with it before. My work went all to pieces, and I went all to pieces. I thought my doom was signed. I thought I should never be fit to earn my living again. And I had reason. It had been coming on me steadily since my last year in Wales, and here was the finish at last. My hospital knowledge told me the meaning of my symptoms, and I was quite played out. For the first time I despaired of my health. And then (thank God!) I was thrown across a remedy—or at least a palliative. It has not failed me since.

I have come round with a rapidity which astonishes myself, seeing how deadly ill I was; and not only so, but my digestion keeps better than ever it has done for many a year. Such upsets as the present are due to other causes than my food going wrong with me. My journalistic power is returning to me. I almost hope (no, I daren't say it!) my creative power may gradually return. Even in this poem, poor mechanic thing though it be, I have felt something like faint distant stirrings of the forgotten power. I should be almost at peace of mind, but for my money-anxieties.

That brings me to the fact that Mrs. Maries tells me you have paid part of the great sum which has got piled up against me during my two illnesses. It is hard to say what I feel—perhaps better not to try. But I find five pounds something are still owing (that is, when Mrs. Maries spoke to me, I don't remember the date) after handing over to her the *Illustrated* cheque. And I don't see my way out of it. All I can manage is to pay the last month's due. The debt has got beyond all possibility of effort. For the future, I have at least the advantage of restored health, of renewed ambitions, of all which is symbolized by my actually carrying through a long poem, however bad. But the past is a weight impossible to lift.

However, these things I designed to talk over with you. I wish I could come in to-night. Any-way, God bless you, dear Wilfrid, and all happy wishes to yourself & Mrs. Meynell & the children. At any rate I will see you to-morrow after Mass.

Yours ever,
Francis Thompson

P.S. I send you a trifle I found among my papers.

The "little play" was *Napoleon Judges,* unpublished until it was printed in *The Man Has Wings* in 1957. *Saul* was a similar effort, unfinished and still unpublished; the manuscript is in the Boston College Collection. The poem for the *Academy* (December 29, 1900) was *The Nineteenth Century.* The "*Illustrated* cheque" may refer to a review of Yeats in the *Illustrated London News,* September 1901. The "trifle" is unidentified.

137. To Wilfrid Meynell

28 Elgin Avenue,
Sunday [? late 1900]

Dear Wilfrid,

I intended to call in to-night, but was taken sick at the critical moment.

I saw what I concluded was Rook at the *Academy* on Wednesday; but we did not even exchange a look, for Hind did not introduce us. So I left, convinced that Hind meant to get out of the Academy by hook or by C. Rook. If Rook *had* spoken, I should have expected him to quote Brutus to the Romans;—

"Hear me for my caws."

And I should instantly have answered with Othello:—

"It is the caws, it is the caws, my soul!"

Perhaps his silence, in fact, was owing to some caws or impediment in his speech.

His appearance differed from my expectation. I expected something like the enclosed sketch. I should explain that this singularly original drawing represents Sir Rook in the act of refreshing himself with a draught of ink. The problem stated underneath may be answered in several ways, but hardly in one move. A conceivable solution is as follows.

1. Hind takes umbrage.
2. Hind checks Rook.
3. Rook takes hat *en passant*.
4. Rook takes hook.
5. Hind to—blazes.
6. Hind cheques Rook.
    Chequed-Mate

I trust to drop in when Tuesday is over.

Yours ever,
F. Thompson

Sir Rook, you observe, has his portcullis raised, for convenience of quaffing the coal-black wine.

> Clarence Rook was a former assistant to Hind on the *Pall Mall Budget*. The "enclosed sketch" shows a knight in armor with a helmet in the shape of a castle tower; underneath is a line from *Troilus and Cressida*: "Stand fast, and wear a castle on thy head."

138. To Charles Lewis Hind

28 Elgin Avenue,
Tuesday [? late 1900]

Dear Hind,

I muddled up the time altogether to-day. How, I do not now understand. I started off soon after 2. Thinking I had time for a letter to the *Academy* which it had been in my mind to write, I delayed my journey to write it. When I was drawing to a conclusion, heard the clock strike 3 (as it seemed to me). I thought I should soon be finished, so went on to the end. A few minutes later, as it appeared, the clock struck again, and I counted 4. Alarmed, I rushed off—vexed that I should get in by half-past 4, instead of half-past 3, as I intended—and finished the thing in the train. I got to the *Academy*, and was struck all of a heap. There was nobody there, and it was ten past six! How I did it I do not even now understand. That time flies when I am writing, I know; but I cannot conceive how I could miscalculate the striking of the clock *twice running*. I will be with you in good time to-morrow. But that cannot make amends to myself for such a *fiasco* & waste of time. I must have spent not far short of 3 hours and a half over that beastly letter—which you will probably not think worth insertion after all.

Yours,
F.T.

139. To Wilfrid Meynell

28 Elgin Avenue,
Wednesday Night [January 1901]

Dear Wilfrid,

I have just got home. The Imperial & Colonial Magazine asked me to submit "one or two poems" of an Imperialist nature. I sent them one, as you know. They have rejected it. If the poem sent through you is also rejected (as I expect) I shall give up & go back to the streets. I cannot go on here—or anywhere else—under these circumstances. Try as I will, all doors are shut against me, while the veriest rubbish by others—who have not even my name—finds acceptance. I cannot go on. It is hopeless. If your poem mis-carries, that is the end. My last resource for lifting the dead weight from my shoulders is gone.

Yours ever,
F.T.

I thought this one was safe, having been asked for.

> The *Imperial and Colonial* magazine began publishing in No-
> vember 1900 and lasted for seven monthly issues. No Thompson
> poem appeared in it. The few verses it did carry are mediocre
> but strongly imperialistic. No indication can be found as to
> which poems Thompson refers to here.

140. To Wilfrid Meynell

[January 1901]

. . . Things have become impossible. B—— did not outright refuse me an advance on my poem, but told me to call again and "talk it over" . . . The only thing is for me to relieve you of my burthen—at any rate for the present—and go back whence I came. There will be no danger in my present time of life and outworn strength that I should share poor Coventry's complaint (that of outliving his ambition to live) . . . For the reverse of the medal, you have Ghosh

who has just been promised £220 odd for a series of tales . . . For
the present at any rate good-bye, you dearest ones. If for longer—

> Why, then, this parting was well made.
> Yours ever, and whatever comes,
> Francis Thompson

Quoted from EM, pp. 316–17. The date is conjectural, but it
seems to fit this particular period of economic despondency.
S. K. Ghosh was a fellow-lodger at 28 Elgin Avenue, as well
as an acquaintance of the Meynells. He set down some mem-
ories of Thompson in his quasi-novel *The Prince of Destiny*,
published in 1909.

141. To Wilfrid Meynell

[February 12, 1901]

Dear Wilfrid,

Here is the 19 Century article. Will you please forward it, and
also the accompanying letter to the Editor, for which I have no
envelope. And would you enclose stamps to him for return? I have
had to write the last part in pencil—I hope that will not prevent its
acceptance?

I trust Hind's article will go to him to-night, and then I shall
have done what I can. God help me in the struggle which now begins, for I see the conditions will be much harder than before, and
I have reason to dread the worst.

God bless and thank you and yours, dear Wilfrid, for your
long and heroic kindness to me.

And remember if ever you want to communicate with me, the
Poste Restante Charing Cross will find me. I shall make a point of
going there every now and then, in case such an occasion should
arise.

Ever and in all fates yours,

Francis Thompson

I wish I had thought to make my will before I left. You ought
to have it. But now it cannot be done.

See the following letter and note.

142. To the Editor of the *Nineteenth Century*

Care of W. Meynell, Esq.,

47 Palace Court W.,

Feb. 12, 1901

Dear Sir,

The enclosed is a narrative of personal experiences as an outcast in the London streets. I submit it to you in the hope you may think it of interest to *Nineteenth Century* readers. Perhaps you may know my name, since the late Mr. Traill had an article on my poems in the *Nineteenth Century* during 1893 or '94.

Will you kindly return to the above address in case of non-acceptance?

Yours sincerely,

Francis Thompson

Editor Nineteenth Century

> From the above two letters it is clear that Thompson completed his "narrative of personal experiences as an outcast in the London streets," and forwarded it to the *Nineteenth Century* magazine through Meynell. It was never published and the manuscript has disappeared; perhaps Meynell dissuaded him and the article was never submitted. Many fragments scattered through Thompson's notebooks show that it was essentially a very frank literary autobiography, in the manner of De Quincey's *Confessions of an English Opium Eater*. Its disappearance and the fact that it is not mentioned in any of the Meynells' writings on Thompson may indicate it was destroyed. Helped and encouraged by Wilfrid Meynell, Thompson did not return to the streets.

143. To Everard Meynell

28 Elgin Avenue,

Paddington W.,

Tuesday Night [August 14, 1901]

Dear Ev,

I hoped to have seen you to-night, but have been so late at the Academy that it is not possible. So I am obliged to make my proposal by letter.

Would you, and could you, join two or three of us in a quiet game of cricket to-morrow? If you could, we should be very pleased to have you. It is only a bit of quiet practice, for amusement's sake; no match. There will only be Browning, Bryant, and myself. "Meet" at Elgin Avenue, about eleven, if you can manage it. We will wait for you till half-past eleven, if you do not turn up; but after that we shall conclude you cannot come. You will find a very decent ground—with net and all necessaries,—including lemonade or Kola, if you like to purchase them. (The drinks, I mean, not the cricket requisites, which will be all right). We had a game on Friday, my first for over eighteen years—from which I am still somewhat sore and stiff. I enjoyed it: though Bryant was dead on the stumps—my personal and fleshly stumps—which he peppered freely; finishing with a trimmer on the knee-cap (causing it to swell), and a beautiful ball on my left temple, which cannoned off a yard or two behind the wicket. My hat saved me. Bryant thought I was hurt, till I reassured him by a bad joke.

Yours,
F.T.

> Everard Meynell accepted the invitation and briefly recorded the activities: "Of seven men and boys who met there, six had made some compromise with the conventional costume of the game; they could boast a flannelled leg, soft collar, or at least a stud unfastened. . . But he was dingy from boot-laces to hat band. Timorously excited and wonderfully intent upon all the preparations, he stiffly awaited his turn to bat. When it came he remembered he had no pads on and stayed to strap them . . . then, supremely grave, he batted." (EM, p. 44.)

144. To William Archer

28 Elgin Avenue,
Paddington W.
[summer 1901]

Dear Mr. Archer,

It will give me great pleasure that you should make use of any of my poems which you may require for your book, to which I wish every success.

I owe you thanks for your kind advice with regard to the little dramatic effort which I sent you. Personal trouble and ill health prevented my acknowledging it at the time, as I wished to do. It was to me most useful and authoritative.

Apologising most regretfully for this late recognition of your kind trouble on my behalf,

Believe me,
Yours most sincerely,
Francis Thompson

William Archer's *Poets of the Younger Generation* was published in 1902. It included a number of poems by Thompson and a short biographical sketch. The "little dramatic effort" was *Napoleon Judges*.

145. To Charles Lewis Hind

28 Elgin Avenue W.,
Wednesday [November 1901]

Dear Hind,

I caught fresh cold yesterday, and have been laid up to-day in consequence, preventing me from carrying out my programme at the Brit. Mus. Had my materials been at home, I could have done my work none the less, since my head is clear, and only my body ill. As it is, I have occupied myself in preparing this week's book, and further revising the *Lang*. Coming to read it over, I was not satisfied that it would meet your wishes. *Now* I trust it may. I have taken out about half of the original article, and added near as much—in the sense I understood you to desire, so far as I found myself able.

I knew I was queer on Tuesday, but did not know I was off my head, as I must have been. I missed giving you, not only one, but the last three pages of the *Dream* article. I forward with the *Lang* the other two pages (*one* I gave you on Tuesday) which I found to my consternation to-day.

Yours affectionately,
F. Thompson

I find I have no stamp, so must get this to you to-morrow myself. It is beastly rheumatism which is knocking me up; a thing I never had since my childhood till late years. It attacks my knees especially —a sign, one of my old medical chiefs said, of insidious rheumatic fever, liable to react on your heart. But let us trust that is not always the case; and besides it is question whether a man of forty, and a professional hermit, retains such an organ as a heart. I hope your vaccination goes on all right—Whitten told me you had gone through it. I am afraid of it, till I pull round from these afflictions sore.

> Thompson's review of Andrew Lang's *Alfred Tennyson* appeared in the *Academy*, November 23, 1901. His review of *Dreams and Their Meanings*, by H. G. Hutchinson, was in the *Academy*, November 30, 1901.

146. To Wilfrid Meynell

28 Elgin Avenue,
Thursday [fall 1901]

Dear Wilfrid,

I meant to have come in last night, but could not. I am upset with a bad cold, and rheumatism in the knees, so that I clump down stairs of mornings like the elephant, who—

"has knees
But none for bending."

I feel very pulled down and weak, for the cold has lasted since Saturday, lifting a little on Sunday afternoon and Monday, only to return worse on Tuesday. In the interval I shoved through my work (of which Gerard will have told you, and Thorpe, if it were too great a stretch of confidence to rely on Bastian) and I think got it in ahead of the other judges. I await now the decision of the competition.

I feel very *done*, and hardly can foretell what day may give me a look at you. It seems to me as if I had caught fresh cold to-day—

I trust I may be wrong. It breaks me up so, I never was used to these long colds before.

Love to all, and I hope none of you are victims.

Yours ever,
Francis Thompson

"Thorpe" (Thomas Thorp) was a fellow lodger at 28 Elgin Avenue and a friend of the Meynells. "Bastian" was Sebastian, eldest of the Meynell children. The "competition" was a friendly verse-writing contest, of which nothing further is known.

147. To Wilfrid Meynell

Monday [December 24, 1901]

Dear Wilfrid,

I was struggling all last week under the double burden of ill health and the endeavour to work off the arrears which have come upon me through the Academy's fault rather than my own. I have been working up to the last minute, and have just come in—defeated, at least partially. But these things we can talk about when I come in to-morrow, as I will gladly do. Tuesday and Wednesday, as it happened, I was crumpled up altogether, or I would have answered dear Monnie's letter, as I have day after day intended to do, and been defeated by the struggle to get my work straight before Xmas, complicated by persistent illness. I wanted to see you long ago, but kept delaying with the hope of getting my Academy arrears straight first of all, so that things might be ready for the conflict with the A., on which we shall certainly have to enter. And you know, I think, how oblivious I am to the procession of time; which is to me long when I am unoccupied, and a mere flash when I am preoccupied. I have only just failed to clear off things with the A.; and should feel equal-minded had I nothing else to worry me. My bout of ill health (the result of cold and the abominable vicissitudes of weather) I began to emerge from on Sunday night. Not unnaturally, I have suffered this winter as I have never before done so early; because we have never before had such weather so early in the winter. February or March is usually the time when I get ill. But this winter I have had attacks of rheumatic cold quite unusual for me. I really think, however, I am beginning to get acclimatised, though naturally rather pulled down.

Of course I will come in to-morrow night. Did I not you might be sure I was knocked off my pegs altogether, and I should feel that the world had gone off its hinges. I have never missed seeing you at Xmas save when I was at Pantasaph.

Every happy wish to you, dear Wilfrid, and may God be as kind to you as you have ever been to me.

Yours affectionately,
Francis Thompson

> The nature of the "conflict" with the *Academy* is not known; it could not have been serious, however, since he continued and even increased his work for the magazine.

148. To Monica Meynell

Monday [late December 1901]

Monicella Mia Soavissima,

A very happy Xmas first of all. In the second place, thank you for your kind note, which was a bright spot in a rather dismalish birthday. I was very unwell all week, and particularly ill Tuesday and Wednesday. I was made no better by the fact that I could not stay in and nurse myself, but had perforce to go out in the bitter weather, catching fresh cold, so that when my work was done I was fit for nothing but to go to bed. I hoped to come in on Saturday, when I began to get better, but had a fresh lot of books poured upon me, pegging me down so that to this moment I have not finished my work. I have just come home after a fruitless attempt to get in at any rate the most part of my work before Xmas, very cold and wet and tired. But I shall see you at any rate to-morrow night, I trust. I must run up with these notes for you and your father before I go to bed, since I want you to have them on Xmas morning, and I am too late for the post.

This weather crumples me up. My blood is not fit to bear; and the corpuscles—frozen hard—are sliding over it: you could hear them, with a megaphone, *tinkle-tinkle* like a shoal of mother-o'-pearl fish—such as we used to have for card-counters when I was a child.

Until I can see you, I lend you this young gentleman, who is more about your own age, to supply my place. You have seen him before, though I doubt you will not recognise him. You were a child when he was introduced to you, and of course he was much older then.

with best wishes dear Monnie,
your affectionate friend
Francis Thompson

The date of Thompson's birthday is disputed: it was probably December 18 but could have been December 16. "This young gentleman" probably indicates a photograph of himself.

149. To Wilfrid Meynell

28 Elgin Avenue,
Saturday [May 1902]

Dear Wilfrid,

I could not come in to tea with Blunt and Yeats, for I had to go down to the Academy, and was back much too late. Had I known on Thursday, I would have altered my arrangements so as to accept your invitation, for I should very much have liked to meet Yeats, whom I have long wished to see. You know I heartily admired his work, which in its consistent contempt for popularity and research of what is fine and delicate appeals to my own soul. Nor (despite his championship of certain French poets as the last word of present poetic tendency) has he, like other poets who aspire to delicacy, made himself an echo of Paris. He has followed English —or Celtic—literary tradition, in which I think is the truest inspiration for a poet of the English tongue. This I account to him for righteousness, when others have sterilised themselves by repeating Verlaine and other Parisians,—as though there were not more poetic sap in a hundred branches of our English tree, than in the whole trunk of France. Better Italy, if we are to go abroad at all.

Yours always, dear Wilfrid,
F. Thompson

The manuscript of the letter has been altered by cutting and pasting; a notation in another hand on it gives the date as May 1902. Thompson had met William Butler Yeats ten years before, briefly, at a meeting of the Rhymers' Club in the fall of 1891.

150. To Charles Lewis Hind

Thursday [June 1902]

Dear Hind,

I was so unwell yesterday that I could not come—neuralgia in the eye. I am the more sorry because the *Watson* was ready to bring with me, as you desired. The acute pain drove it out of my head, nor could I see to write an explanation of my absence. Today, when I remembered the unsent article, I thought it of course too late to be of use to you this week. So my eye being still weak, I decided to bring it (not the eye) tomorrow, with personal explanation. But getting your telegram, I send it herewith. A really fine ode—though closely imitated (in point of style) from my *Nineteenth Century* Ode in the *Academy*. Thorpe perceived it, without any "lead" from me, so it is not merely my own fancy. But it is so admirably imitated as to be, on the whole, a better poem than the original. Second time he has paid me such rather left-handed compliment. If all made such fine use of the model, I would not mind imitation.

Yours in haste,
F. Thompson

Thompson's review of William Watson's ode on the coronation of Edward VII appeared in the *Academy*, June 28, 1902. Thompson's poem, *The Nineteenth Century*, had appeared in the *Academy*, December 29, 1900.

151. To Charles Lewis Hind

[September 1902]

Dear Hind,

I was taken sick on my way to the station, not having been to bed all night, and having been working a good part of to-day; and though I came on as soon as I could pull myself together again, I was too late. So I leave the *Dumas* article, which I brought with me, and will be down to-morrow morning, when I am told you will be here.

Yours,
F. Thompson

P.S. You had another very interesting article last week; but I had qualms whether your art of artistic romance, or of the Thing Seen, or the Thing which ought to have been seen if it wasn't, was taking us in again with its realism more real than fact.

> Thompson's review of *Alexander Dumas (Père): His Life and Works*, by A. F. Davidson, appeared in the *Academy*, September 6, 1902. "Things Seen," written by Hind, was a feature in the Academy.

152. To Monica Meynell

28 Elgin Avenue,
Saturday [late 1902]

Dear Monica,

I would have answered you long since, if I had not been so worried with work that I do not know how to get through it; while at the same time I have been in very bad health, suffering from neuralgia for nearly four weeks without relief, so that it grew worse instead of better. Having got rid of my poem, I have taken a little rest from work to which I had no right, and my neuralgia seems happily to have got better—though I am almost afraid to say so; for I still feel very weak and jaded, so that it might easily return. Therefore I take this moment to write to you.

Most warmly and sincerely I congratulate you, dear Monica, on what is the greatest event in a woman's life—or a man's, to my thinking. I sympathise with you in your happiness, and hope it will be the beginning of a life-long happiness with the lover you have chosen—I say lover, for I hope you will always be lovers, despite dinners and servants and other inevitable, not to say wholesome prose of marriage. Your future husband, of course, I have barely seen, and that but once. But that he is your choice is enough for me, enough to make me regard him as a friend, and extend to him, if he will allow me, the affection which you once—so long since— purchased with a poppy in that Friston field. "Keep it," you said (though you have doubtless forgotten what you said), "as long as you live." I have kept it, and with it I keep you, my dearest. I do not say or show much, for I am an old man compared with you, and no companion for your young life. But never, my dear, doubt I love you. And if I have the chance to show it, I will do.

I am ill at saying all I doubtless should say to a young girl on her engagement. I have no experience in it, my Monica. I can only say I love you; and if there is any kind and tender thing I should have said, believe it is in my heart, though it be not here.

My dear,
Your true friend
Francis Thompson

P.S. Would you give the accompanying note to your father?

> Monica Meynell became engaged to Caleb Saleeby in the latter months of 1902. They were married on June 14, 1903.

153. To Alice Meynell

Tuesday [December 1902]

Dear Mrs. Meynell,

Excuse this pencil, and the absence of note-paper. I have to snatch a moment to write where and how I can. I have been so unwell for a fortnight that my work is all behind; and I am almost in despair how to pull off the arrears before Christmas. I have not a moment to myself scarcely, and have missed my sleep a lot, which upsets me. But for this, I should have answered your kind note at once.

I shall have great pleasure in accepting your invitation for Christmas Day. In case I should not be able to write again before Christmas, I wish yourself, Wilfrid, and the children all the happiness of the season. With love to all,

[signature cut out]

> The illness and the arrears of work might seem to place this letter in December 1901, but Alice Meynell at that time was on a lecture tour in the United States. It is written in pencil on a leaf torn from a notebook.

154. To Alice Meynell

Sunday [December 27, 1902]

Dear Mrs. Meynell,

Thank you for your kindness in remembering my birthday—better than I did myself. I fully intended to have been with you on Xmas Day; but I was taken sick in the afternoon, & indeed was unwell all yesterday as well. I have been very upset since last I saw you—have not been so pulled down any winter for a long while as I have been this, especially a week or so ago. But I hope to see you, to-morrow if possible—that is, if I only keep better.

With all best wishes of the season to yourself, Wilfrid, and the family,

Yours affectionately,
F. Thompson

155. To Wilfrid Meynell

28 Elgin Avenue,
Saturday [May 1903]

Dear Wilfrid,

I have been anxious to see you, but everything has been against my seeing anybody. At last I trust I can manage it, to-morrow evening. I should have done so tonight; but I had long since been asked, & unable, to call on Miss Tobin; I had failed to join her birthday party to which she kindly asked me, & even to answer her letter in time for her birthday. So, sending a hasty note of warning yesterday, I called on her this evening by way of amends—only to find she was at Torquay. I am not sorry; for I was caught, lightly clad, in a thunder storm, & so long delayed that I was ashamed to go on to her at all. It was therefore for the best; but it spoilt my chance of seeing you to-night. Tomorrow will make amends, I hope, for I want to see you as soon as I can, on a matter of advice, besides that I have not seen you since you came back from your long absence; & that this Xmas (the first time when I have been in London) I spent ill in bed instead of with you.

Yours always, Dear Wilfrid,
Francis Thompson

Quoted from a copy in the hand of Mrs. Sowerby. Agnes Tobin was a California friend of the Meynells on a visit to London; she is remembered for her translations of Petrarch's sonnets.

156. To Monica Meynell

Westbourne Grove, 12:30 p.m.
Wednesday, June 14, 1903

Dearest Monica,

You were a prophetess (though you needed not to be a sibyl to foretell my tricks and manners). I reached the church just ten minutes after twelve, to find vacancy, as you had forewarned me. A young lady that might have been yourself, though her cavalier was not like Mr. Saleeby, approached the church by the back entrance, just as I came away, but on inspection she had no trace of poppy-land. There must have been other nuptial couples about, I think.

So I can only wish by letter you and your husband all the happiness God can imagine for you. It seems but the other day, my dearest sister (may I not call you so? For you are all to me as younger sisters and brothers—to me, who have long ceased practically to have any sisters of my own, so completely am I sundered from them) that you were a child with me at Friston, and I myself still very much of a child. Now the time is come I foresaw then,—"Knowing well, when some few days are over, you vanish from me to another." You may pardon me if I feel a little sadness, even while I am glad for your gladness, my very dear.

But that is enough for me. May you have the happiest of bridal days—and the sun has come back to look at it and you.

I was designing to call last night, till I learned from you that you would be occupied with your wedding-party. Then I hoped I might have got to you to-night, instead; but could not manage it. So, to my sorrow, I must be content only to write. Had I known before, I would have called in on Sunday, at all costs, rather than defer it to (as it turns out) the impossible Wednesday.

My dearest love and congratulations to your father and mother. I shall be with you all, at any rate, in spirit.

Yours ever dearly, my dear,
Francis Thompson

> Invited to Monica's wedding, Thompson arrived at the church too early and, thinking he was late, went home. The quotation, inaccurate, is from *The Poppy*.

157. To Wilfrid Meynell

28 Elgin Avenue,
Monday [October 1903]

Dear Wilfrid,

The interview last Friday landed me a doubtfully hospitable Shore. All articles to be cut down to a column. Immediate result, fifteen shillings for this week. Since have received more books, bringing it up to the usual 30 shillings (through Andrews' action, I conjecture). But takes 5 books & 5 articles to reach this result— all to be done by to-morrow. Don't know what to do; & therefore cannot venture to see the chappie again (which would be of necessity a *committing* interview, one way or t'other) till I have seen you. Yet can draw no money till I see him. Therefore am

waiting anxiously for your return; when I may explain all the complexities of the situation (which I cannot do by hasty letter), and
arm myself for the decisive encounter by deciding explicitly what
I can accept, & what cannot—how far I can go, & no farther. At
present most perplexed & anxious. Do not cut short your holiday:
yet I *do* need to see you by Wednesday at latest. It is very worry-
ing, & more complex than I can here expound.

Hoping for sight of you & timely, most needful advice.

Yours ever,

F.T.

Then *signed* articles of a column apiece! I don't, *don't* trust
him; & Andrews would like to see you. Am at a standstill till I can
see you.

> In October 1903 C. L. Hind resigned as editor of the *Academy*
> and was replaced by Teignmouth Shore. Thompson continued
> to write for the magazine, though his contributions were re-
> duced in length and quantity. At the same time he began re-
> viewing for the *Athenaeum*, a connection arranged by Wilfrid
> Meynell.

158. To Everard Meynell

June 23, 1904

Dear Ev,

Am perplexed what to do. Your boy says you left a message you
would meet me at P.C. to-night. So I suppose you are not returning. I had brought you second vol. Sir T. Browne. But further, if
I am to go to D. of S. to-night (on which point I was referred to
you) I want pair dress-slippers (besides trousers, for which I must
trust you). And I have left my ticket at home. Don't know if it be
indispensable. But it all puts me in a muddle, not knowing what has
been decided. Perhaps I had better go back for ticket, get shoes, &
go to P.C. on spec.

F.T.

> "P.C." was the Meynell home in Palace Court. "D. of S." was
> the Duchess of Sutherland, a friend of the Meynells, at whose

house, evidently, a party had been planned. It is not known whether Thompson attended. The Duchess later used one of his poems in an anthology, *Wayfarer's Love*, published in 1904 for the benefit of crippled children.

159. To Wilfrid Meynell

28 Elgin Avenue,
Wednesday [January 1905]

Dear Wilfrid,

After ordering breakfast on the table at 9, and setting my alarum for half-past 8, I foolishly forgot to pull back the check. Of course it did not go off, and I got down to cold tea at noon—having been late in bed. I can only call to-night, and ask for another appointment, when I will get Mrs. Maries to call me—as I should have done last night. But I am so used to calling myself by the alarum when I want to rise early, that I never thought of it. I can only express my sincere sorrow. So forgive me, seeing it was an accident, not intentional neglect on my part. And by the simple precaution I speak of, I can ensure it shall not happen twice.

Rather seedy, but will see you to-night.

Yours ever,
F.T.

160. To Everard Meynell

28 Elgin Avenue,
Tuesday [January 15, 1905]

Dear Everard,

I was too exhausted & shaken to see you to-day, after dreadful time last night. Will you please have the remaining ten shillings ready for me to-morrow morning (Wednesday),—the morning when you should get this note? I will be at the shop before one. I trust you to have it for me by then.

Am not at all well to-night. Good-bye till I see you to-morrow. Love to all.

Yours ever,
F. Thompson

Everard Meynell had opened a small store, The Serendipity Shop, dealing largely in rare books and manuscripts, located at first in Westbourne Grove. Here, during the spring and summer of 1905, Thompson regularly delivered portions of the manuscript of his life of St. Ignatius and collected money from Everard for his daily subsistence. Wilfrid had arranged for his son to give Thompson one pound for every three pages of manuscript.

161. To the Editor, *The Academy*

28 Elgin Avenue,
Maida Vale W.,
February 5, 1905

Dear Sir,

Since your request is so sudden as to leave no time for intercommunication, I will do what you ask *now*. But I confess I am surprised. Since the change of proprietorship I have had no communication that my services were further required; and have supposed, therefore, that my connections with the paper had lapsed with that change. If I am wished to do anything further, I should desire first to know what my position is to be in regard to the paper, and on what terms. At present I am not even informed whether I am desired to be a regular contributor to the paper, or a contributor at all. I desire some understanding on these matters before I do anything else for the *Academy*—if I am wished to do anything. At present your sudden request is the first intimation I have had of any continued connection with the paper.

Yours sincerely,
Francis Thompson

See the following letter and note.

162. To Wilfrid Meynell

Monday [February 5, 1905]

Caro Mio Guilfrido,

(Short for "Wilfrid" Italianate; hope not villainously wrong!) *Ignatius* to-morrow night (Tuesday), when trust to see you. Delayed by sudden request from *Academy*: fear wrong impulse, so hold my (already written) letter to *Academicians* for your inspection & advice on said morrow-night. *Riled*, quite apart from delay to *Ignatius*: perhaps no reason for *riledness*—we shall see, or *you* shall see, for are you not (by high official appointment) keeper of Our Poetic Conscience in these matters below the moon? Seriously, I want your advice before I venture to send the letter—should you think fit for me to send it at all.

Anyway, it results in giving you prolonged notice, "ample verge and room enough" (I trust) for the *Ignatius*: so good comes from it, if no other way.

So sorry this prevented me coming in (as I designed) for dear Everard's birthday. May the good goddess Fortune fall deep in love with him, & prove for once no jilt!

Ever yours, F.T.

> The two letters above are preserved in an envelope, on which is pencilled the following note by Wilfrid Meynell: "When Hind [i.e. Shore] was succeeded in the editorship of the *Academy* by Lord Alfred Douglas, F.T. had not at first any exchange of communication. But, shortly, a request for a book review came, in reply to which FT wrote the letter here enclosed, asking my advice on its suitability. I advised a new and more friendly version, which he adopted and which resulted in friendly arrangements for future work. W.M." "*Ignatius*" refers to Thompson's biography of the Saint; he was probably submitting portions of it for Meynell's opinion.

163. To Everard Meynell

Monday [May 2, 1905]

Dear Everard,

I will be at the shop to-morrow morning as early as I can—'twixt ten & eleven, if possible, hoping you will be there.

I missed you to-day, unluckily. Just as I was starting I found my coat was decorated with candle-drippings, and it cost me over half-an-hour's delay to scrape the grosser traces away, by which time I was too late. I then made a shot for half-past three, as about the time you might return; & it should seem got there just as you had left. Deceived by a notice on the door, I waited till your assistant (I never recall his name) turned up about five. From his kindness I had a shilling, which enabled me to get a little to eat, & go up to the *Academy*, where I had a belated article to deliver. It was unlucky; but I should have got off earlier to begin with. Of course I could not get to Palace Court afterwards without sacrificing the last shred of a wasted day.

The *Academy*, in a review of Pierre Loti's new book, gravely talks about "Commandant Loti." Why not Captain Linesman, & Mrs. George Eliot? We *have* had Madame Sand, I think. Cannot we leave the monopoly of these things to the French? It seems natural that young *struggle-for-lifers*, experimenting in *bif-stek* & *schmoking-jackets*, should make these *schoking* mistakes. And after all, it was an Italian (Metastasio, I think) who—knowing, as Canning says, that roast-beef was our national dish, & that the charter of our Liberties was won at Runnymede—brought on the stage that Englisch Milor of name so representative, Lord **Runny-beef**. Whence Canning was inspired to create Beefinstern & Puddencrantz.

Love to all,
Yours ever,
F. Thompson

164. To Everard Meynell

28 Elgin Avenue,
Tuesday [June 12, 1905]

Dear Ev,

This to remind you I shall be at the shop, whereof the name is mystery, which all men (mostly women) seek to look into, & in the mouth of the young man Aloysius doubtful is the explanation,— yea, shuffleth like one that halteth by reason of the gout; in the forehead & forehand of the blind & infant day, yet swaddled in the sable bands of the first hour and the *pre-diluculum*. For the Wodensday, a kitten with its eyes still sealed, is laid in the smoky basket of night, awaiting the first homoeopathic doses of the morn's tinctured euphrasy. (Even as *euphrasia* once cured an inflammation of my dim lid—*don't* mistake the vowel in "dim," it is *not* "a.")

Alas! cricket recedes: my foot was worse going home. The disease has too surely, I fear, come to stay; breaking out in one when it abates in the other foot. It has lasted so long & continuously, I have small, if any real hope of an eventual cure. I must resign, I doubt, to its habitual companionship henceforth. It is a sore thing to me, whose one physical pleasure & resource against ill-health lay in my freedom and activity of foot.

Love to all & yourself, dear Everard.

Yours affectionately,
Francis Thompson

Pardon the dirty note-paper; I could no better.

165. To Everard Meynell

28 Elgin Avenue,
Friday [July 8, 1905]

Dear Ev,

I told your father I should be at the shop to-morrow morning, but I send this line to *mak siccer,*—as the lover of artistic completion said who revised Bruce's *Murder of Red Comyn*. It is interesting to see the tentative beginnings of the James school in Bruce, already at variance with the orthodox methods upheld by his critical collaborator. The critic in question considered that Bruce had left off too soon. But to Bruce's taste (evidently) there was a suggestion in the hinted tragedy of "I doubt I have killed the Red Comyn" more truly effective than the obvious ending substituted by his *confrère*. History, by the way, has curiously failed to grasp the inner significance of this affair.

I am quite run down to-night, my foot so crippled I can scarcely bear to put it to the ground after a painful walk home. Your father didn't look the thing, either.

Love to him & all,
Yours ever,
F. Thompson

166. To Everard Meynell

28 Elgin Avenue,
Friday [July 22, 1905]

Dear Everard,

I write to remind you I shall be at the shop to-morrow. I think, despite my disappointments, I shall make a final effort to see Lancashire's second innings—though I know it will be a failure. I will try this time to get there before lunch—the third time pays for all, & I trust my third effort to get out early will succeed. I think it will.

Feet *etc.* worse again to-day; but the swelling never really goes, even when the pain does. I want to get to bed. Good night, with love to you all, especially the poor invalids.

Yours affectionately, dear Ev,
Francis Thompson

I did not go to Lord's. Could not get there before lunch; & getting a paper at Baker St., saw Lanc. had collapsed & Middes. were in again. So turned back without getting my ticket—luckily kept from another disappointing day.

167. To Everard Meynell

28 Elgin Avenue,
Thursday [July 24, 1905]

Dear Ev,

I will not ask you to see me at the shop before eleven to-morrow, after to-day's experience. I will only ask you to do so as soon as you conveniently can; since I certainly shall start off to the shop as soon as I wake or am wakened—whichever happens first—& I dearly want not to miss the resumption of Spooner's & Poidevin's innings. I don't think I shall fail twice running.

As to the note you asked. The Latin *simplex* is from *plecto* (or rather its root) meaning "I entwine", & some root allied to the Greek *sun*, "together." Its root-meaning is therefore "twined together," & it primarily means that which has *synthesis* or unity, as opposed to that which is confused or perplexed by lack of oneness. When Wordsworth (is it not?) somewhere speaks of a being "simple & unperplexed," consciously or unconsciously he uses the word *mainly* in this original sense, though few even thoughtful folk explicitly so grasp it. It is degenerated in the common mouth to the meaning almost of "elementary." Milton, saying poetry should be "simple, sensuous, & passionate" (is that the third word?), by *simple* means *synthetic,*—opposed to prose (especially, doubtless, he had in mind *philosophic* prose) which is *analytic.*

Love to all, & kindest wishes for the invalids.

Yours affectionately,
Francis Thompson

Athenaeum cheque not come. Sorry for my landlady, & am perplexed about it—don't understand it at all.

168. To Everard Meynell

28 Elgin Avenue,
Wednesday [July 27, 1905]

Dear Everard,

I write to remind you of tomorrow. Thank you very much for leaving me supplies today. I was upset, having been up till four *a.m.* in an attempt to finish my book. I will not be so foolish tonight, & will get to the shop in good time. I was sorry to find Olivia worse. May the nurse bring her round.

Haven't Yorks. & Lancs. had a good time of it at Old Trafford? What about Brearley in the Tests *now*? Next comes Yorks. *v.* Lancs., & don't I wish I were there! One of the York eleven at the Oval said they were "getting ready for Lancashire"—remembering Whit Monday at Old Trafford; & the Lancs. comment on his saying is, "Wigs on the green! hurroo!"

We shall be ironed out, Ev.!

Love to all.

Yours affectionately,
F. Thompson

169. **To Everard Meynell**

28 Elgin Avenue,
Wednesday, Aug. 2, 1905

Dear Everard,

Being better than I have been the last two days, I will be at the shop to-morrow between twelve and one—I would be there earlier were there any chance of seeing you. And I ask you, as an act of kindness (I do not pretend any claim on you) to be there before one. I have urgent need to finish work to-morrow (it should have been done today, had I not been so weak and exhausted to start with), & I cannot begin it till I have had a full meal, being still weak though my feet seem better. I must seize every hour my health & strength may leave me to clear arrears finally out of the way in this next two days. Do not refuse me the aid you can give, which I cannot do without. All things else have failed me: give me that at least for a time.

This is, I think, the last letter I shall write you, since they have seemingly ceased to be of any avail. So far as I can see, it may— I am reluctantly driven to believe—be very near the end with me altogether. This ignominious life cannot, as I think, go on many days further. Did it affect none but myself, I should (please God) keep patience & wait till the end, whatever it might be, since I believe that one should always "try the last" & play out the game, not despairing of Providence. But I have no right to involve others in loss which there are no reasonable, no foreseeable means of preventing or repairing. And those means on which I had justifiable & sufficient cause to depend have helplessly failed me. A day or so will put a final term to my long suspense. But virtually any expectation has already left me. In that day I must put through my work, before the night come in which (perchance) I can work no more. Even for this I must rest on you. Do not be wanting to me in that which you can. Your own dark day may come, dear lad; who think it now as little as I once thought it—though I had never your light-

ness of heart, was never without sad overshadowings of the hurry-
ing calamity.

Love to all, especially the dear invalid, & Viola.

> Yours ever most affectionately,
> Francis Thompson

"The day cometh, also the night;" but I was born in the shadow
of the winter solstice, when the nights are long. I belong by nativity
to the season of "heavy Saturn." Was it also, I sometimes wonder,
under Sagittarius? I am not astronomer enough to know how far the
procession of the equinoxes had advanced in '58 or '59. Were it so,
it would be curious; for Sagittarius, the Archer, is the Word. He is
also Chiron, the Centaur, instructor of Achilles. The horse is *intellect* or *understanding* (Pegasus = *winged intellect*). He is the
slayer of Taurus the Bull (natural truth & natural or terrestrial
power & generation, the fire of unspiritualised sense) which sinks
as he rises above the horizon. Ephraim, the type or symbol of the
Word, (as Judah of the Father & the Priesthood), was an *archer*,
or symbolised as such. (See Jacob's dying & prophetic blessing of
his sons, wherein each has a symbol proper to his character & that
of his tribe, indicating his place as a type in the Old Church, & in
the foreshadowing of the New). But this is very idle chatter, & I
don't know how I fell upon it when my mind is serious enough,
indeed. Perhaps as the mind wanders, tired with heavy brooding.

170. To Everard Meynell

> 28 Elgin Avenue,
> Thursday [August 3, 1905]

Dear Everard,

I am very sorry I missed you to-day. Doubtless through the sudden rain & cold, my feet were so bad I could not get my boots on
till after bathing them some time with hot water.

I am told you wanted to see me. I will be at the shop to-morrow
morning, & wait for you. I am better in body, though not in spirit—
or spirits.

I have but just time for the post, having been writing to your father. Will you give him the accompanying letter; for I have only the one envelope for both?

Love to all,

Yours very affectionately, dear Ev,

F. Thompson

Thank you warmly for the money to-day. Please do not fail to see me, if you can help, since you will be away on Saturday to Monday. I am sorry I wrote you so gloomily—though there was & is cause enough. But I should not have troubled you with it.

171. To Everard Meynell

28 Elgin Avenue,

Monday [August 8, 1905]

Dear Ev,

I trust by tomorrow, when this note reaches Granville Mansions, you will have come back from your walking-tour. I am sorry I missed you on Friday. But unexpectedly the cheque came; & equally unexpectedly I found myself baffled in cashing it. This kept me running about a large part of the day, & unsuccessfully in the end; so that I was upset in my appointment with you. When I started out I had no idea but what I should cash it, or some fair proportion of it, at once & go straight on to my appointment with you. Instead I was driven from pillar to post (as the saying is).

The cheque was unexpectedly large, giving me enough to discharge what I have understood to be my landlady's bill, & six-and-sixpence over—nearly enough to cover the Friday, Saturday, Sunday & Monday during which I have been unable to see you. But it leaves me only a shilling for today, & nothing for to-morrow. I should not have that, had I not—dreading accidents in connection with your departure—pinched myself to keep a sixpence over from Thursday, which makes up the shilling for today. So I hope to see you at the shop to-morrow.

Then we shall, I trust, hear your adventures & renew the *cordial intent*—which is the *Evening News'* translation of *l'entente cordiale*. Twice in the course of a leader it evinces its knowledge of the

French tongue by that boldly original rendering. If the French squadron have to encounter much cordial understanding of their language on a par with this, let us hope Providence will gift them with a miraculous & *cordial intent* of it. Otherwise the Tower of Babel will be a bad second to the meeting of the fleets. *Cordial intent* is good, as Polonius says,—excellent good.

To our cordial intent—& bring with thee of the mammon of iniquity, O Everard-bar-Wilfrid!

I cannot look in tonight to learn whether you are returning to your haunts to-morrow, having been unwell the last two days, so that my work is belated.

Love to all.

Yours everest,
F. Thompson

I am not all right, in fact, & wish I could have joined you in your healthy holiday. I feared to risk the break-down of my feet. That is a sore obstacle to the one thing which has ever been life-giving to me. Without exercise I cannot get well. But my ill-health deprives me of exercise. It is a vicious circle,—*vicious* in every sense. If I have failed to explain myself in this letter, I will do so when I see you—it has been rather a complex business.

> In the spring of 1905 the Meynells moved from the Palace Court house to a flat over the offices of the publishers Burns and Oates at 4 Granville Place, just off Oxford Street. Some time before this, Wilfrid Meynell had been appointed director of the firm.

172. To Everard Meynell

28 Elgin Avenue,
Friday [August 12, 1905]

Dear Ev,

I will be at the shop good time tomorrow morning; & I trust you will be able to let me have the full amount. I know you will if you can, & am very grateful to you for the regularity you have shown towards me for some while past.

Short time to catch post. My dearest love to your father, & I hope he may have the benefit from his week which he has for a good while past needed to get. I have not liked to see him looking so weary.

I am in low spirits about my own nearing departure. I know it is good for me—nay, needed very much. But I feel depressed at going away from you all just when you are all going away from me—it seems like a breaking with my past, the beginning of I know not what change, or what doubtful future. Change, *as* change, is always hateful to me; I am a born Conservative. Yet my life has been changeful enough in various ways. And I have noticed these changes come in shocks & crises, after a prolonged period of monotony. In my youth I sighed against monotony, & wanted romance; now I dread romance. Romance is romantic only for the hearers & onlookers, not for the actors. It is hard to enter its gates (happily); but to repass them is impossible. Once step aside from the ways of "comfortable men," you cannot regain them. You will live & die under the law of the intolerable thing they call romance. Though it may return on you only in cycles & crises, you are ever dreading its next manifestation.

Nor need you be "romantic" to others: the most terrible romances of to-day (indeed, of any day) are inward, & the intolerableness of them is that they pass in silence. I know the "romances" of lives that to the world are commonplace, or are held "romantic" for their least notable features. One person, indeed, told me that my own life was a beautiful romance. "Beautiful" is not my standpoint. The sole beautiful romances are the Saints', which are essentially inward.

But I never meant to write all this. Love to all.

Yours ever, dear Ev,

F. Thompson

In order to care for Thompson's worsening health and to do something about his increasing dependence on drugs, the Meynells arranged for him to spend some time away from London. He was to stay with a local family near the Franciscan monastery in Crawley, Sussex.

173. To Everard Meynell

28 Elgin Avenue,
Sunday [August 14, 1905]

Dear Ev,

I was so very unwell yesterday, I could not get to see you at all: & knowing you would be at cricket today, it was useless to come to the flat as I should otherwise have done. You may be sure I shall be at the shop in good time tomorrow, for I have been two days without anything but bread, & am anxious to get supplies again. So I hope you will be able to let me have the full amount, as you can well conceive.

I thank you for the parcels. But you sent only one of the two things I asked for. I asked a night and a *day-shirt*—you sent only the night-shirt. The day-shirt is yet more needed—indeed, an absolute necessity for my going—away.

Love to all.

Yours most affectionately,
F. Thompson

The letter was accompanied by the following, on a separate piece of notepaper:

Expenses this Week.
(Up to Wednesday inclusive).   *d.*

Meth. Spirits	5
Tea (¼ lb.)	3½
Sugar (2 lbs.)	4
Bread	6
Tobacco	2
Matches	½
Candle	1
Envelopes & Notepaper	1
	1:11
Mid-d. Meal Tuesday	1:0
” ” ” Wednesday	1:0
TOTAL TO WEDNESDAY	3:11
(incl.)	
Received from W.	5:0
	3:11
BALANCE IN HAND	1:1

174. To Everard Meynell

28 Elgin Avenue,
Tuesday [August 16, 1905]

Dear Ev,

Though I was dropping with sleep last night, the wretched rat kept me awake till long past dawn. As a result, I slept (when I did at last get peace from throwing boots at it) clean through the day, only waking about 6. I had been awake so many nights, you see.

Consequently, I am like to be up at an unearthly hour tomorrow morning, & to be at the shop unusually early, when I trust to see you at last. Since I not only badly need supplies, but want to see you about several things—especially the day-shirt.

Love to all.

Yours ever, dear Ev,
F. Thompson

175. To Everard Meynell

28 Elgin Avenue,
Wednesday [August 17, 1905]

Dear Ev,

I will be at the shop tomorrow morning. I called at the flat tonight about half-past nine, thinking to have seen you & learned how you had sped with my landlady; but found all a-bed, save (I conjecture) your worshipful self. Nathless, I could not wait there for you with no one up, & the servant one that knew not Thompson. She was timid of me as it was, when I only asked a couple of envelopes. So I must wait to learn from you tomorrow; having no mind to meet my landlady's wiles without first knowing things from you (if possible).

Love to all. Most awfully sleepy & tired.

Yours ever, dear Ev,
F. Thompson

A few days after writing this note Thompson departed for Crawley.

176. To Wilfrid Meynell

c/o Mrs. Gravely
7 New Road, Crawley, Sussex
[August 31, 1905]

Dear Wilfrid,

I am surprised to hear you are off to Italy to-morrow, without having communicated with me. What am I to do with the poem when I have finished it?

What am I to do when the month is out? Madam, I know, wants me to stay here for the winter. But a worse place for a rheumatic man than Sussex when the rain & cold set in I cannot imagine. These last days I have been sitting shivering in my overcoat, and wishing for fires and town. I sampled Crawley before in late autumn, and got out of it as soon as I could. Besides, my lodgings in town are running on, all my things there. A minor matter is that I want the address of the *Windsor Magazine*; there is no getting it in this out-of-the-way corner.

Yours affectionately,
F. Thompson

Best love to Mrs. Meynell and everyone. I hope you will have the sun in Italy which has forsaken us here. All my clothes, I may add, are left in London, save what was barely sufficient for the month.

> Quoted from a copy in the hand of Alice Meynell. The poem mentioned was *Ode to the English Martyrs*, which had been commissioned by the *Dublin Review*.

177. To Wilfrid Meynell

c/o Mrs. Gravely
11 Victoria Road, Crawley, Sussex
Friday [December 1905]

Dear Wilfrid,

Herewith goes the rest of the poem. At the best, too manifest is its sore inequality; at the worst—I would rather not surmise the too possible worst. . . .

x x x x x x x x x x x
These signs (dotty & starry) denote the receipt & arrival of your letter. It is a plain case of telepathy! As you perceive from what I had already written, Mrs. Meynell will not be tried. If she could articulate the rough draft, she is cleverer than I, who even with the unfair advantage of being the author found it a mysterious problem in anatomy—having had time to forget my own design when I flung down the scattered & *disjecta membra* like a handful of dominoes or a child's box of "bricks." She has had a blessed deliverance, I promise you; & I have no faith that even she could have wrought the marvel you so gaily pledge her to.

As to one passage in the verses (I will not repeat the temerity of calling them a poem!) I am sorry I cannot recall the utterers of the two fine & Shakesperean sayings quoted. I had a note of their names, but know not where I made it, nor can remember wherein I read the thing. It must, I fancy, have been at Pantasaph, or even earlier.

I am sorry I should have hurt you by a careless passage in my former letter. It was certainly unmeant either as joke or sneer; but as a serious though passing explanation. You could not (since I said nothing of it) have known the peculiar conditions & necessity under which I was at the time; & so it seemed to me natural you should conceive extravagance. The matter being suggested by the course of my narrative, I interjected an explanation I was now able to give (whereas before I had felt debarred): but it had so little importance in my mind that I did not pause to consider my words; & how I may have put it to create so unintended an impression on you I cannot tell. That is the worst of letter-writing: what the comment of voice and manner would save from misinterpretation is taken askew in black & white. It is a main reason why I detest on principle all letter-writing:—& how consolatory to think that in one matter at least I fully act up to my principles! Even with so frank, sweet-natured, & swiftly sympathetic a girl as K. D. King I did not always escape these quicksands of familiar & unguarded correspondence; & more than once protested the risk she held me to. As last I backed out; excusing myself for long silence on the plea that I *had* written, but was too wise to send what I was foolish enough to write. I held over my letter till morning, re-read, &

burned it. Once, I think, two successive letters were posted in this *fiery* fashion. Yet after all, but a few months before her marriage, I had to follow a letter with a swift & prompt *palinode*, before she had time to answer it. Anyone else would have lost patience & temper with me. *Moral:*—to those about to write a letter; "Don't."
I don't.

Since I understand Ev. is to collect & forward my precious & anxious papers, he is going to have an anxious & admonitory letter on the subject—as soon as I can find time. Here I must end for the present. Love to Mrs. Meynell & the chicks (who are all cocks & hens now).

I just manage to get on when it's not cold, & have a horrible time when it is. I get better food than I ever had in lodgings since Storrington, & keep shut up in a nice warm room, or else—but for these things—I should go to pieces. O for Spring! & not the fraudulent substitute which of late years has been rather worse than winter.

Yours ever, dear Wilfrid,
Francis Thompson

I doubt Anselm's being here much—if any—longer. Not that I know. I don't see him, he being so busy & much away, I so shut up; so it won't make any difference in society should he go.

> The *Ode to the English Martyrs*, edited by Wilfrid Meynell, appeared in the *Dublin Review* for April 1906.

178. To Mrs. Elizabeth Blackburn

Tuesday [mid-January 1906]

Dear Madam,

I were indeed ungrateful if I were not ready to accept advice, correction, or if you thought I merited it, reproof; from so old a friend, to whom I am indebted for so much and such constant kindness. But there is a manner, even in reproof. And this is the second time you have used towards me a manner against which I have, I think, a right to remonstrate; and before even more hastily than in the present case. I will not say more; since I think you will, on reflection, yourself admit I am not unreasonable in this. As to the substance of your letter. My conscience acquits me of having done anything to bring on my illness, or altered my habits for the worse in any way since I came here. I wish my illness were attributable to the cause you allege; for then I should have the remedy in my own hands, and could readily apply it. As it is, it is not. I am suffering from the same illness as last winter; brought on by the exhaustion from my long and dangerous relapse into influenza, which at one time I had almost thought would make an end of me. But ill though I am, I am far from being so ill as I was last winter in London. With regard to myself and my affairs I would ask you, if you can get out, to see Fr. Anselm; before whom, having to consult him about a letter from Wilfrid, I laid both that and your own letter. The matter needs too much discussion for a note, and I dare not at present venture out—indeed I was scarce able to get to him. I can only say here that Wilfrid seems to have decided on keeping me here. I promised Anselm to refer you to him.

As to having lost touch with me, you should surely know now, dear Madam, that it is illness alone which has kept me from seeing you. I did not reproach you for not having been to me through my long illness, but took it for granted you were not well enough to go out. Could you not extend a like charity of belief to one you have known so long? But there is no danger, dear Madam, that I shall forget your true goodness, despite the tendency to "say in your haste" which you share with another person of old who was "after God's heart."

> I am, dear Madam,
> Yours affectionately,
> Francis Thompson

Despite Thompson's denials, it is obvious that his domestic difficulties at this time were at least partly due to his drug-taking (laudanum was mailed to him by a London chemist). His erratic habits, accentuated by the drug, were inevitably irritating to his landlady. On January 30, 1906, Mrs. Blackburn wrote to Meynell forwarding the above letter: ". . . the poet is more than ever a nightmare to me. I remonstrated with him about a fortnight ago and he wrote the enclosed letter. He is worse than ever and his landlady called last night to ask how long he intended to stay. I was too ill to see her but she left a message that she found the strain too much for her, as he stays in bed all day and for a fortnight has never gone out of the house, not even to mass, which at all events on Sundays gave her an opportunity of not having to do his room at night. She spoke to him about it but he has taken no notice. No one can do anything with him, not even Fr. Anselm . . . I shall be very glad when he is gone . . . If he is ill really (I don't think he is) he ought to go to a hospital."

179. To Wilfrid Meynell

c/o Mrs. Gravely
11 Victoria Road, Crawley, Sussex,
Tuesday [early February 1906]

Dear Wilfrid,

Madam (perhaps partly because she is, as I hear, ill with influenza, for which reason I abstain from seeing her about this matter, lest I should catch a fresh attack myself) Madam, I say, seems to have acted with her usual amazing precipitation, without waiting to consult me, Anselm, or anyone. I understand she has written you that I am very ill, & must go into hospital or see a doctor at once.

It is all baseless nonsense. I told you in my last letter how I was, & am like to be till Spring relieves me. But I am, thank God, far from being so bad as I was in London last winter, and should have been again, or rather worse, had I been exposed to the conditions of my life in London and its horrible fogs and smoke, which are killing to me.

The whole trouble (as Madam could have ascertained had she consulted me, or got Anselm to do so) is simply about my lying late in bed; which, as you know, has nothing to do with illness, & was a difficulty at Pantasaph as it is here. If that were removed, my landlady has no objection (she says) to keep me. I have arranged, therefore, that she shall try coming into my room in a morning & making sure that I am really wakened. She has agreed to try that plan for a month longer, and if it succeed in getting me up, she will then not object to my staying on, she says. Here is the whole substance and extent of the matter, and such is the agreement I have come to with her. I do not doubt of the plan succeeding, as it succeeded when I got the O'Connors to try it. For the bother is just that I answer automatically to the call at my door, without really waking. But why Madam will write off in these wild spasms of fanciful exaggeration, without taking time to learn the true facts of a matter. She did not even see my landlady or her husband, but put her own hasty interpretation on what had been said by my land-lady to Madam's landlady—a ready method for the distortion of facts. My landlady declares she never meant to say she wanted me to go; but only to represent that she could not go on under the inconvenience of my late rising, & to arrive at some understanding on the subject. As it is, you understand she agrees to keep me here a month further "on approval" (so to speak), to try the effect of the plan stated; & if it succeed in removing the difficulty of my late rising, will not then object to my further stay. I think the difficulty will be overcome;—practically, I am *sure* it will. But the worry I have had with Madam's sporadic outbreaks into sudden & ground-less letters or action, whenever some unforeseen & unforeseeable thing makes her boil over!—it is like living at the foot of Vesuvius.

As for any new cause for anxiety about my health, it is baseless moonshine—apparently caused by the notion that late rising means serious illness. My trouble of health is just what I expected & was bound to go through during the winter, & was made doubly sure by so long & exhausting an attack of influenza. The wonder is it has not been much worse after that—but for my conditions of life here, which are as favourable as they could be—far better than any I have had since Storrington—it certainly would have been. So far, since Xmas I have escaped the acute colds & the rheumatic gout from which I suffered so badly in London last winter.

> Yours in haste,
> F. Thompson

Madam (need I say?) hasn't seen me, & as usual evolved every-thing out of her fertile brain, seemingly on the strength of my landlady's communication repeated at second hand. My landlady said to me: "I never said you were ill; I should have told her, if I had been asked, that I thought you were rather better!" I was going to see Madam on Sunday; but Anselm (on whom I called on Sat-urday) advised me not to do, since she had a bad cold which I ought not to risk catching. I now hear it is influenza—truly or falsely; so that I still more keep away. She always catches it if there is a chance: she did even at Pantasaph poor Madam!

Wednesday. This was too late to go last night: so I add a line, this morning. We put the new plan in practice this morning, and it got me up *instanter*—I knew it would, from past experience.

But I want to ask you this. There are, as I have been told, four *Athenaeum* books waiting for me at my London lodgings. I am afraid to ask the people there to send them, lest they should burgle it and the books be lost, as happened before. Could Everard get them for me, and forward them to me *at once?* I am most anxious to have them and get them done *now*, or they will soon be too antiquated for insertion, and I shall lose a lot of money—they are already very late. The books I have here I shall soon have finished, and I want to do those others—want most pressingly to get all my Athenaeum work in by the next fortnight at latest, or there will not be time for all the reviews to appear this quarter, and my cheque will be largely diminished. If Ev. can do it, please let me have them *immediately.* If he cannot, please send me word he cannot, *at once* (a post-card with that sole message will do); since I must then risk telling my London people to send them, and that I must do without further delay. Am sorry to trouble you or Everard about it; but you see the matter is of urgent importance.

Am much better and full of work to-day. But the latter I have been the last fortnight. Love to all.

> The difficulties at his lodgings blew over and Thompson re-
> mained at Crawley until the start of May. He did little writing
> however; only four book reviews appeared (in the *Athenaeum*)
> between February and May.

180. To Wilfrid Meynell

[late February 1906]

... My landlady leaves all such things to her husband, who does nothing right if he can do it wrong, & who hates me into the bar-gain—I didn't admire his poems, & ignored his paintings.

But as to my verses—I shrink from calling them a poem—unless some miraculous change takes place in my health, *they will have to stand as they are.* I just put them through, by a terrible dead-lift, & I can do no more. The last reserve of power I could husband was discharged into them, & I can summon up no more. Any attempted change would but make bad worse. Such as they are, they must suffice. One quite certain thing is, the *Dublin* might go further & fare a great deal worse. Even in my ashes, I think there lives a little more fire than in any other Catholic versifier of whom I know. Yea, even K.T. would (I think) be wanting in a matter of this kind. It is not her line. I say this as a matter of commercial justice, not as a brag—God knows I have little indeed left to brag of!

And now, dear Wilfrid, I know there are other things I had in my mind to write; but this letter was begun primarily as a serious exposition of my affairs & condition, for your serious consideration; & has grown so hypertrophied, taken so long to write, that I must leave anything else to another occasion. I will only say that, with the cessation of extreme cold, the symptoms of which I spoke have abated—for the present. And with warm love to Mrs. Meynell, yourself & all, remain,

Yours ever,
Francis Thompson

P.S. I should perhaps add (what I ought to have added in its due place & connection), that of course my identification of the disease from which I suffered last spring but one with *beri-beri* (devoutly though I hold it) may be quite wrong without affecting the practical point in the least. By any other name 'twill smell as ill. It is a point of purely medical interest; even as Saleeby, refusing to call a disease gout, treats it precisely like the man who *calls* it gout. The undoubted fact is that 'twas a deadly disease caused originally by mal-nutrition; springing from failure of heart & circulation; presenting the symptoms described; & bringing me into imminent danger.

Another point I would note (lest you should mention the matter to Saleeby or another medical man). *Paralysis* was perhaps a misleading word in some ways: I used it because the correspondent describing the malady of the Japanese armies used it. But we are apt to associate it with waste of tissues or disease in the nerves themselves. I should rather, perhaps, have said loss of power in & of control over the legs. Again, "beginning from the ankles & *spreading upward*" was misleading. It might seem to imply a gradual & slow progression. I should rather have said "*striking* upwards." The first attack (& worst, since I at once adopted precautions, & began next day the process to which I owed my gradual recovery) was sudden & comparatively rapid. First, a giving & loss of power at the ankles; then—perhaps in about half an hour—it struck suddenly upward, so that only by powerful effort of will did I keep from falling, & to some extent shake it off. This striking upward came on at intervals till I with difficulty crawled home. So to speak, the wires were cut between the lower part of the leg & the brain; I could neither dispatch orders to it nor receive intelligence *from* it which would enable me to direct those orders intelligently. I can only describe the horrible sensation in one way—it felt as if my leg were *swooning away*. The only premonitory signs were the dreadful exhaustion & the peculiar sickening tremor & twitching of the nerves in the part first affected. Even this last summer, when the only thing present was the swelling of my feet, I could *produce* that horrid tremor by *stroking* the muscles or tendons of the foot. So much for medical accuracy, & I have done with an unpleasant subject.

I suppose you are all electioneering in London. Elections have long ceased to interest me: I so early perceived that the country was pretty equally misgoverned by both parties. John Bull, unteachable John, still believes he can improve the government by sending the Outs in & the Ins out. That is because he confounds *government* with *legislation*. The only things materially affected by party change are legislation & perhaps foreign policy. The country is not governed by the ministry, but by a permanent administration, whose names nobody ever hears, who are responsible to no censure, & whose sole political creed is that, whatsoever Cabinet shall reign, still *they* shall draw their salaries. That is the corrupt, effete, routine government which goes on for ever, unaffected by elections; & no minister or ministers can alter the misgovernment of the land. It has its roots deep in either party; neither party dares more than *play* at reforming it; & nothing short of a revolution will ever tear that many-tentacled polypus from its rock. The only thing of more alarming growth is this letter; which shall really develope no more tentacles. *Finis*—& a good job, too, you'll say. For the sake of symmetry, I *might* have completed a thirtieth page. I have really felt obliged to number them.

A lengthy portion (the first twenty-two pages) of the manuscript of this letter is missing. The poem mentioned was the *Ode to the English Martyrs.* "K.T." was Katharine Tynan.

181. To Wilfrid Meynell

c/o Mrs. Gravely
11 Victoria Road, Crawley, Sussex,
Sunday [March 5, 1906]

Dear Wilfrid,

Draw the tooth; this is your hour & the power of darkness—or of the *D.R.* As an article of commerce, do with it what seemeth good unto you. Shouldn't dream of publishing it (in book, I mean). If any poetry *has* got into it, it is a pity; I intended best silver-gilt, & *that* is wasteful—brass much cheaper, & preferred for commercial purposes.

Sorry I can't tell you I am rioting in health—no use hoping it till winter ends & sun comes—if there's any left. But have certainly been better last three weeks or four—I can't calculate time here. Been well enough for work anyway. Not so well last 2 or 3 days, but think mainly stomach. While cramp still knocks now & again at door, though doesn't come in, and noises in ears at times—not often, must keep in wholesome fear. But certainly much more capable of work, & on the whole been certainly better.

Athen. work done: had 2 proofs, but none since,—which makes me anxious. Still, only 2 weeks delay, & others may yet come.

The new scheme has answered, and I have got up and downstairs regularly of a morning. So I think all trouble as to my lodgings is blown over. The only thing which might give trouble is if we should not be able to pay them regularly; since I am afraid they are not in a position to purchase supplies for me, or get them on credit, if they should have to wait for their money. It is the money-question that—as ever—puts me in fear for the future.

I cannot offer you a lively Crawley if you come down, though it would be good to see you again. Anselm is away, & will only return to leave altogether in about a week after his return. The other friars mostly know us not: Cuthbert seems seldom here. And Crawley in winter is not lovely. I myself am as I say. I have not yet reached the ideal depicted in the enclosed remarkable drawing, which Ev.'s jealousy will probably exclude from exhibition at his studio. With warmest love to Mrs. Meynell, the children, and not least yourself,

Yours in haste,
F. Thompson

Meynell had asked permission to edit the *Ode to the English Martyrs*; it was finally printed with a long opening passage (some forty-seven lines) deleted. The Meynells visited Crawley sometime in April. The drawing has been lost.

182. To Wilfrid Meynell

c/o Mrs. Gravely
11 Victoria Road, Crawley, Sussex,
Monday [May 1906]

Dear Wilfrid,

Next Saturday I shall have to leave here and sample London life again. The consolation is that I shall once more be within reach of you. You took all the fine weather with you: it has been bitterly cold and wintry since—hail yesterday, some stones very large, and rain to-day; but always miserably cold.

What you say about the disadvantage of my going out in bad weather is true, but is unaffected by the question of my boarding in or going out for my meals. If I boarded at my lodgings I should have to go out during the day to do my work. And if I could stay in the house to work, it would be very unimportant that I went out just to get my meals. But to work indoors means either a sitting-room with a fire—and *that* means extra expense which I could not live up to; or a bed-room with a fire during the day, in which I should be allowed to sit all day, merely turning out while it was cleaned in the morning. And *that* means extra expense. It is Ghosh's arrangement, but he paid a good deal more for his room than I did. No London landlady will stand a lodger in his bed-room all day without having it made well worth her while by extra payment. Their ideal is a man who turns out early in the morning and only comes back at night. They can get plenty such lodgers; therefore will have no others without increased payment for the inconvenience. And that I could not afford: experience shows it is hard enough to maintain regular payment without it.

The question of meals is therefore quite apart from this un-doubted but inevitable drawback. And I am resolute I will not again board with a London landlady. It is a semi-starvation, espe-cially for a dyspeptic. Restaurants are far from ideal, but I get better fed, and they are cheaper in the end. The other means get-ting in extra food for yourself; as nearly all of us did in the "colony" at Elgin Avenue—save Benson, who had an ostrich-stomach, & would eat chopped shavings if you put on him red spectacles & said it was hash. He said Mrs. Maries was a good cook, who by common consent was the roughest cook we had ever met. Whenever I have had meals at a London lodgings I sorely repented it.

There is no news here, & if there were at the week-end, I should be able to give it you in person. With best love to Mrs. Meynell, yourself, & whoever else is at home,

Yours ever, dear Wilfrid,
F. Thompson

Thompson left Crawley for London early in May, returning to his former lodgings at 28 Elgin Avenue.

183. To Wilfrid Meynell

Wednesday [May 9, 1906]

Dear Wilfrid,

You must be wondering whether, like the illustrious Breitmann's "Carty," I have—

"Gone afay mit der lager-peer
Into de ewigheit!"

No; I am hulling at Elgin Avenue, considerably battered & water-logged, making short cruises to get my sea-legs after a winter of "sailing upon dry land." I have been with you mightily in spirit, but the flesh has been parlously weak. In the simple & direct speech which critics vainly desire of me, I have been too ill & exhausted to get to see you. My journey exhausted me very much, and walking tries me after being shut in the house all winter; while a cold & pain in the chest, which I had had for several days, became worse and—conjoined with my general seediness—troubled me a good deal. Today I think I have somewhat improved, or I am getting more used to the disruption of a sedentary life. Anyway, I attempted to get to you, but at the Bayswater Rd. found it was a quarter to eight—too late for your dinner-hour—& being threatened also with a *soupçon* of cramp, concluded to await to-morrow; when I have no doubt I shall see you. For to-day, I think, I have begun to shake down after the pressure and nerve-worry of my removal from Craw-ley. Train-travel, even in my best days ("best" by figures & com-parisons), always knocked me up. I dislike all vehicular travel, & trains I hate as the gates of Hades. "So, till to-morrow eve, my own, adieu!"

And you may add the next line, if you will. Best love to Mrs. Meynell & all. Yours ever,

F. Thompson

Is Ev. back? I have picked up an old Phil May number I thought he might like—only process-work, of course.

> The lines Thompson quotes are from Charles Leland's *Hans Breitmann* ballads.

184. To Everard Meynell

Wednesday [summer 1906]

Dear Ev.,

Character counts, even in cricket!

This morning I was looking at a *D. Mail* photo. of the S. African team for the coming cricket-season. One of the faces instantly caught my attention. Some time ago I had read that one of the S. African bowlers had the Bosanquet style; though I had forgotten his name with those of all the others (having no special interest in the team). "Well!" I said to myself. "If character count for anything in cricket, *this* should be the Bosanquet bowler. He has just the peculiarly sly look which struck me in B.'s photos, as curiously corresponding with his tricky bowling." But having made the observation, I thought no more of it: since Hall Caine is no Shakespeare, *Plonplon* was no soldier, & neither the Tsar nor the Prince of Wales are Thompsonian poets. Great then was my surprise when tonight I read the accompanying article (which I had not time to read this morning), and found that the fellow *was* the Bosanquet bowler. Facial character was for once, at least, justified in resemblance. Can you, I wonder, identify the man? I send you the photos., and I think you should be able to spot the S. African Bosanquet. The likeness of expression must be patent to you as to me. I will ask you when I see you again.

Yours ever,
F.T.

Thompson fancied that he bore a facial resemblance to both Czar Nicholas and the Prince of Wales (Edward VII).

185. To Everard Meynell

Clarence House, 128 Brondesbury Road,
West Kilburn, London N.W.
[fall 1906]

I am aweary, weary, weary,
  I am aweary waiting here!
Why tarries Everard? sore I fear he
  Has forgotten my shirting-gear!
Ah, youth untender! Why dost thou delay
  With shirts to clothe me, an untimely tree
Unraimented when all the woods are green?
  But thou delay not more: unboughten vests
Expect thy coming, shops with all their eyes
  Wait at wide gaze, and I thy shepherd wait,
In Tennysonian numbers wooing haste.

Cannot this melt you, O Libbell, to purchase & send with fiery utmost speed those day & night-shirts for the which I long, and ever long in vain? Not all thy promises to thy father made, nor all my meek petition & dire need, awake thee from oblivious lethargy? And I, to haste thy motions all unapt, here with foot tumid and dilacerate, cry—"Shirts, shirts, shirts! O for a shirt, ye gods!"

Buy, send, with wingèd expedition send; or be for ever recreant!

Also unto thy sire revered relate, how I to-morrow to his hospiteous tent cannot my pledgèd and preparèd foot direct, for that I housel me (great thing by me forgot!) if forth I go; and doubtful is it if I forth can go, whereas in my already swollen foot, out of mere weakness and enfeebled strength, I, from his tent hospiteous homeward bound, the thongèd tendon brake. Yea, in the instep where some summers past, in like wise feebled, I the sinew strung brake, I re-brake it; that, more swollen by thrice, it doth my painèd loveliness immure, and I keep forcèd house.

In plain words, I am very weak, & my foot so swollen & painful in walking that I cannot much more than limp across road to the post. Please send the shirts, I want them badly, to-morrow being the day for changing my things, and I have none to change.

Yours ever, dear Everard,
F. Thompson

Love to mother, father, & the dear chicks who cackle singularly like hens. Lest you think it nonsense, I add clearly; that I broke a tendon in the instep, broken some years ago, so the more ready to give way in my exhausted state.

> Sometime in fall 1906 Thompson took up lodgings in Brondesbury Road; it was to be his last move. "Libbell" was a nickname for Everard Meynell.

186. To Wilfrid Meynell

128 Brondesbury Road,
Thursday [February 22, 1907]

Dear Wilfrid,

It has been a miserable *debacle* with me, & I don't know whether I'm on my head or my heels. I couldn't get my Henry James done for the Athenaeum at the beginning of last week, as I should have done, & they were waiting urgently for it, while another book came in. I specially engaged myself to do the *James* at once. Yet I have been so completely upset by aggravated renewal of diarrhaea & dyspepsia which seemed for a day or so to have cleared off, that with every attempt I have only been able finally to get the *James* through this moment—at four o'clock on Friday morning (for the Thursday at top of this is misleading, I discover). It has been a wretched time, and my legs are so weak I fear to cross street in front of a vehicle, lest they drop me before it. I don't know whether the diarrhaea has now really gone; the dyspepsia certainly hasn't. I will try to call in to-morrow if nothing more happens to prevent me. The remaining Athenaeum work doesn't tie me up; since I have not bound myself to instant execution, & can use some latitude. But the James has been a series of perpetual abortive efforts, frustrated or dragging it forward but a little way, to be resumed same fashion next day. I just jump if the note-paper slips, my nerves are so unstrung. The James was a beast of a book to get through—I didn't know what I was undertaking so light-heartedly.

Yours ever,
F. Thompson

Thompson's review of *The American Scene*, by Henry James, appeared in the *Athenaeum*, March 9, 1907.

187. To Wilfrid Meynell

128 Brondesbury Road,
Thursday [spring 1907]

Dear Wilfrid,

I don't know even now whether it be Influenza or not: but anyway in its *effects* on me it has been worse than my *first* attack at Crawley was. I feel like a wrung-out towel. To-day it has perhaps been somewhat better on the digestive side (though I fear to say so); but cough and cold worse, I think. I am soaked with cold, and something seems now more evidently developing on the chest *apart* from the digestive (or indigestive) pains.

To make things worse, I am at end of my money. It has been

an expensive illness to me in many ways. I am more often than not taken ill when I get a little money in hand, neutralising the hoped-for benefits of it: but this has been particularly severe and unfortunate.

I suppose I must get to you to-morrow, therefore, if anywise possible. But should I not turn up within an hour after dinner-time, could you manage to send me on something? For should I be worse again or the weather too cold or wet, it would be suicidal to venture the journey in my weakened state and the condition of my chest (as it now seems). I am likely, if I do come, to arrive as soon as I can; for I dare not stay out late.

I hope with all my heart you, too, may not be ill (as you were not at all right when I last saw you.)

Yours ever with love to all,
Francis Thompson

> Thompson's health rapidly declined through the summer and fall of 1907, under the double onslaught of tuberculosis and opium. On August 24 he left London for the Sussex estate of Wilfrid Blunt, a friend of Wilfrid Meynell's. He did not, however, give up the drugs; as it was during his stay at Crawley the year before, laudanum was mailed to him by a London chemist.

188. To Alice Meynell

[Newbuildings,
September 14, 1907]

Dear Mrs. Meynell,

You might have added to the *willow* par. the Latin *salex* and the Eng. *sallow*:

> Among the river sallows borne aloft
> Or sinking as the light wind lives or dies!

The English, I should guess, may be from one of the romance tongues; if so all these modern forms are, mediately or immediately, from the Latin. But it is interesting to find the Latin and the Irish really identical (if you neglect the inflectional endings in the former)—salic and salagh. 'Tis but the difference 'twixt a plain and a guttural hard consonant—for connective vowels are unstable endlessly. As for k and g, you see, e.g., *reg-o* evolve *rec-*tum.

Excuse this off-hand note, but your paragraph interested me.

With warm love to yourself, Wilfrid, and all the *quondam* kids who are fast engaging themselves off the face of my earth.

Yours ever, dear Mrs. Meynell,
Francis Thompson

Quoted from EM, pp. 159–60. Thompson returned to London, accompanied by Everard Meynell, on October 16, "so weak he had to be helped into the carriage." On November 2 he entered the hospital of St. John and St. Elizabeth to attempt another drug cure. He showed initial improvement but after about a week his condition suddenly worsened. He died peacefully at dawn on November 13, 1907.

INDEX

Absence, 212

Academy (the A.), 12, 184, 189–91, 194, 195, 198, 205, 213ff., 225ff., 235, 237, 238

Alexander Dumas (*Père*) . . . , 230

Alfred Tennyson, 225

Alice Meynell: A Memoir, 87

American Scene, The, 265

Amphicypellon, 61–62, 83, 125. *See also Sister Songs*

"Analogies between God, Nature, Man and the Poet," 98

Andrews (with publishing firm), 213, 234, 235

Angel in the House, The, 104, 144

Angelo, Father, 21

Annals, 95, 96

Anselm, Father, 93–94ff., 109, 110, 138–39, 140, 143, 148, 153ff., 174, 253ff., 259–60

Anthem of Earth, An, 12, 66, 121, 144, 192

Any Saint, 113, 114

Archer, C., 193

Archer, William, 8, 191–93, 215–16, 223–24

Arnold, Edwin, 135

Arnold, Matthew, 112

Ashton-under-Lyne, 8, 11. *See also* specific inhabitants

Assumpta Maria, 109, 113, 114

"At Monastery Gates," 118

Athenaeum, 12, 114–15, 185, 187, 188, 235, 242, 256, 259, 264–65

Aurea Dicta, 127–28

Austin, Alfred, 144

Before Her Portrait in Youth, 47, 48, 50, 143

Bishop's House, 95ff.

Blackburn, Elizabeth (Madame), 7, 25, 26, 40ff., 51, 68, 72, 83ff., 92ff., 102ff., 113, 114, 120–21, 250, 252–56

Blackburn, Vernon (V.B.), 40, 42–43ff., 48–49, 54, 58, 60–61, 67, 125, 142–43

Blunt, Wilfrid, 12, 89–90, 200, 203, 204, 266

Bookman, 115

Bosanquet, Bernard, 263

Boston College, 92

Brahms, Johannes, 37

Brien, Maggie, 11, 92, 117, 212

Brien family, 95, 129, 130

Brightwell (reviewer), 194

Bronte, Charlotte, 44

Browne, Sir Thomas, 12

Browning, Elizabeth, 34, 44

Browning, Robert, 32, 34, 37, 184, 189, 190

Bruce (*Murder of Red Comyn* by), 240

Buona Notte, 30, 48

Burns, Robert, 201

Burns and Oates (B & O), 12, 50, 51, 246

Burr, Edmund Godfrey, 12, 174

Butler, Samuel, 136

Byron, George Gordon, Lord, 46–47

Captain of Song, A, 132–33, 135, 185, 187, 188

Carlow, Parnell and, 71

Carr, Comyns, 26

Carroll, John, 24, 33–48, 73, 155

Catholic World, The, 145

Century of Revolution, A, 30, 34

Champney, Basil, 215

Christmas Carol, A, 60

Chronicle, 128, 181, 191, 193

Clarke, Robert, 133, 134

Cloud (Alice Meynell), 156, 176–77

Cloud (Shelley), 38

Cloud's Swan Song, The, 137

Coleridge, Samuel Taylor, 192

Colour of Life, The, 140

Communication, Thompson on, 52–54

Compass, Thompson on the, 136, 137
Constable (publisher), 179, 180, 181, 183, 198
Corymbus for Autumn, A, 65
Cousins, The, 141
Cox, Mr., 39
Crashaw, Richard, 28, 146, 195
Crawley, 12, 71ff., 247, 249ff.
Cust, Harry, 146, 147
Cuthbert, Father, 71, 79, 80, 96, 97, 110, 129, 130, 138–39, 144, 260

Daisy, 30, 31, 36–37, 114, 184
Daphne, 30, 47
Danchin, Pierre, 207
Davidson, A. F., 230
De Amicitia, 212
De Quincy, Thomas, 9, 38, 44, 189
Desiderium Indesideratum, 96
Disraeli, Benjamin, 71
Dome, 199
Domus Tua, 100
Double Need, A, 59
Doubleday, Arthur, 182, 183, 185–86, 188, 189, 198–200
Doubleday, Mrs. Arthur, 188
Douglas, Lord Alfred, 238
Dream-Tryst, 23, 28, 34–35
Dreamers, 30
Dreams and Their Meanings, 224, 225
Drugs (laudanum; opium), 7, 11, 12, 28, 33, 86, 90ff., 207, 247, 253, 266
Dublin Review (D. R.), 25, 26, 36, 38, 48, 252, 257, 259
Dumas, Alexandre, 230

Edinburgh Review, 147–48, 154–55
Edward VII, 229, 263
Eleanora Duse, 156
Elevaverunt Flumina, 114
En Route, 182
"Error of the Extreme Realists, The," 28
Essays I, 68
Essays II, 66, 98
Ex Ore Infantium, 103

Eyes, Thompson on, 54, 55, 175–76, 177

Fallen Yew, A, 106ff.
Feilding, Everard, 139–40, 149, 200
Fletcher, Father Philip, 34
Ford, Clarence, 96
Fortnightly Review, 80, 114
Francis de Sales, St., 58
Franciscans, 70–71. *See also* specific locations, members
From the Night of Forebeing, 117, 134

Gale, Norman, 194
Garvin, J. L., 119
Ghosh, S. K., 220–21, 260
Ghost-chasing, 139–40
Gladstone, William, 103

Hake, T. G., 51, 52
Hans Breitmann, 261, 262
Hayes, Alfred, 8, 182, 183, 194–95
Head, Dr., 139
Health and Holiness, 12
Heard on the Mountain, 186
Henley, William Ernest, 42–43ff., 58–59, 79, 203, 204; letter to, 65–66
Hennessy, Pope, 71
Her Portrait. See Before Her Portrait in Youth
Hind, Charles Lewis, 8, 189–90, 193, 195, 200ff., 210, 213–14, 218, 219, 221, 224–25, 229–30; resignation of, 235
Hobby-Horse, The, 94
Hound of Heaven, The, 11, 40–41, 48, 49, 110, 121
Hugo, Victor, 38
Hunt, Leigh, 58, 97–98
Hutchinson, H. G., 225
Hyde, William, 196–98
Hymn to Snow, A, 64

Idylls of the King, 27
Ignatius, St., 12, 68, 237–38
Illustrated London News, 217
Imperial and Colonial, 220

In Her Paths, 84
Indiana University, 212
Intimations, 117

James, Henry, 264–65
Jesuits, 63. *See also* Ignatius, St.
Johnson, Lionel, 124
Judgment of Heaven, 81, 111

Kaufmann, Angelica, 139
Keats, John, 64
King, Katherine Douglas (Katie), 8,
    12, 173–74, 177, 180, 206, 207,
    211, 212, 251
Kingdom of God, The, 12
Kingsford, Anna, 143
Kipling, Rudyard, 42, 58, 184
Krudener, Mme. de, 96

Lane, John, 79, 98, 99–100, 106,
    110ff., 125, 130, 137, 141, 145,
    148–49ff., 179–80, 199, 200; letters
    to, 122–24, 125–26
Lang, Andrew, 224, 225
"Language of Religion," 95–96
Lanier, Sidney, 184
Le Galliene, Richard, 104, 111, 112,
    121–22, 123, 124, 127, 128, 130
Leland, Charles, 262
Life of St. Ignatius, The, 12. *See also*
    Ignatius, St.
Lilly, W. S., 29, 30, 34
"Literary Coincidence," 28
Literary Criticisms, 48
Little Jesus, 11, 92, 96, 103
London, 9ff., 188ff., 261ff. (*See also*
    specific inhabitants); projected
    work on, 197
Love and the Child, 145
Love Declared, 151
Love in Dian's Lap, 211, 212
Love Thy Neighbor, 99
Ducas, Winifred, 173
*Lux in Tenebris. See From the Night
    of Forebeing*

"Macbeth Controversy, The," 26
McLeod, Fiona, 189, 190
Making of Viola, The, 66, 75–77, 78

Man Has Wings, The, 217
Mann, Father H. K., 118–19
Manning, Cardinal, 74, 75, 77, 141
Marianus, Father, 93, 94, 103–4, 116
Meredith, George, 76–77, 153, 155,
    177ff., 181, 183, 185, 192
Merry England, 11, 23ff., 70, 96, 173–
    74. *See also* specific contributions
Meynell, Alice (A. M.), 26, 37, 40ff.,
    50, 61, 67–68ff., 104, 106ff., 127–
    50 *passim,* 156, 231–32, 266–67;
    letters to (*See* Table of Contents,
    pp. 13–19)
Meynell, Everard (Cuckoo), 8, 9–10,
    62, 63, 153, 252, 256, 260, 267;
    letters to, 222–23, 235–36, 236–37,
    238–49, 262–64
Meynell, Francis, 66–67, 102, 107
Meynell, Madeline (Sylvia), 152, 153
Meynell, Monica, 36–37, 62–63, 69,
    110, 113, 116–17, 120, 139, 141,
    227–28, 230–31; marriage, 231,
    233–34
Meynell, Olivia. *See* Sowerby, Olivia
Meynell, Prue, 41–42
Meynell, Sebastian (Bastian), 225,
    226
Meynell, Viola, 8, 49, 87, 152, 153
Meynell, Wilfrid, 7–8, 9, 11, 33ff.,
    58, 79, 89ff., 113ff., 122–23, 124,
    147, 177ff., 185, 198, 200, 222,
    246, 253; letters to (*See* Table of
    Contents, pp. 13–19)
Meynell family, 7ff., *See also* specific
    members
Milton, John, 242
Mistress of Vision, The, 137
"Modern Men: The Devil," 66
Moods, 30
Morning Post, 194–95
Morris, Lewis, 59, 60, 120
Mostly Fools, 141
Murder of Red Comyn, 240

Naphali, 200, 202–3
Napoleon Judges, 217, 224
Narrow Vessel, The, 151, 211
National Observer, 66
Nature, Thompson on, 101–2

New Day, The, 52
New Poems, 12, 103, 129, 137, 138, 151, 156, 182, 185, 193, 194–95
"New Poet, A," 111
New Review, 125
Newcastle Chronicle, 119
Newman, John Henry Cardinal, 47, 48
Nicholas, Czar, 263
Nineteenth Century, The (magazine), 75, 217, 222
Nineteenth Century, The (poem), 229
Nocturns, 212

Ode for the Diamond Jubilee of Queen Victoria, 193
Ode to the English Martyrs, 12, 252, 259, 260
Ode to the Setting Sun, 11, 35, 48, 112, 138
Opium. *See* Drugs
Orient Ode, 129, 132
Orison-Tryst, 87
O'Sullivan, Vincent, 111
Our Literary Life, 48
Owens College, 8, 11

"Paganism Old and New," 23–24, 39, 177
Pall Mall Gazette (P.M.G.), 52, 113, 118, 130, 139, 146, 147
Pantasaph, 11, 91–188 *passim*
Parnell, Thomas, 71
Passion of Mary, The, 11, 23, 24, 34
Pastoral, 198
Patmore, Coventry, 7, 8, 12, 67–68, 79–83ff., 90, 95–96, 97, 104, 112ff., 119–20, 130, 181, 183, 188, 191, 192, 213–14, 215, 220; death, 186–87; letters to, 97–98, 127–28, 131–34, 134–37, 142–44, 145–47, 174–77, 178–80, 184–85
Patmore, Harriet, 98, 177–78, 186–87
Perry, Father, 34, 39–40, 47
Poems, 11, 99, 102, 106, 107, 111–12, 114, 115, 119, 123, 153
Poems and Ballads, 36
Poets of the Younger Generation, 224

Poppies, 30, 77, 78
Poppy, The, 152–53, 154, 234
Power Cobbe, Miss, 204–5
Percursor, 97
Preludes, 78–79
Prince of Destiny, The, 221
Probyn, May, 60
Purcell, E. S., 140, 141

Raleigh, Sir Walter, 204
Randolph, E., 141
Raphael, Father, 139
Realm, 124, 130
Religio Poetae, 97, 98
Rethel, Alfred, 70
Review of Reviews, 116
Reynolds, J. H., 64
Rhymers Club, 73, 229
Rhythm of Life, The, 46, 56
Robert Burns and Mrs. Dunlop, 201
Rock, Clarence, 218–19
Rossetti, Christina, 44
Rossetti, Dante, 34, 44, 104, 184
Ruskin, John, 44, 58, 70

Sagittarius, 244
St. James, 112, 114
Saleeby, Caleb, 231, 257
Sargent, John Singer, 127
Saturday Review, 130, 135, 137
Saul, 216, 217
Savoy, The, 152
Scarisbrick, Archbishop, 103
Scots Observer, 43ff., 66
Scott, Bell, 104
Sebastian, Father, 147
Seneca, 54
Sequoia, The, 185
Sere of the Leaf, The, 30, 48, 75
Set, 136
Seven Seas, 184
Shakespeare, William, 105, 136, 192–93
Shamrocks, 77
Sharp, William, 32, 33, 34, 38
Shelley, Lady Mary, 47
Shelley, Percy Bysshe, 11, 28, 30, 31, 36ff., 44, 46–47, 48, 104, 189, 190
Shore, Arabella, 204–5

Shore, Teignmouth, 235
Shrewsbury, Bishop of. *See* Carroll, John
Sister Songs, 11, 12, 48, 51, 56, 59, 62, 125, 129, 130–31, 138, 153, 155, 177. *See also* Amphicypellon
Song of the Hours, 35, 48, 58
Songs Unsung, 120
Sowerby, Mrs. Olivia, 118, 153, 233
Spenser, Edward, 184
Stanford University, 185
Star, 130
Storrington, 11, 25ff.
"Story of a Conversion," 70, 133, 134
Stream's Secret, 184
Suicide attempt, 11
Sutherland, Duchess of, 213, 235–36
Sweets, 77
Swinburne, Algernon Charles, 30, 36, 42, 44, 57, 76, 104, 184
Symons, Arthur, 115, 130

Tablet, 36, 39, 40, 42, 43, 48, 67, 68
Tempo rubate, 76–77
Tennyson, Alfred, Lord, 27, 144, 189, 190
Testament of Calvary, The, 75
Thompson, Dr. (father), 11, 12, 107, 147, 148, 150, 151
Thompson, Mrs. (mother), 11
Thompson, Edward Healy, 8–9, 34, 48
Thompson, Margaret, 8, 46, 47
Thompson, Mary (Polly), 46, 47, 48, 147, 148, 201–2
Thompson, Norbert, 8
Thorp, Thomas, 225, 226
"Threnody of Birth, A," 65–66
Tile, straw, 74–75
Tit Bits, 142
To a Dead Astronomer, 30, 47
To the Dead Cardinal of Westminster (on Cardinal Manning), 74, 75, 77
To Monica Thought Dying, 106–7, 115
To My Godchild, 67
To a Poet Breaking Silence, 48, 50, 102–3

Tobin, Agnes, 233
Tom O'Bedlam's Song, 198, 199
Toole, Canon, 35, 36, 46, 48
Traill (reviewer), 114, 115
Trelawney, Edward John, 46, 47, 104
Troy, 61, 62
Tuberculosis, 12, 266
Tynan, Katharine (K. T.), 30, 36, 47, 48, 115, 257; letter to, 75–78

Unknown Eros, 144, 149
Ushaw, 8, 11
Ushaw Magazine, 75, 109, 119

Vaughan, Cardinal, 141
Venus Fly-Trap, 73
Vie et l'Oeuvre d'un Poète, La, 207
Vision of Saints, A, 60
Vita Nuova, 211

Wanderings of Oisin, The, 52
"Wares of Autolycus, The," 118
Watson, William, 229
Watts, Theodore, 44
Waugh, Arthur, 195
Wayfarer's Love, 236
Weekly Register, The, 11, 30, 34, 48, 49, 52, 60, 69ff., 83, 90, 96, 103, 148
Weekly Sun, 121
Wendell Holmes, 79
Westminster Gazette, 121–22, 123
Westminster Press, 122
Whelan, Bernard (Brin), 70, 71
Whitten, Wilfrid, 8, 190–91, 213–15, 216
Why Wilt Thou Chide?, 130
Wilde, Oscar, 44
Wilkinson, Father Adam, 109
William Archer, 193
Williams, Jane, 46
Winds of the World, 156
Wiseman, Cardinal, 39
Wordsworth, William, 117, 189, 190, 242
Wyndham, Thompson on, 203, 204

Yeats, W. B., 51, 52, 217, 228–29
Yellow Book, The, 142, 151